SAMS
PUBLISHING

M T W T F S S **24**

Using the *Teach Yourself in 24 Hours* Series

Welcome to the *Teach Yourself in 24 Hours* series! You're probably thinking, "What, they want me to stay up all night and learn this stuff?" Well, no, not exactly. This series introduces a new way to teach you about exciting new products: 24 one-hour lessons, designed to keep your interest and keep you learning. Because the learning process is broken into small units, you will not be overwhelmed by the complexity of some of the new technologies that are emerging in today's market. Each hourly lesson has a number of special items, some old, some new, to help you along.

Minutes

The first 10 minutes of each hour lists the topics and skills that you will learn about by the time you finish the hour. You will know exactly what the hour will bring with no surprises.

Minutes

Twenty minutes into the lesson, you will have been introduced to many of the newest features of the software application. In the constantly evolving computer arena, knowing everything a program can do will aid you enormously now and in the future.

Minutes

Before 30 minutes have passed, you will have learned at least one useful task. Many of these tasks take advantage of the newest features of the application. These tasks use a hands-on approach, telling you exactly which menus and commands you need to use to accomplish the goal. This approach is found in each lesson of the *24 Hours* series.

40 Minutes

You will see after 40 minutes that many of the tools you have come to expect from the *Teach Yourself* series are found in the *24 Hours* series as well. Just a Minute Notes and Time Saver Tips offer special tricks of the trade to make your work faster and more productive. Cautions help you avoid those nasty time-consuming errors.

50 Minutes

By the time you're 50 minutes in, you'll probably run across terms you haven't seen before. Never before has technology thrown so many new words and acronyms into the language, and the New Term elements found in this series will carefully explain each and every one of them.

60 Minutes

At the end of the hour, you may still have questions that need answered. You know the kind—questions on skills or tasks that come up every day for you, but that weren't directly addressed during the lesson. That's where the Q&A section can help. By answering the most frequently asked questions about the topics discussed in the hour, Q&A not only answers your specific question, it provides a succinct review of all that you have learned in the hour.

Teach
Yourself

MICROSOFT®
WORD 97

in 24 Hours

Teach Yourself

MICROSOFT®
WORD 97

in 24 Hours

Linda Jones
Ruel T. Hernandez

SAMS
PUBLISHING

201 West 103rd Street
Indianapolis, Indiana 46290

Copyright© 1997 by Sams Publishing

FIRST EDITION

International Standard Book Number: 0-672-31115-1

Library of Congress Catalog Card Number: 97-66670

2000   99   98   97   4   3   2

Interpretation of the printing code: the rightmost double-digit number is the year of the book's printing; the rightmost single-digit, the number of the book's printing. For example, a printing code of 97-1 shows that the first printing of the book occurred in 1997.

Composed in AGaramond and MCPdigital by Macmillan Computer Publishing

Printed in the United States of America

Trademarks

President, Sams Publishing   Richard K. Swadley
Publishing Manager   Dean Miller
Director of Editorial Services   Cindy Morrow
Managing Editor   Kitty Jarret
Director of Marketing   Kelli Spencer
Product Marketing Manager   Wendy Gilbride
Assistant Marketing Managers   Jen Pock
                                    Rachel Wolfe

Acquisitions Editor
Cari Skaggs

Development Editor
Brian-Kent Proffitt

Production Editor
Kate Shoup

Copy Editor
Nanci Sears Perry

Indexer
Chris Barrick

Technical Reviewer
Alexandria Haddad

Editorial Coordinators
Mandi Rowell
Katie Wise

Technical Edit Coordinator
Lynette Quinn

Resource Coordinator
Deborah Frisby

Editorial Assistants
Carol Ackerman
Andi Richter
Rhonda Tinch-Mize

Cover Designer
Tim Amrhein

Book Designer
Gary Adair

Copy Writer
David Reichwein

Production Team Supervisors
Brad Chinn
Charlotte Clapp

Production
Carol Bowers
Mike Henry
Brad Lenser
Carl Pierce

Overview

Contents

Acknowledgments

Linda Jones

Foremost, I wish to thank Cari Skaggs at Sams Publishing for giving me the opportunity to write this book. The great production staff at Sams deserve a hats off for their feverish work in pulling this project together.

As you will learn in the pages of this book, people read bulleted lists more readily than paragraphs, so here's a bulleted list of the others I want to acknowledge:

- My husband, Harry, and our four children, Harry, Pat, Amy, and George—thanks for these months of sacrifice! Without your help and support, this would have been impossible.
- To my boss, Pat Smoker—thanks for allowing me extra time from my job to tackle this project. I appreciate the sacrifices that were made to pick up the slack in my absence.
- To Cindy Meister, a private consultant, who volunteers her qualified responses to the Microsoft newsgroups—my thanks. Cindy was instrumental in solving a couple of questions that cropped up in the writing of this book.

Ruel Hernandez

Ruel wishes to thank the editors at Sams Publishing for their guidance, and to acknowledge his sisters, his parents, and the family dog for their encouragement in the writing of chapters for this book.

About the Authors

Main Author

Linda Jones is a Management Information Systems Software Training and End-User Support Coordinator at Purdue University. Linda spent seven years as a Communications Specialist, writing professionally and providing computer support in a large office setting. Linda has a Bachelors degree from Manchester College in North Manchester, Indiana. She also has a Masters degree from Purdue University in Educational Computing and Instructional Design. Linda lives in West Lafayette with her husband, Harry, and their son, George. They have three other married children and two grandchildren.

Contributing Author

Ruel Hernandez is a former instructor who taught computers and word processing to government employees. Ruel has practical experience teaching computers and understands the need to provide a friendly and simple approach to introducing computers to people who have never used them before. He has had published articles on "ECPA and Online Computer Privacy," "Computer Electronic Mail and Privacy," and a couple of articles in the *Byte Buyer* magazine (now called *ComputerEdge*). He is also a contributing author (covering the use of multimedia with PowerPoint 97) of *Teach Yourself PowerPoint 97 in 24 Hours* by Sams Publishing.

Tell Us What You Think!

As a reader, you are the most important critic and commentator of our books. We value your opinion and want to know what we're doing right, what we could do better, what areas you'd like to see us publish in, and any other words of wisdom you're willing to pass our way. You can help us make strong books that meet your needs and give you the computer guidance you require.

Do you have access to CompuServe or the World Wide Web? Then check out our CompuServe forum by typing **GO SAMS** at any prompt. If you prefer the World Wide Web, check out our site at `http://www.mcp.com`.

JUST A MINUTE

> If you have a technical question about this book, call the technical support line at 317-581-4669.

As the team leader of the group that created this book, I welcome your comments. You can fax, e-mail, or write me directly to let me know what you did or didn't like about this book—as well as what we can do to make our books stronger. Here's the information:

Fax: 317-581-4669

E-mail: Dean Miller
        `opsys_mgr@sams.mcp.com`

Mail: Dean Miller
        Comments Department
        Sams Publishing
        201 W. 103rd Street
        Indianapolis, IN 46290

Introduction

You've made an investment in Office 97 or the standalone version of Word 97. It takes a lot of time and effort to familiarize yourself with any new software package, and sometimes the "experiment until you learn" method doesn't get you where you want to be. In fact, you may miss out on some of a program's best features because you never take time to explore what the program can do.

If you're new to Word, give yourself 24 hours with Word 97 and this book. Play as you go and experiment with the features in your own environment. The examples in this book give you a starting point to learn the basics of Word 97. If you're an old pro at Word, you'll find that Word 97's new features add enough spice to keep things more than a little bit interesting.

Microsoft issued its first quarter report for 1997 with statements such as, "...the strongest quarter ever for Microsoft Office," and "...sales have averaged one license of Office 97 per second." As of the first quarter, eight million copies of Office 97 licenses had been sold. Microsoft claims that 70 percent of Fortune 1000 companies are either now using or actively evaluating Office 97.

The shift to the new Office 97 suite has come as a surprise to many, but those who have had their hands on the package aren't willing to give it up. Word 97 is an integral part of this package.

How To Use This Book

This book is designed to teach you topics in one-hour sessions. All of the books in the Sams *Teach Yourself* series enable the reader to start working and becoming productive with the product as quickly as possible. This book will do that for you!

Each hour, or session, starts with an overview of the topic to inform you what to expect in that lesson. The overview helps you determine the nature of the lesson and whether the lesson is relevant to your needs.

Main Section

Each lesson has a main section that discusses the lesson topic in a clear, concise manner by breaking the topic down into logical component parts and clearly explaining each component. Embedded into each lesson are Step-Ups, Cautions, New Terms, Keyboard Shortcuts, Just a Minutes, Time Savers, and other elements that provide additional information.

Step-Up

Step-ups show you features of Word 97 that did not appear in earlier versions.

CAUTION

Cautions point out a problematic element of the operating system. Ignoring the information contained within the Caution could have adverse effects on the stability of your computer. These are the most important informational bars in this book.

 NEW TERM New Term elements offer a quick-and-easy way to beef up your Word 97 vocabulary.

KEYBOARD SHORTCUT

Keyboard Shortcuts show you the quick and easy way to complete tasks without using your mouse.

JUST A MINUTE

Just a Minute elements offer notes and asides about the topic at hand.

TIME SAVER

Time Savers show you tips to beat the clock and accomplish your tasks in Word 97 more quickly.

Q&A

This section of each lesson provides questions and answers that reinforce concepts learned in the lesson and help you apply them in new situations. You can skip this section, but it is advised that you go through the questions and answers to see how the concepts can be applied to other common tasks.

PART
I

Word: The Tool and How It Operates

Hour

Hour 1

Word 97—
A Multipurpose Tool

This hour explains the history of the tool called a word-processing application. It includes an overview of some of the uses you might have for Word 97 and suggestions as to when other software choices might be more appropriate for certain tasks. You will also look at some of Word 97's exciting new features that make it worthy of the best-seller list.

The highlights of this hour include

- [ ] How word processing has changed the way business is done
- [ ] What your documents say about you
- [ ] How to decide when to use a word-processing application
- [ ] What Word 97 has to offer

The Evolution of Word Processing

Over many centuries, the need to communicate in writing has taken various forms. From carving inscriptions in rock, to pen and paper, to the modern age of typewriters and personal computers, people have shared their thoughts and ideas in printed form.

Nothing has increased the volume of printed matter as dramatically as the advent of personal computers. While computer folks are trying to get us to conserve paper by putting many of our communications *online*, people are still generating mountains of publications of all types. The reason is that it has never been easier to create documents. You have the tools right at your fingertips to generate documents and publications that once would have taken a full production staff to create.

 Putting a document *online* refers to making it available on computer rather than in printed form. Online help, for example, works within a software program to give quick access to help with the program.

Many documents are available on the *Internet*; these are considered *online* publications also.

 The *Internet* is the glue that holds the thousands of individual computer networks around the world together so they can talk to each other. Using special cables, wires, and/or telephone lines, we can connect computers to what is often called the *Information Superhighway*. Hour 24, "Working with the Web," discusses how to get on the Information Superhighway.

Today's word-processing software can no more be compared to the typewriter than the first airplanes to today's jetliners. We're talking a whole different class. Even the early word-processing software was a far cry from what we have today in programs such as Word 97.

When was the last time you got a typewritten letter or report with erasures or correction fluid? Can't remember? The age of the typewriter is all but gone. Small mistakes used to be ignored or corrected by hand if it meant retyping the whole document. Now, mistakes are easily and quickly corrected when you use a program like Word 97. Text can be deleted or shifted from one place to another.

Changes can be made so easily that we've come to expect almost instant production of documents. Even with the speed at which documents can be created and corrected, it is still important to proofread the document to ensure that it is of high quality.

One of the prime concerns for businesses is that the documents they produce not only accurately convey the right message, but that they look like they come from progressive, professional organizations. Individuals, too, are judged by the documents they produce.

Employers will tell you that the resumés and cover letters they receive from job applicants fall far short of what they would expect from professionals. Most colleges are now dedicating at least part of a course to job interviewing and writing resumés. How you look in print may determine whether an employer ever sees you face-to-face.

A *word processor* is the tool that can produce those great-looking documents that make people sit up and take notice. Each generation of word-processing software adds more glitz to what can be produced in print. Now, many of the same techniques used to create printed documents are being applied to electronic transfer of information. Hour 24, "Working with the Web," discusses some of Word 97's capabilities for generating electronic documents that look good.

 Word processing is the term applied to typing and manipulating text before sending it to print or some other medium.

Another term closely associated with word processing is desktop publishing. Software programs like Word 97 combine text, page layout, and graphic capabilities in ways that rival the work of professionals. Hence, the term desktop publishing: The whole process of typing content, adding graphics and photos, laying out the pages in creative ways, and dashing it off to a printer (either your own or that of a professional printing company) is all done with a desktop computer.

Word-Processing Uses

What would you use a word-processing application for? The answer has changed as word-processing applications have gotten more sophisticated. The first word-processing programs were designed to type letters, generate reports, and produce other types of standard business communications. Although this is still the primary function of a word-processing application, there are so many other features packed into a program like Word 97. So what would you use a word-processing application for?

- ☐ Brochures
- ☐ Newsletters
- ☐ Flyers and booklets
- ☐ Signs
- ☐ Reports and proposals
- ☐ Advertisements
- ☐ Resumés and cover letters
- ☐ Catalogs with pictures
- ☐ Business directories

☐ World Wide Web pages

☐ Visual aids

☐ The book you're writing

I think you get the idea. There is no end to what you can do with a word-processing application!

Using the Right Tool for the Right Job

The fine line between what different types of applications can do these days causes some major confusion. A word-processing application can act as a *database* program, or it can do some of the things a *spreadsheet* program might do. It has many graphic capabilities and could be used to create illustrations or visual aids for presentations. How do you decide which program to use?

NEW TERM A *database* is an information-management system. It is a way to store related information for easy retrieval. For example, your address book (electronic or paper) is a database; it contains the name, address, and phone number for each person listed. A recipe file is another kind of database.

NEW TERM A *spreadsheet* program is an electronic ledger with columns and rows, used primarily for entering numbers and performing calculations on the entries.

Databases

Database programs such as Microsoft Access, a part of the Office 97 Professional Suite, are good at keeping records of lots of similar information. You might use a database to keep a company's client list, an inventory list, an employee information file, a product catalog, and so forth. Databases can sort all that information out for you in chunks as big or small as you need.

Spreadsheets

A spreadsheet is the best application for numbers and calculations. Microsoft Excel, a component of both the Office 97 Standard and Professional Suites, is a prime example. Whenever using complicated formulas or tallying long columns of numbers is important, a spreadsheet is the program of choice. Automated functions are built into spreadsheet programs to allow them to work efficiently with numbers. Spreadsheets are used for everything from keeping corporate financial records to tallying bowling league scores.

Presentation Design Programs

Newer on the scene than word-processing applications, databases, or spreadsheets are presentation design programs such as PowerPoint 97, another Office 97 ingredient. The

objective of presentation programs is building effective oral or electronic presentations, audience handouts, and speaker's notes for use during a presentation. Animation and sound have been integrated with text and graphics to teach and present in a more interesting format.

Word-Processing Applications

Typically, you think of word-processing applications when dealing with text and publication. Words are the primary component; graphics may add some spice. But Word can also act as a database. It can be used to keep track of information as a database does. As you'll discover in Hour 15, "Mail Merge," Word allows you to keep an information file that can later be used to create letters, reports, envelopes, and labels.

Use Word's table feature to enter columns of figures, and use the AutoSum feature to add the numbers for you as you would with a spreadsheet. Word's Formula function allows you to perform other calculations, even very complicated ones. You'll learn about Word's table features and AutoSum in Hour 14, "Working with Tables."

Visuals can easily be created in Word 97. The exciting new graphic features make it simple to create overhead transparencies or audience handouts that look professional.

If Word can do all the things that other programs can do, how do you decide which tool is right for a job? It's a matter of scale and features. Large databases that contain information that must be sorted or extracted in specific ways are more appropriate for a database program. Heavy-duty accounting or number crunching is done better by a spreadsheet program. Full-blown visual presentations with animation and other visual effects can be done more easily with a presentation design program.

On the other hand, if you had to choose one program, Word 97 *could* do it all.

What's New in Word 97

Word 97 is packed with new features that make it different from earlier versions. There is something new for everyone. Create your own Web page, use the new drawing tools, take advantage of the new editing features, and coordinate your projects with the excellent integration between Word and the other applications in the Office 97 suite.

Artificial Intelligence?

Who's in there doing that? I didn't type that word; the computer just started typing by itself! Why does that animated paperclip on the screen (see Figure 1.1) keeping nodding at me? It acts as though it wants me to do something! Hour 4, "Help?! There's Lots of It in Word 97" discusses Office Assistant and the many other Word help features.

Figure 1.1.

*The Clippit Office
Assistant.*

With each new version of Word, you see more of what I call "read my mind" features. Microsoft has termed it IntelliSense. It doesn't quite read your mind and transfer what it read to the computer, but it does sense when it can do something more easily than you are doing it, or when it can clean up after your mistakes.

Several of these IntelliSense options start with *Auto* because they automate several tasks. AutoComplete, AutoCorrect, AutoFormat, AutoText, and AutoSummary round out the Auto functions.

AutoComplete is a feature that looks at AutoCorrect, AutoText, and other information sources to fill in the blanks. When AutoComplete sees something familiar in its memory bank that matches what you're typing, a message pops up showing what it thinks you're after. Pressing the Enter key automatically completes the typing with the suggestion. You can ignore it if it's not what you want or turn off the feature completely.

AutoText was around in earlier versions, but has added dimensions in Word 97. As with many other functions, it now has its own *toolbar* (see Figure 1.2). AutoText can be one of your best friends if you have repetitive typing tasks or frequently need to insert a graphic such as your company logo or your electronic signature. You can store paragraphs, full pages, graphics, or signature blocks as AutoText entries that you assign to shortcut names. These entries then are stored for future use and can be placed in documents from the list of entries you have in the Insert | AutoText menu. You'll learn more about AutoComplete and AutoText in Hour 16, "Automating Tasks."

Figure 1.2.

The AutoText toolbar.

 A *toolbar* is a group of *buttons*. The buttons in one toolbar usually perform related tasks.

  Buttons are the small pictures that, when clicked with the left mouse button, initiate some action. In the margin is the Printer button from the Standard toolbar. When you click it, it sends a message ordering the printer to print your document.

AutoCorrect searches for and changes common misspellings as you type. For example, it will change *alwasy* to *always*. There is a raft of words people commonly mistype, and AutoCorrect is already preprogrammed to catch and correct them as you type. Your own problem words can be added to the list of misspelled words that AutoCorrect automatically detects and fixes for you. Find out more about AutoCorrect in Hour 21, "Bookshelf and Word's Editing Tools."

1

AutoFormat is a feature that hands a final document over to Word and says, "Take a look at this and do any special formatting that would help this document." AutoFormat applies styles (unless you tell it not to), smart quotes, and other formatting. AutoFormat does all of this in the background while you create a document. You tell Word what you want formatted and what you don't. Hour 12, "A Matter of Style," shows how AutoFormat works.

AutoSummarize looks at the major topics (frequently used words and phrases) in a document and builds a summary of the document. Use AutoSummarize for an abstract or executive summary. You specify how involved the summary gets by telling Word what percentage of the original or what level of detail to include in the summary.

New Navigation Tool

A great addition to Word 97 is the capability to move quickly from one place to another in your documents using Document Map. Document Map adds a sidebar to the left of your document that shows major headers in the document. You can click one of the headers to get there instantly. Document Map even has its own icon on the Standard toolbar (see Figure 1.3).

Figure 1.3.

The new Document Map feature.

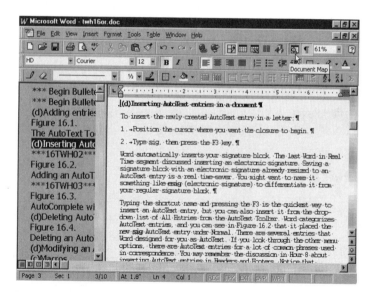

Everything Graphic

The expanded graphic capabilities may be the biggest draw to taking the plunge into Word 97. Enhancements such as the text rotation tool, special Photoshop-type effects, fancy text-wraps around graphics, and 3D objects give Word 97 the power of a full-fledged desktop publishing program.

Not only do the graphic and drawing tools allow more graphic creation, but Word lets you work graphically. More buttons and added toolbars give you point-and-click control over many of Word's functions. You can even create your own toolbars. Hour 11, "Customizing Word to the Way You Work," includes instructions on building toolbars.

If you've used WordArt in previous versions of Word, you'll be surprised by its new 3D effects. Titles become works of art with WordArt. Hour 17, "Working with Graphics," shows the advances made in the WordArt feature.

You can even draw tables with Word's new Draw Table feature. Tables can be any size or shape when you use this new drawing tool.

Exploring the World Wide Web

Connectivity is a common buzzword; Microsoft is doing its best to get a big piece of the action. Connecting computers with the Internet was one of the underlying design strategies for the creation of the entire Office 97 package. Every application gives you shortcuts to go directly to a *Web browser* such as Microsoft Internet Explorer or Netscape Navigator.

Not only can you connect to the Web, you can create documents that can be viewed on the Web. Nearly every major business or corporation now has a presence on the Web, and they have Web programmers creating the documents used on their Web sites. Regular Word documents can't be viewed on the Web. They must be converted to a format called HTML. You don't need to know how to write HTML code; Word 97 can automatically convert your Word documents to HTML. You'll get the scoop on Web tools in Hour 24.

 A *Web browser* is a software program that lets you connect to and view information from the World Wide Web.

Summary

This hour introduces the term *word processing* and what word processing can do for businesses and individuals. Word-processing applications are better suited at some jobs than others. Database, spreadsheet, and presentation design programs each have their specialties.

Word 97's new features make it worth the investment in both money and learning time. As you polish your skills in upcoming chapters, you will appreciate the work of a whole fleet of programmers who asked and answered, "How do people want a word processing application to work?"

Hour 2, "Begin at the Beginning: Installing Word 97," will give you the skills you need to start new documents, and to open files that have already been saved. You'll also be introduced to Word's wizards—tools that automate the process of creating great letters and other documents.

Q&A

Q No one else in my organization has upgraded to Word 97. Will I have trouble sharing documents with someone who hasn't upgraded?

A With the properly installed converters, you should be able to save your documents in an earlier version of Word. Word 97 has some enhancements over previous versions; the converters try to match the features as closely as possible. You may want to shy away from using some of the special graphic effects if the document must be shared and modified between versions.

Q I clicked the Web browser tool, but I didn't connect to the Internet. What did I do wrong?

A Simply having a Web browser is not enough to get connected. You must have either a modem that is connected to a phone line or a connection through lines maintained by your business or organization. If you're connecting through a modem, you will need to subscribe to an Internet service provider (ISP) such as America Online or CompuServe, or have a dial-up connection for direct Internet access. Hour 24 explains more about this process and lists several ISPs.

Hour **2**

Begin at the Beginning: Installing Word 97

This hour explains the essentials you'll need to know about installing Word. You don't have to be a computer expert to install Word; Windows 95 has tools to simplify software installations.

The highlights of this hour include

- ☐ The easy steps to installing Word 97
- ☐ Whether to choose the Typical or the Custom installation

Installing Word 97

Installing software used to be a frightening process, and most people found themselves calling the professionals when it came time to put new software on their systems.

Some people remember those days, but today installations are a simple process. Before you pay a professional or bother a neighbor, give it a try! Whether you're installing the entire Office 97 package or Word 97 by itself, the steps are the same.

Almost every installation requires you to know two things:

☐ Whether you have enough room on your hard drive to install the program

☐ What drive you're installing from

Is There Enough Space to Install Word?

If you're installing the complete Office 97 Professional Suite, the program calls for 191MB (megabytes) of free hard drive space. If you are installing only Word 97, you'll need about 32MB of free hard drive space. When you perform the installation, Word will warn you if you don't have enough disk space for the options you choose.

There is also an easy way to find out whether you have enough free space before you head into the installation process. Most people install to the primary hard drive C:. To find out whether there is enough space on C: to install Office or Word, complete the following steps:

1. Double-click the My Computer icon on the Windows desktop.

NEW TERM   To *double-click* means to press the left mouse button twice very quickly. The term *click* refers to pressing the left mouse button once.

2. When My Computer opens, all the drives on your computer appear as icons (see Figure 2.1).

Figure 2.1.

My Computer shows all the drives on your computer.

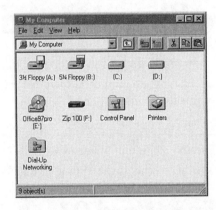

3. *Right-click* the [C:] icon. This brings up a pop-up menu with the Properties option at the bottom.

NEW TERM   *Right-click* means to point to an item and click it once with the right mouse button.

When you click Properties, a chart appears giving you a visual image of the amount of free and used space on drive C:. You need to look at the chunk of free space to see whether it is enough for your installation. Figure 2.2 shows that there are 41.9MB of free space on this system. There would be enough space to install Word, but not the entire Office suite.

Figure 2.2.

*The [C:] Properties
dialog displays the
amount of free disk space
on the c: Drive.*

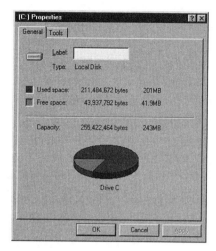

CAUTION

You always need some free space on your hard drive for programs to
operate properly. When calculating whether you have enough space for
an installation, allow for at least 10MB more than the program requires.
For example, if Word 97 requires 32MB of space, you should add
another 10MB for a total of 42MB to do the installation and still have
enough free space to operate. If you don't have enough free space, you
may want to check with someone about installing a larger or second hard
drive. This system shows 41.9MB free, which is probably enough space to
make it work.

If you're tight on disk space, you can always do a Custom installation for a slightly trimmed-
down version of Word or Office that doesn't include every available option.

After you determine that you have enough space on your hard drive, it's time to begin the
installation process. When installing from a CD-ROM, place the Office 97 or Word 97
CD-ROM in the CD-ROM drive. For floppy disk installation, place disk 1 in the 3½"
floppy disk drive.

TIME SAVER

Before starting an installation, it is a good idea to close any programs you
have open. Do not exit Windows, however. You must be in Windows to
perform the installation.

Starting the Installation Through the Control Panel

The instructions included here are for installing Word 97 as an individual software package, but the full Office 97 installation works the same way. With Office 97, you have a few more choices to make.

1. Insert the Word 97 CD-ROM in the CD-ROM drive or disk 1 of the 3$^{1/2}$" installation disks in the floppy drive.
2. Select Settings from the Start menu and choose Control Panel (see Figure 2.3).

Figure 2.3.

The first place to go is Control Panel.

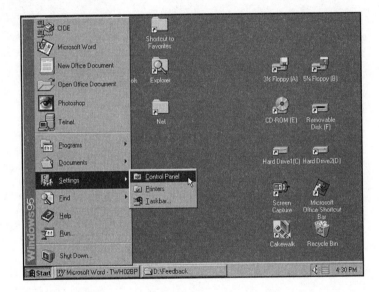

3. Double-click Add/Remove Programs.
4. Select Install from the Install/Uninstall tab.
5. You are asked to insert the first installation floppy disk or CD-ROM. If you have already done so, click Next. If not, insert the disk or CD-ROM, then click Next.

   Windows looks first in the floppy drives and then in the CD-ROM drive to see where you have a program to install (see Figure 2.4). In this example, Windows found the file in the CD-ROM drive—that is the E: drive on this computer. Windows searches your CD-ROM or floppy disk to locate the file that runs the installation.

6. Click Finish.
7. You will get a message that the Setup program is starting.

2

Figure 2.4.

Windows looks for the file it needs to install Word.

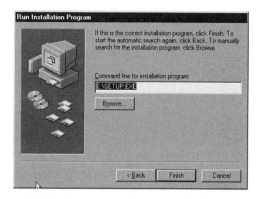

Identifying Yourself

In this stage of the installation process, Word asks questions about you and your software. After the Welcome screen appears, click Continue to start into the next phase of the installation.

You are asked to type your name and, if applicable (and you feel so inclined), the name of your organization. Do so and then click OK. The next screen asks you to verify your software purchase by entering the CD Key, as in Figure 2.5. This number can be found on the back of your Word 97 CD case. With floppy disk installation, you'll be prompted for a serial number. Check the materials that came with the disks for your serial number.

Figure 2.5.

Identifying your software.

The installation program then identifies your product ID number. You should write this number down in case you ever have trouble getting Word to start. The number is available in Word's Help menu under the About option. This is a number Microsoft asks for if you call for product support.

Putting Word Where You Want It

Now that Word knows who you are, you need to decide where to install it. Figure 2.6 is the
next screen that comes up in the installation process. A drive and folder are suggested for the
location of the Word program. If that's where you want Word, you're all set to go. You may
have other plans, however.

Figure 2.6.

*Choosing a place to
install Word.*

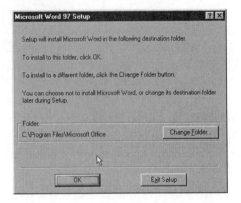

If you have two hard drives and your advanced checking revealed that you don't have enough
space on the proposed drive (usually C:), you can specify another location to install Word.
Click Change Folder. Inside the Change Folder dialog, you can select another drive from the
drop-down list under Drives or select a different folder from the Folders list shown in
Figure 2.7.

Figure 2.7.

*Changing Word's
installation location.*

Weighing Your Options

You've made it this far, and now the critical choices begin. You are asked to choose between
the Typical and the Custom installations (see Figure 2.8). Some of the decisions will be based
on how much room you have on your hard disk.

2

Figure 2.8.

Choose the Typical or Custom installation.

Typical Installation

In a Typical installation of Word 97, here's what you get:

- ☐ Program files needed to run Word
- ☐ Microsoft Graph 8.0
- ☐ Clip Gallery
- ☐ The spelling and grammar checker
- ☐ Some of the converters and filters
- ☐ Some of the help files
- ☐ Some of the wizards and templates
- ☐ Some of the Office tools

Here's what you don't get:

- ☐ WordArt
- ☐ Web page authoring tools

If you want a quick and easy installation, the Typical installation is your best bet. The most commonly used features are added and consideration is given to minimizing the amount of disk space required for Word. You can always go back and add features at another time. If you need features that are not available in the Typical installation, such as the Web page authoring tools, you may want to move on to the Custom installation to avoid having to install them later.

Custom Installation

In the custom installation choice, the benefits are

- ☐ Full control over what options are installed
- ☐ The chance to select all of the Word options for a full installation

The Custom installation method is the only way to get the whole package. If you have enough hard disk space, you'll probably want to choose Custom and opt for Select All. If you don't have space, you'll need to be a little more selective. Figure 2.9 shows the options that come up when you click the Custom button. The preset options are the same as those in the Typical install.

Figure 2.9.

Custom install options.

Describes a selected feature

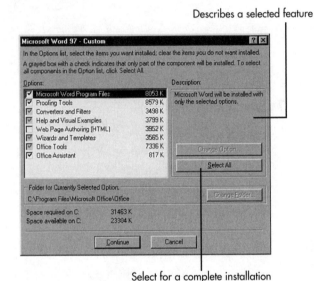

Select for a complete installation

The checkboxes are for groups of features that Word will install. If you click a box that is checked, the check is removed. Click an unchecked box to place a checkmark in it. Only options with checks beside them will be installed. As you begin adding or removing options, you get a tally at the bottom left of the Custom install screen that notes space required and space available. This refers to hard disk space. If the space required exceeds the space available, you're trying to install more options than you have hard disk space for.

In Figure 2.9, some of the boxes are checked, but they are slightly grayed. This means that some of the features under these options will be installed but others won't. To see what other options you have to choose from, do the following:

1. Click an option's name (not the checkbox). For example, click Converters and Filters.

2. Click the Change Option button.

3. Two more grayed boxes appear for the Text Converters and Graphics Filters options.

2

4. Click one of the option names (for example, Text Converters), then click the Change Option button.

5. The Text Converters options are displayed. Check the ones you want to install. Uncheck the ones you don't need.

6. Click OK to set these options and return to the previous screen where you can then repeat the process for Graphics Filters.

Converters and Filters

The Converters and Filters option is grouped into Text Converters and Graphics Filters. This is one place you can save yourself space if you have an idea what kind of files you will use in Word. The following are standard with the Text Converters option if you leave it as is:

- ☐ Word 6.0/95 Export Converter
- ☐ Microsoft Excel Converter
- ☐ Word 6.0/95 for Windows/Macintosh
- ☐ Word 97 for Windows/Macintosh
- ☐ Recover Text Converter

Converters are like foreign language translators. If you don't know the language and don't have a translator, you can't read or write in that language. The same applies to Word. It needs translators to read WordPerfect files and to write Word files in WordPerfect language. In addition to the ones already selected, you can choose from any or all of these converters:

- ☐ Word for Windows 2.0
- ☐ Word for Macintosh 4.0–5.1
- ☐ Works for Windows 3.0 and 4.0
- ☐ WordPerfect 5.x and 6.x (the x stands for every version such as 5.1, 5.2, and so on)
- ☐ Lotus 1-2-3
- ☐ Lotus Notes
- ☐ Text with Layout
- ☐ HTML

If you are moving to Word from one of the other word processors listed, you definitely want to install the converter for that program so you can use your old files.

Perhaps you work with others who use WordPerfect or Word for Macintosh, and you need to share files. You'll need to install converters for these programs if you want to read and write in their languages. If you're going to create or read Web documents, be sure to include the HTML converter so you can speak the language of the Web.

When you've made all the necessary changes to the Text Converters option, click OK. You'll be returned to the Converters and Filters screen where you can select Graphics Filters. Click the Change Option button to review and change the Graphics Filters options.

Graphics Filters are much like text converters in that they translate graphic (picture) files so Word can recognize them. Half the fun of Word 97 is using the new graphic capabilities. Many of the standard graphic file types are included in the Typical installation, but you can install them all by clicking the Select All button, or you can include any of these additional filters:

- ☐ Truevision Targa
- ☐ AutoCAD DXF
- ☐ Micrografx Designer/Draw
- ☐ CorelDRAW
- ☐ Computer Graphics Metafile
- ☐ PC Paintbrush PCX
- ☐ Kodak Photo CD

Almost certainly, you will want to include the PC Paintbrush PCX option. This is one of the most commonly used graphic formats. The Windows Paint program can create PCX files.

More and more collections of photographs are being produced on CD-ROMs. Many of these are in Kodak Photo CD format. There are even photo developers that convert your personal slides, negatives, or photographs to a Photo CD. If you anticipate using photographic inserts, this is an option you might want to include.

Help and Visual Examples

Word gives you its own help under the Typical installation. If you're a WordPerfect convert or if you plan to use Word's new Visual Basic programming language, WordPerfect and Visual Basic are two additional help options you can select from Help and Visual Examples.

Web Page Authoring (HTML)

The Web Page Authoring option is not available unless you select it. There is sure to be someone in your household or office who will expect to find these features on your computer—it's one of the biggest draws of Word 97. Of course, if you have no interest in the Web tools and you don't have to share your computer, it's completely up to you whether you include these features.

Wizards and Templates

Word has several wizards that guide you through the process of creating a letter, a memo, or other types of documents. Hour 3, "Getting Around in Word," will show you how wizards automate building documents and publications. They dress the documents up with just a little help from you. Word's templates also help make document creation a snap. Hour 12, "A Matter of Style," discusses templates and how to use them. In the standard setup, you get the following templates and wizards:

☐ Faxes

☐ Letters

☐ Memos

☐ Resumes

You can also add templates and wizards for reports, Web pages, and newsletters.

Office Tools

If you have the space to select all of the Office tools, you will probably want to. Options like Microsoft Graph and Microsoft Photo Editor are programs that take up a lot of space, but are great enhancements that you'll appreciate. Again, it's a matter of choice and space. Read the Description box to find out what each option does (see Figure 2.10). When you finish making all of the option choices, click OK.

Figure 2.10.

A description is provided for each option.

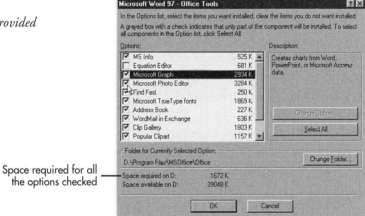

Space required for all the options checked

If you decide later that you didn't install all the features you need, you can use the Add/Remove Programs option or run Setup again to add or remove Word features.

JUST A MINUTE

It's a Wrap!

The installation process begins to copy files to your hard drive. If you're installing over a previous version of Word, the installation program tries to retain your previous settings such as AutoText entries and macros.

You may get a message that says the installation needs to modify your Autoexec.bat file. Click OK, and the installer takes care of the rest. A message will appear saying that Word was successfully installed.

You're ready to start Word and create your first documents. Hour 3 shows you how to do that.

Summary

This hour explains how to install Word 97 from disks or CD-ROM. You don't have to be a computer expert to install your own software.

The next hour shows you how to start a new Word document, open an existing Word document, and navigate in Word 97's new interface.

Q&A

Q If I have Office 95 on my computer, will Office 97 replace Office 95 when I install it?

A Yes. During the installation, Office 95 will be replaced. You will have only Office 97 when the installation is complete. There are ways to get around this if you think you need both versions. Install Office 97 in a directory other than the default directory. It is not advisable, but you can do it.

Q Will I need as much free hard drive space if Office 97 is copying over Office 95?

A No. It will take up more space than 95 did because of the added features, but you will not need an additional 191MB. If you are not sure whether you have enough free hard drive space, go ahead and start the installation. The installation program looks at your hard drive and tells you whether you have enough space to install the program.

Q A computer guru in our office installed my Office 97, and I can't use the ClipArt Gallery. I get some kind of error message about missing components. How can I get the clip art?

A You may, indeed, be missing the components needed to run the ClipArt Gallery (now called the Clip Gallery because it also includes photos, sound, and video clips). Run Word's Setup and use Add/Remove to pick up any components that weren't installed the first time. As for the Clip Gallery, you'll find it under the Office tools. You'll probably also want to make sure that Popular Clipart is checked if you want more graphics.

2

Q **I'd like to use Word 97, but I just don't have the hard drive space to install it. Is there any other way to run it?**

A If you have the CD-ROM version, you can run Word directly from the CD without installing it. This is a great solution for laptops with a CD-ROM drive but limited hard disk space. If you have a slow CD-ROM drive, it may run too slowly to be tolerable, but it's worth a try. Just follow these steps:

1. Insert the Word 97 CD in the CD-ROM drive.

2. Double-click the My Computer icon on the desktop.

3. Double-click the icon for the CD-ROM drive.

4. Double-click the Office folder.

5. Double-click the `Winword.exe` file.

Word will start and you can do everything you could if it were installed on your hard drive. Just be aware that anything you run from a CD will run much slower than it would from a hard drive.

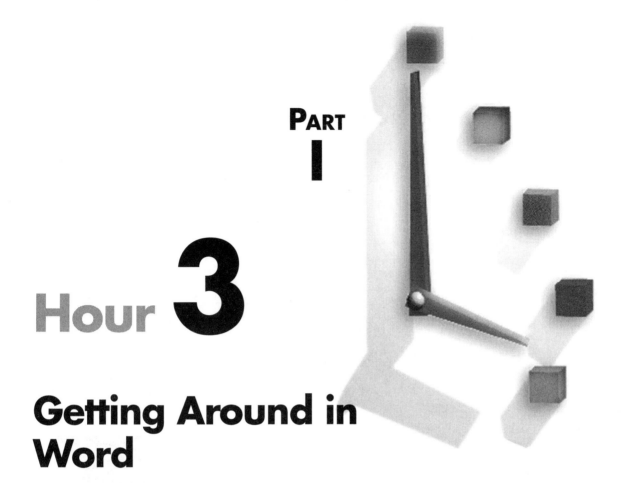

Hour **3**

Getting Around in Word

In this hour, Word 97's new face is introduced. You'll find instructions on starting new documents and opening previously stored documents. One of the easiest ways to get started is by opening and using one of Word's wizards. Word 97 offers toolbars, icons, rulers, scrollbars, and other visual clues to help you get your work done. The revamped look of Word brings order and consistency that make it easy to use.

The highlights of this hour include

- ☐ Choosing your favorite way to start Word
- ☐ Creating a new document
- ☐ Opening a stored document
- ☐ How wizards help you build professional-looking documents
- ☐ How Word 97's face is different from previous versions
- ☐ Why you might use a menu command or shortcut keys instead of the toolbar icon that does the same thing
- ☐ How to move quickly from place to place in a long document
- ☐ When it would help to use the Document Map feature

Starting a New Document

Using the Office Shortcut bar shown in Figure 3.1 is a matter of personal preference. Some people don't like the confusion of having it overlay every application they work in. Others find that the quick access to other programs is worth the loss of screen space. The Office Shortcut bar is probably the easiest way to start Word.

Figure 3.1.

The Office 97 Shortcut bar.

Previous Office Shortcut toolbars showed individual icons for Microsoft applications such as Word and Excel. The New Office Document icon is one-stop shopping for creating a new document in any of the Office applications.

When you click New Office Document from the Office Shortcut bar, you won't find tabs labeled Word, Excel, Access, or PowerPoint. Instead, the tabs are grouped by task types (see Figure 3.2). To open Word and start a new document, click the Blank Document icon, then click OK.

Figure 3.2.

Tabs included in New Office Document.

Document tabs

Just a Minute

The General tab gives you the option of opening a blank database (Access), document (Word), workbook (Excel), presentation (PowerPoint), or binder (Binder). Templates you create also show up as selections in the General tab. Predesigned templates and wizards can be selected from the other tabs.

3

The New Office Document icon on the Office Shortcut bar is also an option in the first tier of the Start menu (called the Startup Group). Selecting New Office Document, as shown in Figure 3.3, brings up Word with a new document ready to go.

Figure 3.3.

New Office Document from the Start menu.

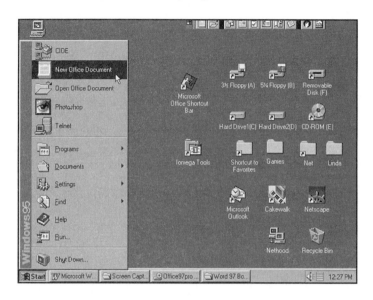

You always have the option of opening Word through the Start menu at the bottom-left corner of the screen and cascading through the Programs menu until you find Microsoft Word. Highlight Microsoft Word, release the mouse button, and Word starts. Figure 3.4 shows how to open Word from the Start menu.

Figure 3.4.

Starting Word from Programs on the Start menu.

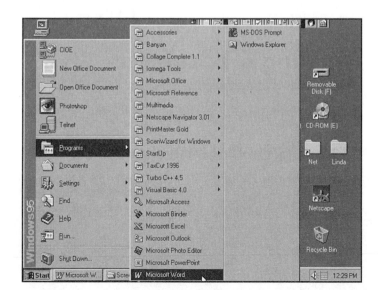

The menu options shown in Figure 3.4 will not match exactly what you see on your computer. Everyone uses different software programs, and only the ones installed on your computer show up under Programs.

Whether you prefer to start Word through the Office Shortcut bar or the Start menu, Word opens with a new blank page onscreen (see Figure 3.5).

Figure 3.5.

Word's startup screen.

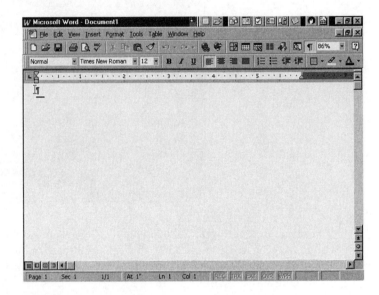

You're ready to begin creating a new document.

Opening a Document

There are several ways to open a previously stored document. You can start Word and then open a document, or you can locate the document and start Word and the document at the same time.

Opening a Document with Word

If you have a document stored on your hard drive or a floppy disk, you can open it in much the same way you start a new document. As with everything else in Windows, there is more than one way to open a document. You can either use the Open Office Document option from the Office Shortcut bar or select Open Office Document from the Start menu.

3

You can also locate the file on your hard drive or floppy disk using My Computer, then double-click it to start Word and open the file at the same time. Say your sister hands you a floppy disk containing a letter she's written to your grandmother and asks you to add a few lines to the letter before mailing it. Follow these steps to add to the document:

1. Double-click My Computer from the Windows desktop.

2. Insert your sister's disk in the A: drive and double-click the icon for the 3^1/$_2$" Floppy drive [A:].

3. Double-click Letter to Granny to open Word and your sister's letter.

Opening a Document After Starting Word

 From Word's startup screen, you can open a document by double-clicking the toolbar icon that looks like a file folder or by selecting Open from the File menu (see Figure 3.6).

Figure 3.6.

*Opening a document
from the File menu.*

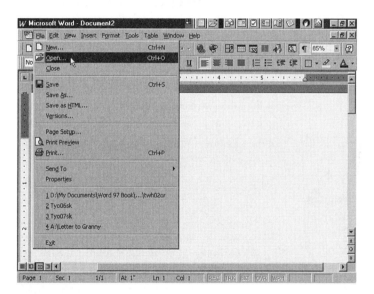

When the Open dialog box appears, you will see the words My Documents in the Look in box, shown in Figure 3.7. When Word is installed, it tells the program to look first in a folder called My Documents to find files. To open Letter to Granny, click the Look in box to display the places other than My Documents that Word can look for files. Select the 3^1/$_2$" floppy (A:) button; Letter to Granny shows up in the list of filenames.

Figure 3.7.

The Open dialog box.

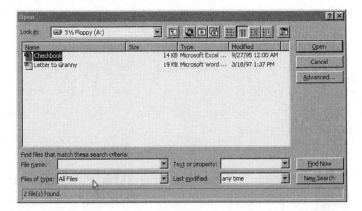

In Figure 3.7, you will notice that All Files is listed in the Files of type box. This allows you to see all the files stored in a location. If you want to see only Word documents, select Word documents from the drop-down list next to the Files of type box.

To open a file from the Open dialog box:

1. Select the drive location from the Look in box.

2. Select the folder where the file is stored on that drive. In this example, the file is not stored inside a folder, so there is no need to look further.

3. Click the filename in the file list and click the Open button, or double-click the filename to open the file.

CAUTION

> The My Documents folder shows only the files stored in this folder. Some people panic and think they've lost all their other files; however, when you're inside a folder, you only see what's stored there. Click the Up One Level button to move out of My Documents. All the folders (directories) on your hard drive show up.

Using Word's Wizards

A great way to create a new document is by using Word's wizards. Wizards automate many of the steps for building a professional-looking document. There are wizards for:

☐ Letters

☐ Memos

☐ Newsletters

3

☐ Reports

☐ Legal pleadings

☐ Fax covers

☐ Web pages

Agenda wizard and Calendar wizard also are available on the Office 97 Installation CD under ValuPak/Template/Word. If you installed from floppy disks, you're not out of luck. These and many other Office enhancements can be accessed from Microsoft's Internet site. Instructions for getting to its site are included in Appendix A, "Additional Resources."

The toolbar button that looks like a blank sheet of paper starts a new document if Word is already running. If you hold the mouse over the icon without clicking it, a ToolTip appears that says New. This is the quickest way to start a new document, but it bypasses the steps to get to the wizards. You'll have to go the long route through File | New. This brings up tabbed folders that include the wizards. The Resume wizard, for example, is under the Other Documents tab.

NEW TERM   *ToolTips* are pop-up messages that tell what a toolbar button does if it is selected.

It is easy to use the wizards. Just follow the instructions onscreen. Figure 3.8 appears when you double-click the Newsletter wizard from the Publications tab. In five quick steps, the wizard builds the framework for a newsletter. Figure 3.8 is the first of the five screens. Click Next to advance to step 2.

Figure 3.8.

The Newsletter wizard.

Step 2 in Figure 3.9 gives you three style choices, Professional, Contemporary, and Elegant, and a sample layout for each style. You can also select whether the newsletter will be in black and white or color. Click Next to move to step 3.

Figure 3.9.
The Newsletter
wizard—step 2.

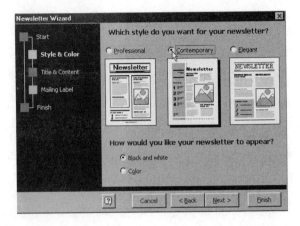

Step 3 asks for a newsletter title and asks whether you want to insert a date, a volume and issue number, or both, as in Figure 3.10. Click Next to go to step 4.

Figure 3.10.
The Newsletter
wizard—step 3.

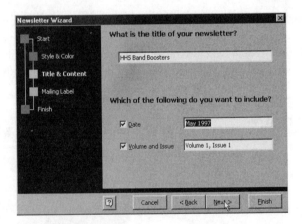

Step 4 allows you to leave a space on the back of the newsletter for a mailing label, as shown in Figure 3.11. Click Next to move to the final step.

3

Figure 3.11.
*The Newsletter
wizard—step 4.*

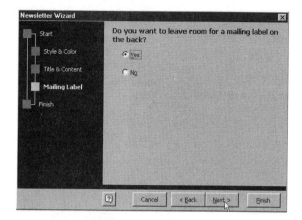

Finally, you've reached the Finish screen. You can click the Back button to move one screen back and make any necessary changes. If everything is correct, click Finish as shown in Figure 3.12.

Figure 3.12.
*The Newsletter
wizard—step 5.*

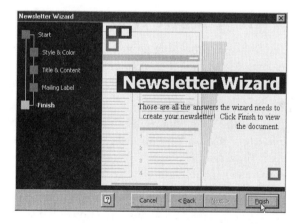

When you have finished all five steps, Word presents you with a newsletter sample as in Figure 3.13. There are instructions in the document on how to lay out the different sections.

Figure 3.13.

The finished framework for a newsletter.

Working with the New Word Interface

The first word-processing programs provided few visual clues to their functions and capabilities. A blank screen usually appeared when you started the program; until you learned a series of keyboard commands, it was pretty tough to figure out what you were doing without the dictionary-sized manual.

One reason that programs like Word 97 don't come with big instruction books is that software companies have learned to harness the power of today's computers to give you as many visual clues as possible. It's not that they didn't want to give you these clues, there just wasn't enough oomph in older systems to do it.

When you start Word 97, the icons help you get started without a manual. Figure 3.14 shows Word's opening screen, with many of the interface's components pointed out.

Title Bar

The Title bar displays the name of the program you're using (Microsoft Word) and the document name. In this case, it says `Document1` because it is a new document that has never been saved. You'll learn how to save and name files in Hour 9, "Managing Your Documents."

3

Figure 3.14.

Word 97 opens with
many visual clues.

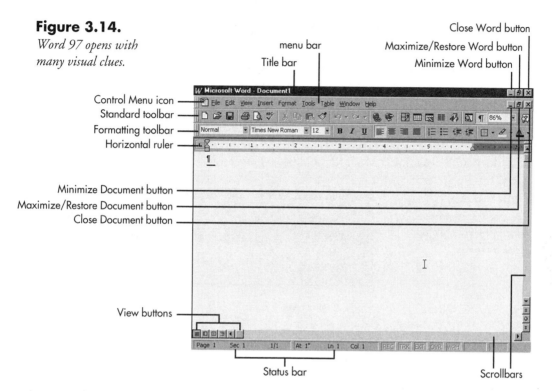

Control Menu icon
Standard toolbar
Formatting toolbar
Horizontal ruler

Minimize Document button
Maximize/Restore Document button
Close Document button

View buttons

Title bar

menu bar

Close Word button
Maximize/Restore Word button
Minimize Word button

Status bar

Scrollbars

Menu Bar

As you click any word on the menu bar, a drop-down list appears, outlining all related tasks
that can be performed under that heading. If you see an ellipsis beside a menu option, it
indicates that clicking this option brings up other options in a separate dialog. An arrowhead
at the right edge of a menu selection indicates that another menu is revealed when you click
this option.

Step-Up

There are additions to the Word 97 File menu that relate to the new connectivity
and file-sharing functions within Word. The Saving as HTML and Send To
options expand Word's capabilities to link to other resources. Versions is a great
editing tool that allows you to save multiple versions of the same document. This
tool is discussed in more detail in Hour 21, "Bookshelf and Word's Editing Tools."

The Control Menu and Control Buttons

As you work with Word, you'll find more than one way to do just about everything. The menu bar is one good example. The Control menu and the Control buttons on either end of the menu bar (see Figure 3.15) can perform the same functions. If you prefer using a menu, clicking a button, or using a keyboard command, you can have it your way.

One of the nice touches that Microsoft added to Office 97 was to coordinate pictures on the menus to match the icons on the toolbars. There are pictures on the Control menu that match the Restore, Minimize, Maximize, and Close buttons.

Figure 3.15.

The Control menu and Control buttons can do the same things.

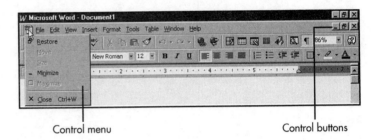

Control menu   Control buttons

Clicking on the minus sign minimizes the document. That just means that it reduces the document to a small window of its own at the bottom of the Word screen. The Restore button looks like overlaying windows. It places a frame around each open document and reduces its size so the open documents do not fill the entire Word work area. This allows you to view more than one document at a time, and to resize the documents. To resize the document, do the following:

1. Move the mouse across any edge of a document window. A double-sided arrow appears (see Figure 3.16).
2. When the arrow is visible, click and drag the edge of the window toward the center of the screen to make the window smaller, or drag it away from the center to make it larger.

To arrange the documents so they are all visible, select Arrange All from the Window menu. This tiles the document windows like puzzle pieces. Click a document's Maximize button to fill Word's work area. The other windows are no longer visible. Clicking the Close button closes the document. If you have not previously saved the file, Word will ask whether you want to name and save the file. If you want to save the document for later use, you should store it and give it a name. If the file has already been saved and given a name, you will be prompted to save any recent changes.

3

Figure 3.16.

The Restore button lets you move and resize document windows.

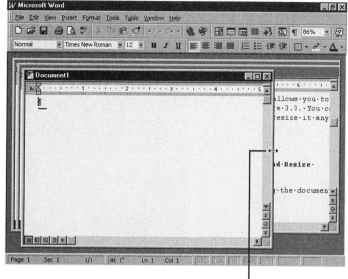

Resizing arrow

CAUTION

Word does not close when you click the Close button on the menu bar. Only the document closes. There is another set of control buttons just above those on the menu bar. These buttons perform the same actions, but apply to the Word program rather than the document in which you are working.

☐ Minimize reduces Word to an icon on the Windows Taskbar (see Figure 3.17). Click the icon one time to bring Word back up to where you were last working in the document.

☐ Restore puts a frame around Word so that you can resize or move it anywhere onscreen.

☐ Close ends your session of Word and closes all open documents.

It can be frustrating to close Word entirely when you want to close only the current document window.

TIME SAVER

The control buttons look and work the same in every Windows application.

Figure 3.17.

*Word is minimized to
the Windows Taskbar.*

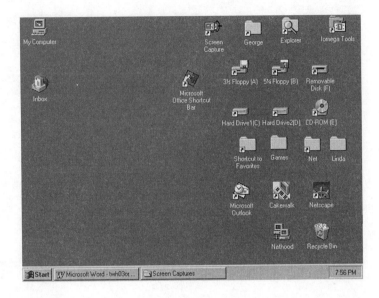

Keyboard Shortcuts

If you see Ctrl and a letter to the far right of a menu option, it signals a keyboard shortcut
for this function. Ctrl+N, for example, starts a new document. For people who work better
without the mouse or are avid shortcut users, keyboard shortcuts can be real time-savers.
Most of the shortcuts use Ctrl and a prominent letter from the option name so they can be
remembered easily. Table 3.1 shows a list of menu options and their corresponding Ctrl key
shortcuts.

Table 3.1. Word's keyboard shortcuts.

Menu option	Keyboard shortcut
File | New	Ctrl+N
File | Open	Ctrl+O
File | Save	Ctrl+S
Edit | Undo	Ctrl+Z
Edit | Repeat	Ctrl+Y
Edit | Cut	Ctrl+X
Edit | Copy	Ctrl+C
Edit | Paste	Ctrl+V
Edit | Select All	Ctrl+A
Edit | Find	Ctrl+F
Edit | Replace	Ctrl+H

3

TIME SAVER

Using the Alt key in conjunction with any of the underlined letters on the menu bar opens that menu. For example, Alt+F opens the File menu. Pressing the underlined letter of an option on the menu selects that option. Pressing Alt+F and then pressing S saves a file. You can select any menu option with an Alt key combination.

CAUTION

When you are using the Alt key shortcuts, do not press the Alt key a second time before typing the second letter. You would not, for instance, press Alt+C after Alt+F to close a file. Just press C.

TIME SAVER

Make a list on a 3×5 notecard of one Ctrl key and two or three Alt key shortcuts. Tape it to your monitor and use the shortcuts during your next few sessions of Word. When you have these memorized, make a new card with new shortcuts and repeat the process. You'll be on your way to becoming a power user.

 A *power user* is someone who knows a software program well enough to get full benefits from its features and can operate quickly and efficiently within the program.

Toolbars

The addition of toolbars has made every application easier to use. Standardizing toolbars so they look similar in every Office 97 application has also lowered the learning curve. Each version of Word brings a new toolbar or two with more visual clues. Every toolbar is grouped by similar tasks. The toolbar that is usually seen under the menu bar is the Standard toolbar, which contains many of the items in the File, Edit, Insert, Tools, and Table menus. The Formatting toolbar, below the Standard toolbar, includes text and paragraph formatting options (see Figure 3.18).

Figure 3.18.

The Standard and Formatting toolbars.

These are by no means the only toolbars. If you select View | Toolbars, you will see a long list of all the toolbars currently available. Click the ones you want to display. You probably won't want to have all of them visible all of the time, as you can see from Figure 3.19.

Figure 3.19.

Too many open toolbars leave little room to work.

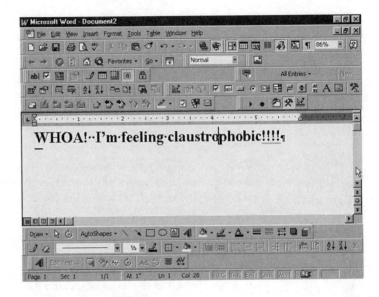

When you first display some of the toolbars, they appear in their own boxes with Close buttons (see Figure 3.20). To place a toolbar in a more permanent location (called *docking*), perform these steps:

1. Click and hold down the left mouse button on the toolbar's Title bar.

2. Drag the outlined image to the top, bottom, or sides of the screen.

3. Release the mouse button. With a little maneuvering, the toolbar can be placed (docked) where you want it.

Other toolbars will automatically dock and may not be completely visible or may cover existing toolbar buttons. If this happens, you can click the double bar at the left edge of the toolbar and drag it to another location or into a box of its own on the typing screen.

Hour 11, "Customizing Word to the Way You Work," goes into greater detail about using and customizing toolbars.

3

Figure 3.20.

*The Drawing toolbar
floating onscreen.*

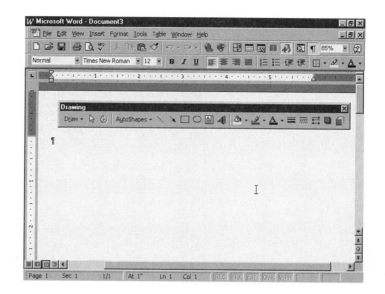

Toolbar Buttons

Toolbar buttons are one of the better visual clues in Word 97. In some cases, the buttons work like on/off switches. An example is the button that activates the Drawing toolbar. Slide your mouse across the Standard toolbar. As you position the mouse over an item, it gives the Tool-Tip for that button. When you click the Drawing button, it appears with a lighted background, and the Drawing toolbar is turned on. It is then visible onscreen. Click the button again, and the switch turns off, making the Drawing toolbar disappear.

Scrollbars

Scrollbars are useful when you work with large documents. The vertical and horizontal scrollbars allow you to see parts of the document that are not currently visible. The single arrows on the scrollbars move through the document (up/down or left/right) in small increments. Dragging the scroll button down on the vertical scrollbar quickly moves to another page farther down in the document (see Figure 3.21). As you drag the button down, a ToolTip reveals the page number location at each position on the scrollbar.

Figure 3.21.

Scrollbars help you move around quickly in a document.

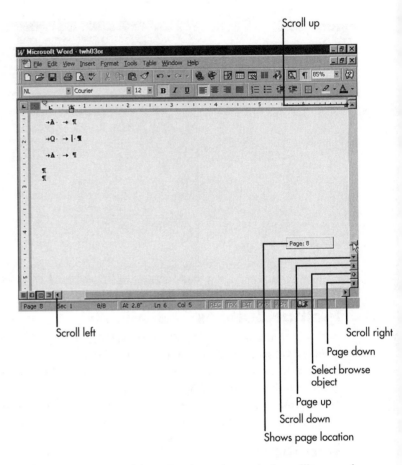

The double-headed arrows (Previous Page and Next Page) on the vertical scrollbar can do more than move up or down a page in Word 97. They can be customized to go places in different ways. The button between the two sets of arrows (the Select Browse object) lets you decide whether you want to move down by page or by one of the other landmarks in the document, such as headings, graphics, and tables. To change the Browse object to footnotes:

1. Click the Select Browse Object button.
2. Select Browse by Footnote, as in Figure 3.22.
3. Click the Previous button or Next button to move between footnotes in the document.

Figure 3.22.

Selecting a Browse object other than Browse by Page.

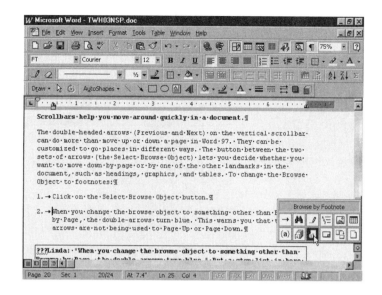

When you change the Browse object to something other than Browse by Page, the double-arrows turn blue. This warns you that the arrows are not being used for Page Up or Page Down.

KEYBOARD SHORTCUT

Ctrl+Home moves to the beginning of a document. Ctrl+End moves to the end of a document.

Document Map

A new feature in Word 97 is the Document Map. It gives yet one more way to wend your way quickly through long documents. Document Map lets you view your document and its outline at the same time. Activate Document Map by either clicking the Document Map icon on the Standard toolbar or selecting View | Document Map from the menu.

There's only one catch: Word looks for paragraphs that are formatted using certain heading styles to build the outline. It tries to pick up headings from documents that are formatted in other ways, but is not always successful in catching headings that were formatted manually or with other styles.

You can quickly jump to another area of your document by clicking one of the headings in the Document Map (see Figure 3.23). With the boundaries set between the Document Map and the document itself, you may not be able to read the entire heading. Holding the mouse over the title reveals the complete heading. Click a heading to jump to that place in the document.

Figure 3.23.

Using the Document Map to jump to another location in a document.

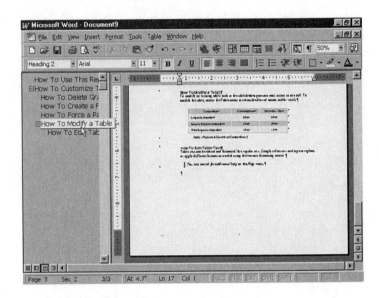

To get out of Document Map view, click the Document Map icon on the toolbar or deselect Document Map from the View Menu.

Summary

This hour explains how to maneuver in Word 97. There are details on starting new documents, opening previously saved documents, and using Word's wizards for quick and easy document creations. Menus, toolbars, and shortcuts let you decide which route to take. Menus are pull-down lists of groups of related tasks. The File menu, for example, lists most of the actions you would perform that relate to a file—such as printing, saving, and closing. Toolbars offer quick, one-step access to many of the menu bar functions. Shortcut key combinations provide a third way to execute commands without using the mouse.

Word 97 has new navigation tools that allow you to get around quickly in long documents. Select Browse Object on the vertical scrollbar to browse one page at a time or to browse by other objects in your document such as footnotes and comments. The Document Map provides a visible outline of your document to the left of your typing screen. Clicking a header in the Document Map takes you to that location in your document.

The next hour explains Word 97's many help features. Online help can guide you through any new task.

Q&A

Q If I reference a page frequently, is there a way to get to that page quickly?

A There are several ways. One is to use Go To from the Edit menu and enter the page number, then press Enter. Another way is to click the Select Browse Object, then click the icon that looks like an arrow. This is a shortcut to the same Go To function you access from the Edit menu.

KEYBOARD SHORTCUT

> Remember: Use the keyboard shortcut Ctrl+G to bring up the Go To option without touching the mouse.

Q I don't like having to use the horizontal scrollbar to see both edges of what I'm typing. Is there any way to view everything in a single screen?

A Select Page Width from the options in the Zoom box on the Standard toolbar. This optimizes the view to allow you to see the full line of type.

Q Can I widen the Document Map area so that I can see more of the headings?

A Yes. Position the mouse over the thick line between the left scrollbar and the document until you see a double-sided arrow that displays a ToolTip with the word Resize. When you see the double-arrow, hold down the left mouse button and drag the line to the right until you see as much of the Document Map outline as you need. Giving the Document Map very much space, however, can really cramp your typing area.

Hour 4

Help?!—There's Lots of It in Word 97

This hour delves into the help features that make Word 97 a winner. Help is just a click away for whatever you're trying to do. It comes in so many forms that you'll have to decide which one works best for you. Chock-full of IntelliSense, Word's online help files are another example of "read my mind" in action.

The highlights of this hour include

- ☐ How Office Assistant steps in to help
- ☐ The difference between Contents, Index, and Find
- ☐ How to use the What's This? feature
- ☐ What context-sensitive help can do
- ☐ Accessing Microsoft's Internet site when the questions get tough

Office Assistant

Word's Office Assistant acts like that person in the office who's always running to your aid when you have a computer problem. Clippit, the new Office Assistant, is at your disposal the first time you start Word (see Figure 4.1).

Figure 4.1.

Office Assistant is always at your service.

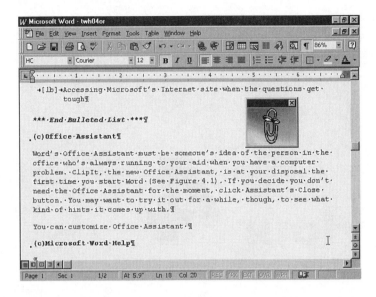

You can customize Office Assistant to offer certain kinds of help and refrain from giving you unsolicited advice. Office Assistant brings up a pop-up menu with an Options selection. If you don't see the menu, click the title bar. When you click Options, you can change some of the ways that Assistant operates (see Figure 4.2).

Figure 4.2.

Change the way Office Assistant works.

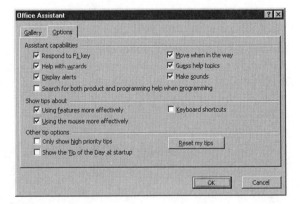

Assistant Capabilities Options

There are many ways to change how Office Assistant operates.

Respond to F1 Key

Nearly every software program uses the *F1 key* to access help. If you check the Respond to F1 key checkbox in the Office Assistant's options, Assistant shows up when you press the F1

4

key. If the Respond to F1 key checkbox is not selected, the normal Help Topics search screens are displayed.

NEW TERM The *F1 key* is one of the numbered function keys usually found across the top of the keyboard. Sometimes the keyboard has an alternate set of function keys either to the right or the left of the standard typing keys. Both sets of keys work in the same way. These keys are preprogrammed by Word to quickly perform specific functions. Other programs may use them for different functions.

Other Assistant Capabilities

Under Assistant Capabilities, you'll find several options that tell Assistant how you want it to function.

☐ Help with wizards—provides help while you're working with most of Word's wizards.

☐ Display alerts—Office Assistant alerts you when it has help to offer.

☐ Search for both product and programming help when programming—offers help when you work with Word's Visual Basic programming, which is the programming behind Word 97 macros.

☐ Move when in the way—scoots Assistant out of the way if you begin to type in the area where Assistant is positioned on the screen.

☐ Guess help topics—lets Assistant figure out what you're trying to do in order to offer solutions.

☐ Make sounds—alerts you with a sound that Assistant has help to offer.

One of Assistant's features that you'll probably disable early on is the Make sounds option. If you're doing lots of things that Assistant thinks it can do better, it will make plenty of noise. People will think you're playing computer games at your workstation, and that's not good! You can keep Assistant working for you without listening to it by unchecking the Make sounds box.

The Guess Help Topics option tells Assistant to watch closely and guess what you're trying to do, then offer suggestions to help you accomplish the task. For example, start typing a letter in a fresh new document. Once you have "Dear So and So," and start to type your opening sentence, Assistant pops up and says, "It looks like you're writing a letter. Would you like help?" as seen in Figure 4.3. If you click the Get help with writing the letter option, you are handed over to a four-step Letter wizard that helps you set up a letter.

Figure 4.3.

Office Assistant watches what you're doing and offers to help.

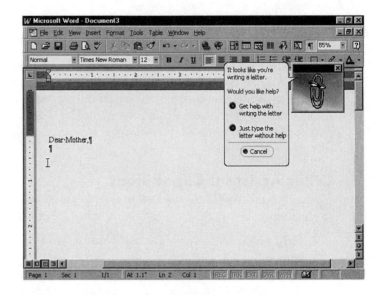

Show Tips About and Other Tip Options

In the Show tips about and Other tip options sections, you can specify what kinds of tips you want Assistant to provide. If you want to see tips on using features more effectively, using the mouse more effectively, or using keyboard shortcuts, check these options.

After you use Word for several weeks and realize you are seeing the same tips over and over at startup, you can uncheck the Show Tips at Startup box. You'll never be slowed down again by the helpful hints unless you reinstate this feature. You can also weed out some of the tips by checking Only show high priority tips.

Changing Assistant's Character

If you're one of those people who changes your screen saver and desktop wallpaper about once a week, you'll like being able to hire a new Assistant when you get tired of Clippit (the animated paper clip). If you have the CD-ROM version of Word or Office and have it in your CD-ROM drive:

1. Click Options in the Assistant pop-up menu and click the Gallery tab. There's an Assistant to fit every taste, from Shakespeare to PowerPup.

2. When you scroll through the options using the Next button and find the one that fits your mood for the day, click OK and Clippit is transformed into your new Assistant.

You can use Assistant as you would any other Help tool. Click Assistant to display a dialog box like the one in Figure 4.4. Type a word or question in the Search box, then click Search.

4

All the entries it can find that might relate to your request are displayed. If you're trying to do a mail merge and need help, you might use Assistant's search in this way:

1. Type How can I do a mail merge? in the Search box.
2. Click Search.

Word is surprisingly quick to respond with a list of possible topics. You will get topics such as

☐ Form letters, envelopes, and labels

☐ Set up a main document for a mail merge

☐ Print or send a mail merge document

Click the one that best answers your question. Assistant reaches out to the Microsoft Word Help database and serves up a Help Topic screen. If you set Assistant to come up with the F1 key, it's just a keystroke away.

Figure 4.4.

Office Assistant is prepared to search.

Type your question here ———

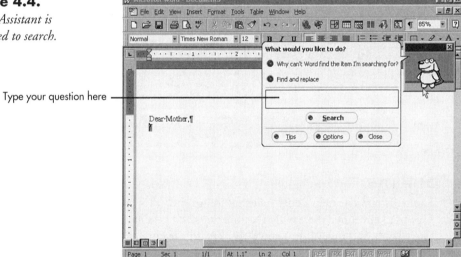

If you decide you don't need the Office Assistant for the moment, click Assistant's Close button. You may want to try it out for awhile, though, to see what kind of hints it comes up with. If you do close it, it is always available from the Help menu under Microsoft Word Help or from the icon at the far right of the Standard toolbar that looks like a talking bubble with a question mark in it.

Step-Up

Office Assistant replaces the Answer wizard used in previous versions of Word.

Help's Contents, Index, and Find

If you're not into animated paper clips or bouncing dots, the traditional help files are still available. From the Help menu, select Contents and Index. This displays a dialog box with three tabbed sections that give you three ways to search, as shown in Figure 4.5. The information you get from help is the same regardless of which way you decide to search, but sometimes it may be easier using one method than another.

Figure 4.5.

Traditional Help with Contents, Index, and Find.

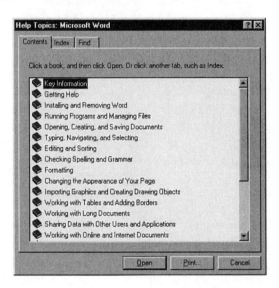

Contents

Contents lays out help under major headings such as Installing and Removing Word or Opening, Creating, and Saving Documents. Each heading has an icon beside it that looks like a book, and indeed, you could think of this feature as a set of help books. When you double-click one of the book titles, the icon appears as an open book with a series of questions listed beneath the title. Some books include subbooks that further categorize the main topic. Double-clicking the question that most clearly matches yours brings up a Help Topics screen.

The Help Topics screens are the real meat of the help information. One of the nice features about help is that you can leave it open while you are trying to do what the Help Topics screen recommends. If the Help screen overlays the area of the screen you're working in, grab the Help title bar by clicking it with the left mouse button and dragging it somewhere else on the screen. Resize the Help window by clicking any of its borders; pull the border in to make the window smaller or pull it out to make the window larger. Grabbing one of the corners and dragging it in or out resizes the window both horizontally and vertically at the same time (see Figure 4.6).

4

Figure 4.6.

Resizing the Help Topics window.

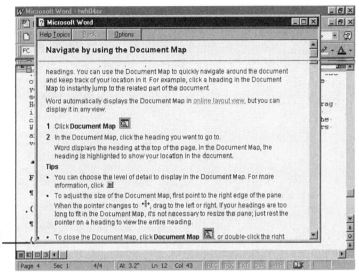

Resize horizontally and vertically from any corner

Help uses a method called *linking* to branch from the Help Topics screen to further information on the subject. The links might branch to

☐ More information screens

☐ Definitions for terms

☐ Show Me demonstrations

☐ Connections to Internet sites

 Linking refers to programming that connects one program to other information, programs, documents, media such as sound, or additional resources. A picture of a hand appears when the mouse is positioned on an icon or word that contains a link. Clicking the link makes the connection, and the additional information appears or an action is initiated. Links are also referred to as *hyperlinks*.

Figure 4.7 shows some of the common elements you might find in a Help Topics screen. Clicking the Help Topics button returns you to the main Help screen. Definitions appear in color with a dashed underline. Links to Internet sites are colored with a solid underline. Show Me instructions have an icon with a bent arrow.

Figure 4.7.

Common elements of the Help Topics screen.

Return to Help Topics

Click for a definition

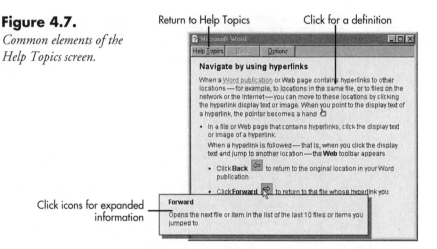

Click icons for expanded information

You can use Contents help feature to get help with mail merge topics. To do so, perform the following steps:

1. Select Contents and Index from the Help menu.

2. Double-click the Assembling Documents with Mail Merge book.

3. Four questions (help topics) and three subbooks are shown in this book. The subbooks contain other help topics. Click one of the topics that relates to your question. For example, click Troubleshoot mail merge to display common problems that people experience when using mail merge.

4. Exit Help Topics by pressing the Esc key or clicking the Close button.

Index

Index works in much the same way as Contents. Instead of grouping related subjects, the words in the search database are indexed. Type the first letter of the term you are searching for in the text box labeled Type the first few letters of the word you're looking for. Index automatically moves to that point in the wordlist (see Figure 4.8). To get a step further down, type the second letter of the word or move down in the list using the scrollbar.

If you know the term or concept you're searching for, Index is an easy way to get there quickly. There is very little difference between Index and Find. After you've tried them both, you may develop a preference for one or the other.

4

Figure 4.8.

Using the wordlist in Index.

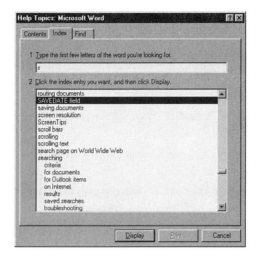

Find

Find looks through every help topic for occurrences of the word you ask it to search for. It might bring up one or several words that contain your search term in one form or another—uppercase, lowercase, parts of words, and so on (see Figure 4.9). It returns a list of all the help topics that contain the word. From the topics list, you get a pretty good idea which one to select to get the answer you want. Double-click the topic to bring it up. You get a more in-depth search with Find, but many of the references may be far afield from what you're after. It might also take you a while to get through the 887 help topics that include the word *document*.

Figure 4.9.

Using Find returns all instances of a word from the help topics.

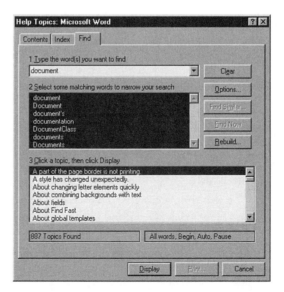

Annotating Help Topics

Regardless of how you get there, while you're in a help topic, you can make notes to yourself for future reference.

1. Select Annotate from the Options menu.

2. The Annotate dialog allows you to make your own notes about a topic (see Figure 4.10).

3. Click Save, and the annotation is filed away for future reference. A small paper clip next to the help topic title shows that there's an annotation stored with this topic.

4. Place your cursor over the paper clip, and you'll notice the picture of a hand. You have just created your own link.

5. Click the hand, and your annotation comes up.

Figure 4.10.

Adding your own help comments with Annotate.

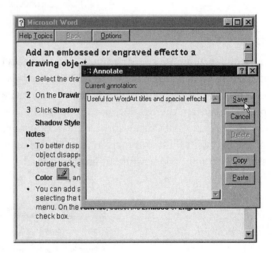

You can also store your favorite help files for quick access. If you find a help topic that you know you will use again, use the following steps to save it:

1. From the help topic you want to reference, select Define Bookmarks from the Options menu.

2. Type in a short name for the bookmark to remind you of what it is; click OK (see Figure 4.11).

3. The next time you want to retrieve this topic, choose Options | Bookmarks from any Help Topic screen, and your list of saved bookmarks is there.

4. Double-click the bookmark you want to see.

4

Figure 4.11.
Saving bookmarks for
favorite help topics.

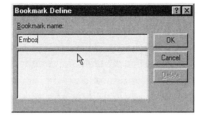

TIME SAVER

You can also print out help topics or copy and paste them into another document from the Options menu.

Context-Sensitive Help

Context-sensitive help means that help is available based on what you're doing at the time or where you are onscreen. Office Assistant won't, for example, ask whether you want help designing a newsletter if you're in the middle of checking the spelling in your document. If it were that *insensitive* to what you were doing, you would turn it off.

In addition to Office Assistant, there is a feature called What's This? that is found in the Help menu. Click it once, and your mouse pointer becomes an arrow with a question mark. Move the pointer to any icon and click. An explanation screen about what that icon can do pops up. Click anything onscreen, such as the scrollbars, control buttons, or menu options, and information appears.

TIME SAVER

Clicking with the What's This? pointer on a typed paragraph presents a pop-up message with information about the paragraph and font formats.

KEYBOARD SHORTCUT

Shift+F1 is a keyboard shortcut to bring up the What's This? feature.

Microsoft's Internet Home Page

If you can't find the help you need from either the built-in help files or this book, you might have run into a bug or a problem that might not be well documented. Microsoft goes to great lengths to make help, resources, and program enhancements available through its Internet site. If you have already logged on, you can connect to Microsoft's site and the most common Microsoft resources from the Help menu (see Figure 4.12).

Figure 4.12.

Access Microsoft's Internet site if you need more help.

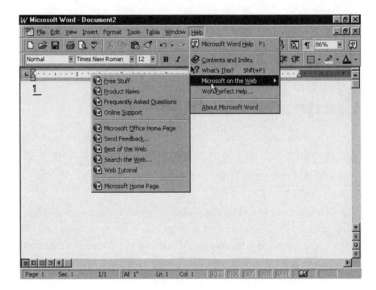

NEW TERM   Being *logged on* means that you are connected either with a modem and a phone line or through a *local area network* to a service that allows you access to resources other than those on your own computer. This often includes access to the Internet. The process of logging on typically requires your name and a password to connect.

A *local area network* (LAN) is a group of computers and other shared resources, such as printers, that are connected by cable and communications software. The computers are usually located in close proximity to each other, usually in a single building or a building complex at the same site. Computers can share information and use common resources when connected in this way.

Microsoft's Internet address is `http://www.microsoft.com`. More information about Microsoft resources is included in Appendix A, "Additional Resources."

4

Summary

This hour explains the vast range of help available to Word 97 users. Office Assistant tells you when you need help, asks you whether you want help, and disappears if you tell it to.

The Contents, Index, and Find tabs allow you to search in ways that fit your needs. Contents offers an outline, Index lists keywords, and Find searches the entire help file for occurrences of a word.

Context-sensitive help brings you what you need depending on where you are. Office Assistant and What's This? are two of Word's context-sensitive help features.

If all else fails and you still have questions, there are volumes of help files available through Microsoft's Internet site.

The upcoming hour takes you to the printed page. Part II, "A Way with Words," explains how word processing leaps past the age of typewriters to a new era in word technology.

Q&A

Q **I went into the Contents tab and selected Technical Support, and when I went back to the Help Topics screen, only a couple of headings were there. Did I lose the help file?**

A No, if you exit help, your search is cleared. Bring it back up, and all of the headings reappear. This doesn't happen under most of the topics.

Q **I searched for several things in Contents and the screen got so cluttered with subheadings that I had a hard time figuring out where to go next.**

A Open book icons are a way of tracking where you have already looked, but it can get confusing finding the main headings with several books open. Double-clicking an open book icon closes the book and all its chapters. All you see is the book's title when it is closed. Close all the open books, and you're back to normal with only major headings showing.

Q **I find a lot of things in Word help files that don't seem to apply to Word. What's happening?**

A Some of the general help files that are available through the Windows help files are also accessible through Word. You get these help files from time to time, especially when you're using Find.

4

RW 1

Word in Real Time

If you have to decide whether to use Word, another application, or a combination of applications for a project you're starting, it is always a good idea to do some advance planning. Before you do a lot of work, there are questions you can ask yourself that will help you avoid restarting the project at some point down the line.

Some basic questions might be

- ☐ What do I need from this project when it's finished? Is it a publication, a report, a presentation, a lookup resource, a form letter that will go to a few people, or one that will go to many people? If you're doing the project for someone else, make sure you know exactly what that person expects from the project. Begin with the output factor and work backward.

- ☐ What kind of information will I be working with—numbers, long lists of names, articles written by several authors, graphics? Begin with the outcome in mind.

- ☐ If there is information that I need to incorporate in my project, can I get it from an existing source rather than re-creating it? Perhaps someone else in the office already has an address file with the needed names and addresses. Your business office may be able to provide an Excel file with needed statistics. The graphic arts department could have scanned graphics or clip-art disks that would work for your publication. Survey the existing resources.

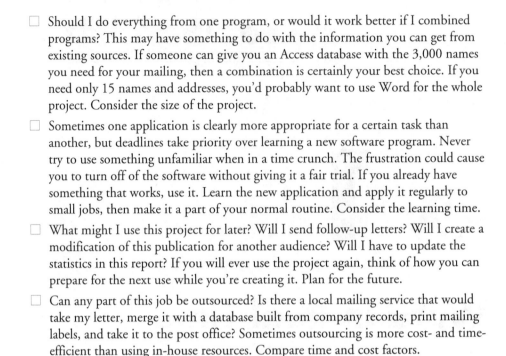

☐ Should I do everything from one program, or would it work better if I combined programs? This may have something to do with the information you can get from existing sources. If someone can give you an Access database with the 3,000 names you need for your mailing, then a combination is certainly your best choice. If you need only 15 names and addresses, you'd probably want to use Word for the whole project. Consider the size of the project.

☐ Sometimes one application is clearly more appropriate for a certain task than another, but deadlines take priority over learning a new software program. Never try to use something unfamiliar when in a time crunch. The frustration could cause you to turn off of the software without giving it a fair trial. If you already have something that works, use it. Learn the new application and apply it regularly to small jobs, then make it a part of your normal routine. Consider the learning time.

☐ What might I use this project for later? Will I send follow-up letters? Will I create a modification of this publication for another audience? Will I have to update the statistics in this report? If you will ever use the project again, think of how you can prepare for the next use while you're creating it. Plan for the future.

☐ Can any part of this job be outsourced? Is there a local mailing service that would take my letter, merge it with a database built from company records, print mailing labels, and take it to the post office? Sometimes outsourcing is more cost- and time-efficient than using in-house resources. Compare time and cost factors.

☐ Have other people in my organization done this kind of thing? Talk to others who have done similar projects to find out which tools made their jobs easier. They may even have sample documents you can borrow.

After you've answered these questions, it will be easier to determine which software applications will give you what you need.

For example, say you have a letter that needs to go out to 150 people. This is, on the surface, an easy project for Word from start to finish. You then determine that you want to track the responses you receive from these individuals. Certainly, you can set up something to handle this project in Word, but the word "track" starts to signal the need for a database.

What if you want to tabulate the responses? Say you're asking for an average household income, number of people in the family, number of dogs on the porch, and so forth. Sounds as if a spreadsheet is needed.

You will probably generate the letter in Word, the text powerhouse. Because you want to do some tracking and calculations, you might decide to take care of the tracking first (entering the names, addresses, and other pertinent information into a database from the return form they'll send back). The database could be used as the file that holds the names and addresses you'll use to generate the form letters.

As the responses come in, the information can be entered in the database. When all the information has been received, the database can transfer the information to the spreadsheet to put the information in columns and make sense of the numbers.

After you learn a suite of applications like Office 97, you have the power to let the individual applications do the work they were designed to do. Your productivity will take a leap forward as you integrate the programs and take full advantage of their strengths.

PART II

A Way with Words

Hour

Hour 5

Working with Words

This hour focuses on putting words on the page. New typing techniques let you run with your stream of consciousness without those annoying carriage returns. This is just one of the ways that typing (or *keyboarding*, as it is called when using a computer) has changed.

Creating a document that is visually pleasing involves using techniques for enhancing text. Creative use of fonts and special accents like bullets and numbering can make all the difference.

The highlights of this hour include

- ☐ How to use the keyboard's advanced typing techniques
- ☐ What fonts are and how to apply them to text
- ☐ How to decide which fonts to use
- ☐ How to automatically add bullets and numbers to lists

New Typing Techniques

There are five key elements that are important to working with text.

- ☐ Keyboarding
- ☐ Cursors and pointers
- ☐ Selecting text
- ☐ Deleting text
- ☐ Formatting text

Keyboarding

You can open a new Word document and immediately start typing. There is a flashing horizontal line at the beginning of the document that tells you everything's ready to go. To get full power from your word processor, however, it helps to know how to use it as more than a typewriter.

A word processor has an important feature that makes it different from a typewriter. It's called *wordwrap*. When you use a typewriter, you press the carriage return at the end of each line. Word processors allow you to type a whole paragraph before you need to insert a carriage return (by pressing the Enter key). Wordwrap knows when it reaches the right margin and automatically wraps around to the next line. The only time you need to press the Enter key is when you want to end a paragraph, end a short line of text, or insert a blank line.

JUST A MINUTE

It may be such an ingrained habit to press the Enter key (carriage return) at the end of each line that you continue to do it. These line breaks can cause a lot of extra work when you begin formatting text. It's a good idea to try to break this habit.

Cursors and Pointers

That flashing mark on the typing screen is called the *cursor*. The cursor helps you keep track of where you can start typing. This is referred to as the *insertion point*.

There are also pointers onscreen as you move the mouse. The pointer changes shapes when the mouse moves to different parts of the screen. It does different jobs depending on where it is. The primary function of the mouse pointer is to select something: a location, text, a menu option, an action from a toolbar icon, or other options on the periphery of the typing screen. It's important to know what the more common pointers do, as shown in Table 5.1.

5

Table 5.1. The mouse pointer's jobs.

Mouse pointer	The pointer's job
The I-beam	Selects an insertion point (appears when the mouse pointer is in the typing screen)
The left-pointing arrow	Selects a toolbar button, a menu, and so on (appears anywhere outside of the typing screen)
The right-pointing arrow	Selects text (appears in the left margin)

These are the three pointers you will see and use most often. Graphics and inserted objects require the pointer to do different things, so it takes on a couple of different forms when working with these elements.

The I-beam, so named because it looks like a large capital letter I, roves the typing screen as you move the mouse. If you want to change the location of the cursor, move the I-beam and click. The cursor moves to the spot where you clicked.

CAUTION

Positioning the I-beam in another location does not automatically move the cursor there. You must click at the position where you want to start typing to actually move the cursor to the new location.

When the mouse pointer takes the shape of a left-pointing arrow, it is ready to perform a Word task, such as printing from a toolbar icon or changing location using the scrollbar.

Position the mouse pointer in the left margin. When the pointer looks like an arrow that points up and to the right, it becomes a text selection tool.

Selecting Text

To do anything with text, it must first be selected. If you want to move it, copy it, delete it, or change the way it looks with fonts and special effects, text must be selected. That's why it's so important to know how to select text.

JUST A MINUTE

Selected text appears as white text on a black background to distinguish it from sections that are not selected.

To select text using the mouse:

1. Click and hold down the left mouse button at the beginning of the text to be selected.
2. Move the mouse pointer to the right and down until the desired amount of text is selected.
3. If you grab too much text, move the mouse back to the left and up.
4. Release the mouse button when the desired amount of text is selected.

If you pick up too much text but have already released the mouse button, hold down the Shift key and use the right arrow key to include more text or press Shift+left arrow to deselect text (one character at a time).

KEYBOARD SHORTCUT

A quicker and more accurate way to select an area of text is to click at the beginning of the selection, then hold down the Shift key and click again at the end of the selection. Everything in between is selected.

There are several shortcuts for selecting text. Table 5.2 is a quick reference for some of them.

Table 5.2. Selection shortcuts.

To select	Shortcut
One character to the right	Shift+right arrow
One character to the left	Shift+left arrow
A word	Double-click anywhere in the word, or Ctrl+Shift+right arrow or left arrow
A sentence	Ctrl+click anywhere in the sentence
A line	Place the pointer in the left margin, and click beside the line (see Figure 5.1)
A paragraph	Click three times quickly anywhere in the paragraph, or double-click beside the paragraph in the left margin
The whole document	Ctrl+A, Ctrl+click in the left margin, or triple-click in the left margin

JUST A MINUTE

When selecting text from the left margin (a line, paragraph, or the whole document), the mouse pointer must be pointing up and toward the right.

5

Figure 5.1.

Clicking twice in the left margin selects a paragraph.

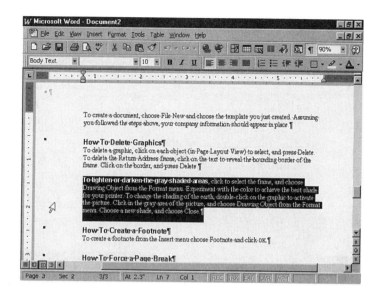

Deleting Text

There are times when you want to delete text. Use the Delete or Backspace key to delete one character at a time. The Backspace key moves the cursor back one space at a time, removing anything in its path. You can delete a block of text by first selecting the text and then pressing the Delete or Backspace key. Use the Ctrl+Delete key combination to delete one word at a time to the right of the insertion point or the Ctrl+Backspace key combination to delete one word to the left of the insertion point.

Formatting Text

Now that you know the basics of selecting text, you're ready to give text a facelift by applying fonts and special effects.

Fonts

The word you hear most frequently when working with text is *font*. Fonts can provide the right tone for the printed message. The important thing to remember is that you must have the text selected before you can change the font.

New Term   A *font* is a set of letters and symbols that bear the same characteristics. The actual font design is called a typeface, though most people don't make a distinction between the two terms. Think of a font as a set of letters in a particular typeface to which you can apply special formatting styles such as boldface and italic.

5

Selecting Font from the Format menu brings up a dialog box that allows you to choose different font characteristics (see Figure 5.2). The Preview box at the bottom of the dialog box lets you see what the selections will look like before you apply them. You have options for:

- ☐ Font
- ☐ Font style (regular, bold, italic, bold italic)
- ☐ Size (the larger the number, the bigger the print)
- ☐ Underline (there are several new styles for underlining; check the drop-down list)
- ☐ Color (if you have a color printer or are creating an online document)
- ☐ Effects (the old standbys like Superscript [3] and Subscript [3] along with some new faces)

Figure 5.2.

Use Format | Font to change font characteristics.

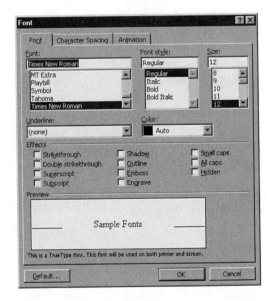

Special Effects

Word 97 includes special text Effects that rival those of the big name desktop publishing packages and graphic editing programs. Format | Font is the place to find them.

To change SALE to **SALE**:

1. Select the word SALE.
2. Select Format | Font.
3. Choose a font that is really bold, such as Arial Black Font.

5

4. Click Bold for the Font style.

5. Change the size to 48 points (or larger if you really want to get their attention).

6. Add a shadow by clicking the Shadow box under Effects (see Figure 5.3).

7. Click OK.

Figure 5.3.

Selecting font characteristics from the Format | Font menu.

Shadow, Outline, Emboss, and Engrave are formatting features that create some great special effects, as outlined in Table 5.3.

Table 5.3. Special effects.

Effect	What it does
Shadow	Creates a shadow effect behind the text
Outline	Gives a hollowed out effect to text
Emboss	Makes text appear raised and lighter, as if it were etched
Engrave	Makes text look sunken, as if carved out

Character Spacing

There are also two other tabs behind the Font tab. Click Character Spacing to change the amount of space between the letters (see Figure 5.4).

5

Figure 5.4.

*Applying special charac-
ter spacing.*

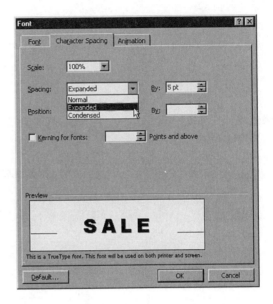

Character spacing lets you:

☐ Resize text horizontally. By increasing the number in the Scale box, text is stretched horizontally but does not increase in height.

☐ Increase space between characters. Select Expanded from the drop-down Spacing list and select a point size in the By box.

☐ Decrease space between characters. Select Condensed from the drop-down Spacing list and select a point size in the By box.

☐ Apply *kerning* for fonts and specify which size fonts to use it with. All fonts larger than the size specified will benefit from the spacing adjustments that kerning applies.

NEW TERM   *Kerning* is a sophisticated feature once found only in professional desktop publishing software. It increases or decreases the space between some letters to make words more readable. It may be indistinguishable in some fonts. In some fonts the spread at the top of a letter, like the capital W, or the bottom of a letter, like a capital A, create an unusual looking amount of space between the letters. Kerning adjusts the spacing between letters to account for the extra space.

Animating Text

In keeping with the multimedia trends that make everything move, the Animation tab lets you apply motion to text. Naturally, if it's going to end up in print, the animation won't do a thing for the text. On the other hand, if you're sharing the document with your boss, you can add a note at the bottom of the page that says I NEED A RAISE and apply a Las Vegas flashing marquee effect to it (see Figure 5.5).

5

Figure 5.5.

Applying animation to text.

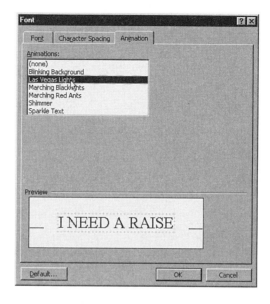

The Formatting Toolbar

You can also apply font characteristics from the Formatting toolbar. The toolbar displays the current font name, size, and styles applied (bold, italic, underline). The arrow beside the font name indicates a drop-down list of other font choices (see Figure 5.6). Click a font name to apply it to selected text.

Figure 5.6.

Choosing a font from the Formatting toolbar.

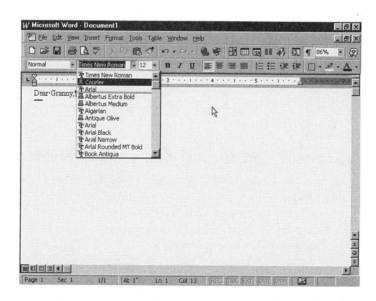

The drop-down list of sizes is rarely smaller than 6 points or beyond 72 points. In general, 72 points is about 1 inch tall. A 12-point font is the standard size for letters and other documents. The drop-down list does not list every size that can be used, or the list would be too long to display onscreen. What you see are the most commonly used sizes.

If you're making alphabet flash cards for your preschooler, you might want 500 points for a letter that fills the whole page. With most TrueType fonts, you can size the font to almost any point size. To specify a font size that is not in the list

1. Make sure that the drop-down font size list is closed (click anywhere outside the list if it's open).
2. Click anywhere in the font size box (the current size will be selected).
3. Type in another font size (for example, 500 for a page-sized letter).
4. Press Enter.

KEYBOARD SHORTCUT

Holding down the Ctrl key and pressing the left bracket ([) decreases the font size of selected text one point size at a time. Ctrl+] increases the point size.

To the right of the Font Size drop-down list on the toolbar are three letters—B, I, and U. You may have already guessed that these letters stand for bold, italic, and underline. Select the text, then click any of the styles to apply them. If you apply bold to a line, the B button is depressed, or lightened. If you decide to take the bold off, select the text again and click the B. The bold is gone and the button on the toolbar is dark again.

KEYBOARD SHORTCUT

Use Ctrl+B to bold, Ctrl+I to italicize, or Ctrl+U to underline selected text.

Some Friendly Advice about Fonts

The rule of thumb that designers use is that there should be no more than two fonts used per publication. That doesn't mean you can't vary the fonts with bold and italic accents, but two font types are enough variety for one document. More than that gives a sense of being cluttered and choppy. If you're typing a letter, you won't want that much variation. A simple letter should be done in a single font.

Specialty fonts are a temptation. The fonts with firecrackers exploding from the tops of the letters or ornate script that emulates fancy handwriting may be tempting, but the font should match your message. The firecracker font may be just fine for the science project poster, but

5

it won't improve your image if you use it in the company's annual report. Scripts are useful for formal invitations, but no one would enjoy reading a long document written in script.

There are several font types. The two most prominent ones are described in Table 5.4.

Table 5.4. Font types.

Font name	Examples
Serif	Times, **Bookman**, Palatino (ornamental ends, or feet and tails)
Sans serif	Arial, **Helvetica**, Univers (straight, or no feet or tails)

All of these fonts were formatted in 14 point. Some look larger even though they are the same point size. Font sizes can be a little tricky. You may decide to set up styles for fonts you use often. Hour 12, "A Matter of Style," discusses how to create and save styles.

Long passages are easier to read when serif fonts are used. They also present a conservative image. Sans serif fonts appear more modern and progressive (*sans* means *without* in French— in this case without ornamentation).

You may, in fact, need a bit of both to appeal to your audience. Use serif for the bulk of the text to make it readable, and sans serif for the title headings to tell your readers you're on the move.

JUST A MINUTE

> Legibility is always the primary concern in using any font. Even when you want a very ornate typeface for a wedding invitation, take a look at the capital letters. Type a line of the capital letters in the font you're thinking about using. People may not recognize the names of the bride and groom because the capital letters may be too distorted in a particular font.

5

Bullets and Numbering

Lists of items can be set apart on the page with bullets or numbers. Adding numbering or bullets to text is a well-known technique for getting people to read things. If you type a paragraph with ten items separated by commas, chances are it won't draw much attention. Put those same ten items in a bulleted or numbered list, and you're almost sure it will be read.

Use bullets or numbers to

- ☐ Emphasize important points you want readers to remember
- ☐ Break down steps in a process

- [ ] Rank order items by importance
- [ ] Provide variety on the page
- [ ] Create a to-do list

AutoBullets and AutoNumbering recognize when you start typing a list and automate the process for you. To build a bulleted list, follow these steps:

1. Type an asterisk.
2. Press the Spacebar twice.
3. Type the listing's text.
4. Press the Enter key.

Word automatically inserts the next bullet for you and tabs over to where the next list item will start. Word continues to insert a new bullet each time you press the Enter key and type a list item. When you want to stop the bulleted list, press the Enter key twice at the end of the list.

AutoNumber works the same way, except you begin with the number 1, then add a period and two spaces. Word recognizes that you are starting a numbered list and enters the successive numbers on each new line until you press the Enter key twice to tell Word you've finished the list.

JUST A MINUTE

Any time you're working with text, the Bullets and Numbering option comes up with the right-click shortcut menu. The right mouse button is one of the most powerful features for working in Word. No matter where you are in a document, when you click the right mouse button, a shortcut menu appears that includes the most common actions that would apply to the job you're doing. If you're working with text, the options are different from the ones that show up when you're using graphics. This is another of Word's context-sensitive features.

To add bullets or numbers to an existing list:

1. Select the list.
2. Click the Bullets or Numbering button on the Formatting toolbar.

To remove the bullets or numbers from a list, follow the same process. The Bullets and Numbers buttons are on/off switches.

You can get very creative with bullets. There are dozens of symbols other than the typical black circle to choose from when adding bullets.

5

Use the following steps to apply a special telephone bullet to a list of instructions for the new receptionist, color it blue, and set the list .4 inches from the left margin:

1. Select the list.

2. Select Format | Bullets and Numbering (see Figure 5.7), or right-click and select Bullets and Numbering from the shortcut menu.

Figure 5.7.

Bullets and Numbering from the Format menu.

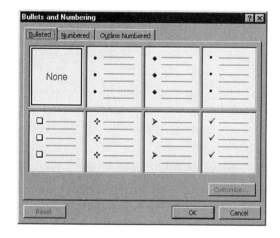

3. Select the Bulleted tab.

4. Click one of the predefined bullets, then click Customize.

5. In the Customize Bulleted List dialog box, click Bullet (see Figure 5.8).

Figure 5.8.

Customizing bullets.

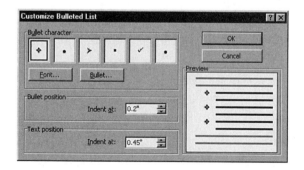

6. In the Symbol dialog box, select Wingdings from the drop-down Font list.

7. The symbols are very small; click a symbol to magnify its picture. When you find the telephone, click OK (see Figure 5.9).

Figure 5.9.

Selecting a new symbol for a bullet.

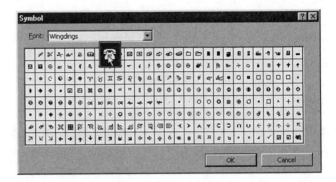

8. In the Customize Bulleted List dialog box, set the Bullet position to Indent at .4 inches.

9. Click Font. Change the font size to 24 points and the font color to blue, then click OK.

10. Click OK again to apply the new bullet.

There are similar, but fewer options when customizing numbered lists. A third tab in Bullets and Numbering, Outline Numbered, lets you select numbering styles for an outline.

Summary

This hour introduces features like wordwrap and selecting text that make typing easy. Fonts give character to the words on the page. Choosing fonts is as important as choosing the words for a document.

Bulleted and numbered lists are excellent tools for creating interest in a document. Word can automatically add bullets or numbers to lists. There are many different styles of bullets and numbers to choose from.

The next hour explores ways to position words on the page. There are tools in Word 97 that make paragraph formatting an easy task.

Q&A

Q Someone in my office got a lot of free fonts somewhere. Will they work on my computer?

A They probably will, but beware of some of the free fonts that are floating around. They can do some strange things like lock up your computer when you try to print a document that includes some of these fonts.

Q I created a document with bullets and gave it to someone else to print from another computer. Why didn't the bullets come out like the ones I put in?

A Unless the other computer has exactly the same fonts, it may not recognize the bullets correctly. It tries to come as close as it can with the fonts it has, but it may not be what you want. This is especially true when working between a PC and a Mac. The fonts are usually not the same, and bullets won't translate correctly. If you have to make this transition very often, experiment and make a list of font choices that work. Hour 11, "Customizing Word to the Way You Work," tells how to include font styles with a document (embedding fonts) so that these characters translate correctly.

5

Hour 6

Formatting Paragraphs

This hour deals with the lines and paragraphs on the page. Word 97 provides many variations in the way lines and paragraphs can be formatted to help a document serve its purpose or make it more attractive. Indents, like bulleted or numbered lists, can inset text to make it more interesting and noticeable.

Using tabs instead of a series of spaces gives the user much more flexibility in the way documents can be set up and edited. Setting tabs is just one of the things that can be done from the ruler. As you explore and use the ruler, it will become your right hand for many tasks.

The highlights of this hour include

- ☐ How to change the spacing between lines
- ☐ What justifying text means and when to use different justification styles
- ☐ How tabs and indents work
- ☐ What to do with the ruler

Paragraph Formatting

When working with paragraph formatting, it is important to know that a paragraph must be selected in order to apply formatting to it. WordPerfect users may be accustomed to having paragraph formatting apply from the cursor forward. This is not the case with Word. The paragraph marker at the end of each paragraph contains the formatting for that paragraph.

Word considers anything with a paragraph marker at the end of it a paragraph. That means that individual lines, items in a list, and blank lines are considered paragraphs.

TIME SAVER

> Paragraph formatting is carried forward with the *paragraph marker*. When you press the Enter key to start a new paragraph or line, the elements that applied to the paragraph before, such as line spacing, bullets, tabs, indents, and alignment, are automatically applied.

NEW TERM A *paragraph marker* is the symbol that shows the end of a paragraph. If you can't see the paragraph markers, click Show/Hide (non-printing characters) from the Standard toolbar to see paragraph marks, spaces, and tabs. Click Show/Hide again to turn off this feature.

Line Spacing

Say you have typed a document, and your boss asks you to double-space it so she can make corrections more easily. Double-space indicates that every line has a full blank line between it and the next line of text.

You might want to change line spacing for a number of reasons. Some single-spaced documents appear too tight for easy reading.

To change the line spacing of a single paragraph:

1. Select the paragraph (triple-click anywhere in the paragraph or double-click in the left margin beside the paragraph).
2. Select Format | Paragraph.
3. Select a line spacing option from the Line spacing drop-down list, as shown in Figure 6.1.
4. Click OK.

Figure 6.1.

*Selecting line-spacing
options from Paragraph
on the Format menu.*

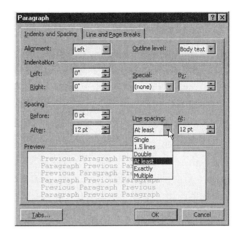

**KEYBOARD
SHORTCUT**

Ctrl+1 single-spaces, Ctrl+2 double-spaces, and Ctrl+5 applies 1.5 line
spacing to a selected paragraph.

There are also options that say At Least, Exactly, and Multiple. In these cases, you enter a
number in the At box. At Least and Exactly call for a point size. In this case, space is measured
in terms of point size just as fonts are. The At Least option allows Word to use more space
than the point size called for. If it needs the space to accommodate anything out of the
ordinary (perhaps a word that has been bolded and increased a couple of font sizes), it can
take a little extra.

Exactly means just what it says. It adds exactly the same amount of space between each line.
If it needs more, it can't have it. There are very few reasons to use this option unless you are
creating a form that must have precise locations for lines or unless you need to match another
document exactly. Multiple lets you select multiples of a single line. Enter a 3 in the At box,
and the lines will be triple-spaced.

Adding just a bit of extra space creates a more eye-appealing and readable document. After
major headings in a publication, it works well to set extra space between the heading and the
rest of the text. The Before and After Spacing options let you set more space either before or
after a paragraph.

The Before and After spacing measurement is in point sizes. Arrows to the right of the Before
and After entry boxes allow you to select space in increments of 6 points, but you can type
any other number in the box to get other spacing sizes. If you're working with a 12-point font,
setting Spacing After to 12 pt gives you about the space of two lines of text between
paragraphs. This eliminates the need to press Enter twice when you want extra space.

Text Alignment

Text can be aligned in four ways. It can be center-aligned. If text is aligned with the left edge but has an uneven right edge, it's left-aligned. Text aligned with the right margin with an uneven left edge is right-aligned. When the edges are aligned to both margins, it's *justified*.

 Justified means that the edges of a paragraph are positioned evenly in a straight line along both margins.

There are buttons on the Formatting toolbar that allow you to align-left, center, align-right, and justify text (see Figure 6.2). Select a paragraph or a whole document, then click any of these buttons to apply an alignment to text.

Figure 6.2.

The text alignment buttons show what they do.

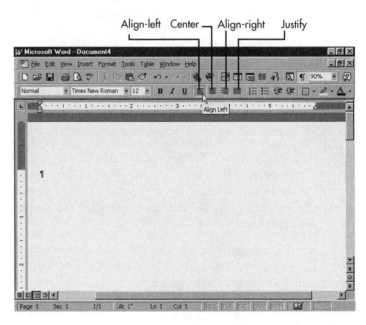

KEYBOARD SHORTCUT

Ctrl+L left-aligns, Ctrl+R right-aligns, Ctrl+J justifies both edges, and Ctrl+E centers selected text.

Left-aligned text is the most readable and is the standard for most things we write. Most books, reports, and other publications use a left alignment. Letters are usually left-aligned.

6

Centered text is primarily reserved for titles, headings, cover pages, invitations, and other documents where short lines of text stand alone. Posters and flyers are good examples.

Right-aligned text is seldom used in regular paragraphs because it is difficult to follow and read. It can be used in small doses for special effect. In combination with graphics, it can be very effective. It is also used in letters to line up dates, inside addresses, or other heading information along the right margin.

Justified (aligned on both edges) text forces more space between some words than normal to spread text out evenly to both margins. This makes it harder to read than left-aligned text, but it works well when a newspaper or dictionary effect is desired that creates a block of even white space between columns. This is considered a formal style.

JUST A MINUTE

Many producers of multicolumn publications have converted to using left-aligned text. It has a relaxed look and, because it is easier to read, is more appealing to the reader.

You can set alignment from the Paragraph option in the Format menu. This takes care of both formats at once. The first option under Indents and Spacing is Alignment, which has a drop-down list with the alignment options.

Tabs and Indents

Tabs and indents are used to position text more precisely than inserting several spaces ahead of text or between items in a list. They are also tools that make editing easier. It is much quicker to adjust tabs and indents than it is to add and delete spaces.

Tabs

Tabs are easy to set in Word. They are used to move text after the cursor to the right a certain amount of space or to line up lists of items precisely. Tabs are also a tool that can help create a table of contents. The terms that applied to aligning paragraphs can be applied to tabs. There are also decimal-aligned tabs. Figure 6.3 illustrates the different types of tab alignments.

Bar tabs are another type of tab. When you set a bar tab, Word draws a vertical line at that tab stop. If you have several lines of text in a table and want to divide the columns, inserting a bar tab creates a vertical line between the columns in the table. If you're creating a table with lines, it is easier to use Word's Table feature than tabs. Hour 14, "Working with Tables," shows how tables work for these kinds of jobs.

Figure 6.3.

Tabs can be centered, left-, right-, or decimal-aligned.

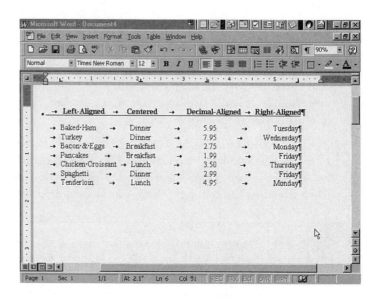

Leader characters can be added to tab stops to make a trail with a dotted, dashed, or solid line leading up to the text at the tab stop. Figure 6.4 illustrates the three types of leader characters.

Figure 6.4.

Using leader characters with tabs.

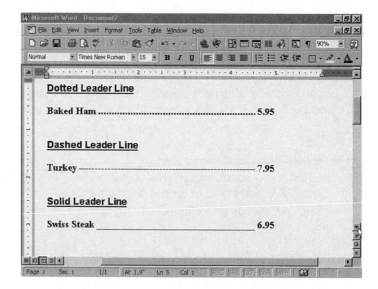

6

Tabs can be set from the Tabs option in the Format menu (see Figure 6.5). Leader characters can be specified as the tabs are set. To set a right-aligned tab two inches from the left with a solid line leader character:

1. Select the paragraphs where the tab will be needed, then select Format | Tabs.

2. Type a 2 in the Tab stop position box.

3. Click the Right button under Alignment and the solid line selection under Leader.

4. Click Set, then click OK.

Figure 6.5.

Setting tabs and options from Format | Tabs.

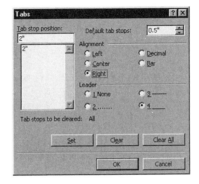

To set several tabs at the same time:

1. Select the paragraphs to which the tabs will be applied.

2. Select Format | Tabs.

3. Type the first tab location in the Tab stop position box.

4. Select one of the Alignment options.

5. Select one of the leader characters, if desired.

6. Click the Set button.

7. Repeat steps 3–6 until you have all the tabs set the way you want them. A list of the tab stops appears below the Tab stop position box.

8. Click OK.

To remove all of the tabs from the selected text, select Format | Tabs and click Clear All. Tabs are set automatically every half inch if no tabs have been set manually. The default half-inch tabs will not appear in the list of tabs set. To change the default tabs to 1 inch:

1. Select the paragraphs where the tabs will be applied.

2. Select Format | Tabs.

3. Change the measurement in the Default tab stops box to 1".

4. Click Set, then click OK.

Indents

Indents set text in from one or both margins. They are set through Paragraph in the Format menu. This is the same place that line spacing is set. To indent a paragraph one inch from both the right and left margins, either type a 1 in the Left and Right option boxes under Indentation, or use the arrows to increase indents in .1 inch increments. Under Special are options for indenting the first line of text or creating a *hanging indent*. You can specify the indent size in the By box (see Figure 6.6).

Figure 6.6.

Setting indents and Special options.

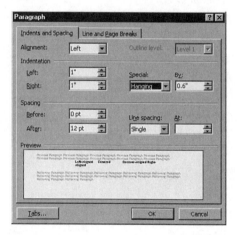

NEW TERM A *hanging indent* indents every line in a selected paragraph except the first line, which remains flush with the left margin. It is often used with numbered lists and outlines to indent the lines after the numbered line. It's also used for agendas and dictionary-style listings. This is an example of a hanging indent:

Day 1   Hike 12 miles, make camp, scout for wood, build a lean-to, purify water, set up markers for plant identification, short hike for animal track discovery.

A quick way to indent selected text is with the Increase Indent button on the Formatting toolbar. This button looks like an arrow shoving a paragraph in from the left margin. Increase Indent moves the paragraph in one half inch from the left margin. Increase the indent further by clicking the button again. Decrease Indent has the opposite effect: It brings the indent further out toward the left margin one half inch at a time.

The keyboard equivalents for the Increase and Decrease Indent buttons are Ctrl+M (increase) and Ctrl+Shift+M (decrease).

Ctrl+T creates a hanging indent. Ctrl+Shift+T removes a hanging indent.

Using the Ruler

Setting both tabs and indents can be done quickly and easily from the horizontal ruler just below the Formatting toolbar. The ruler is marked in inches for ease of measuring. You can change the measurement unit to centimeters, if you prefer. To set this option:

1. Select Tools | Options.
2. Click the General tab.
3. Select centimeters from the Measurement Unit drop-down list.
4. Click OK.

If you don't see the ruler, it may be turned off. Make sure that ruler is selected on the View menu. If there is not a checkmark beside ruler, selecting it checks it and turns the option on.

To set a tab on the ruler:

1. Select paragraphs the tab will apply to.
2. Position the mouse pointer anywhere on the ruler and click.

If you don't like where you put the tab, click and hold down the tab marker and drag it to another location on the ruler. A dotted positioning line appears that goes from the ruler all the way down the page to allow you to position the tab very precisely (see Figure 6.7). When the tab is where you want it, release the mouse button and the tab moves to the new location.

If you set a tab and decide you don't want it after all, drag it anywhere off the ruler. The tab is removed.

Click the Tab Alignment button at the far left of the ruler. As you click, the picture on the button changes to show the different alignment options. The pop-up ToolTip gives the tab name. Centered, left-, right- and decimal-aligned tabs can be set on the ruler by selecting one of the tab alignment options.

6

Figure 6.7.

Moving a tab on the ruler.

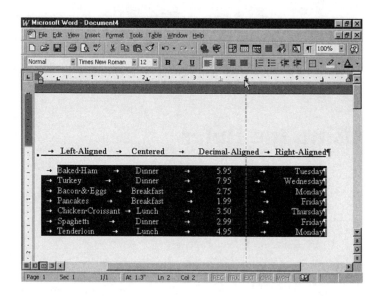

Indents can also be set and moved on the ruler. The small triangles on either end of the ruler are used to set a first line indent, a hanging indent, and left and right indents. A ToolTip is displayed when the mouse is positioned over one of the markers to let you know which indent you're setting. If you click the Left Indent marker (the bar under the two triangles on the left end of the ruler) and drag it further to the right on the ruler, it moves all three markers and sets a larger left indent (see Figure 6.8).

Figure 6.8.

Increasing the left indent using the ruler.

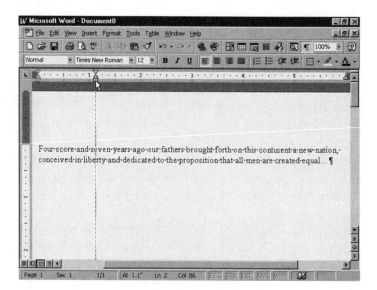

6

Drag the top icon to create a first line indent or the middle icon (that also brings with it the Left Indent icon) to create a hanging indent. A first line indent is the type of indent you would use for normal paragraph indents. With the first line indent set, you don't have to manually tab to indent the first line of each paragraph.

Inexperienced users often try to create a hanging indent by typing the first line at the left margin, pressing Enter at the end of the line, and using tabs or spaces to indent the next line. Every line that follows has to have tabs or spaces at the beginning and a carriage return at the end to create the hanging indent effect. Any changes to the text can throw everything off. Learn to use Word's hanging indent feature for this purpose. Not only will it make things easier to edit, but text will line up more uniformly.

Perhaps you're typing a dictionary-style listing and want the term to be offset from the definition. Setting a hanging indent is a clean way to accomplish this. Follow these steps to set a hanging indent:

1. Type the term.
2. Press the Tab key.
3. Type the definition.
4. Grab the Hanging Indent button and drag it along the ruler to the spot where the definition of the term begins in the first line (see Figure 6.9).

If you need to change the text, the indent is still intact and flows with whatever changes are made. If you want more space between the term and the definition, move the Hanging Indent marker further to the right on the ruler.

Figure 6.9.

Setting off text with a hanging indent.

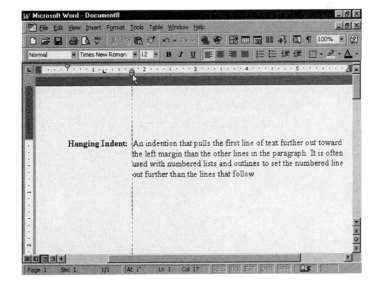

Tabs and indents help create *whitespace* that is an important part of the page layout. White-space gives the eyes a rest and sets off text to make it easier to read. The whitespace between columns in a table allows readers to easily identify what comes under each heading. A long quotation is made more prominent by indenting it from both the left and right margins.

TIME SAVER

Text that is indented from both the left and right margins looks much better when it is justified. Click the Justify button on the Formatting toolbar to apply this alignment to selected text.

Whitespace is a term used in desktop publishing to refer to places on the page where there is no text or typing.

Summary

This hour is an overview of line and paragraph spacing. Line spacing and indents can be set through the Paragraph option in the Format menu or by using the ruler. Paragraph text alignment has an impact on the way the reader perceives the publication. Justified text is considered a formal style, left-aligned text is more casual and readable. Right-aligned text can be used for special effect. Centered text works well for titles and headings.

Decimal tabs are great for working with numbers to line up a column of figures on the decimal point. Tabs set with leader characters can make columns easier to follow. Indents can inset text such as quotations and instructions.

Q&A

Q I got a strange indent that I didn't want. How can I get rid of it?

A Check the paragraph formatting. Right-click anywhere in the paragraph. Click the Paragraph option, then make sure the left and right indents are set to 0 inches. Also, check the Special settings. Select None to get rid of any hanging or first line indents.

Q I changed the Indentation and Special settings, but something is still putting in the indent.

A If you can't track the problem in the paragraph formatting, try to find another paragraph in your document that is indented (or not indented) the way you want it. Highlight the paragraph, then click the Format Painter icon. This copies the paragraph formatting to the paintbrush. Move to the offending paragraph and drag the paintbrush over the entire paragraph, including the paragraph marker. The indents should change to match those of the paragraph you picked up with the paintbrush. You can also remove all paragraph formatting by selecting the paragraph and pressing Ctrl+Q.

Q Can I set up a right indent from the ruler?

A Yes. There is a marker on the right side of the ruler that looks like the Hanging Indent marker on the left (these are visual associations to the slide bars on a typewriter that set the margins). Drag the Right Indent marker to the left as far as you want the indent.

6

Hour 7

Manipulating Text

This hour shows the freedom you have to rearrange your documents any way you want. You can take entire paragraphs or pages and move them around in your document. You can move sections from one place and put them in another. You can copy text and reuse it in other locations or in other documents.

Nearly as powerful for manipulating text is Word's Find and Replace feature, which allows you to replace a word you have used incorrectly throughout a document. You can also globally replace formatting options such as font styles.

The highlights of this hour include

- ☐ How to use the clipboard with the Cut, Copy, and Paste features
- ☐ How to copy a section of text
- ☐ How to use drag-and-drop to move text
- ☐ How to use the Find and Replace features

Cut, Copy, and Paste Functions

In the days before word processors, writers would create an outline, then type a document. They might take the pages and cut them up and rearrange sections to create a more logical or effective order. With tape or paste, they would reassemble the document in the new order and retype it with the changes.

Word processing applications have automated all of that with the Cut, Copy, and Paste functions. To understand how these functions work, it is important to understand what's happening behind the scenes.

Windows 95 has a feature called the clipboard. Cut and Copy use the clipboard as a temporary storage space for selections that have been cut or copied. The Standard toolbar contains the icons for Cut, Copy, and Paste (see Figure 7.1). Paste takes whatever is stored on the clipboard and places it where you want it. These are powerful tools that have revolutionized the way we work with documents and between applications.

Figure 7.1.

The Cut, Copy, Paste, and Format Painter icons on the Standard toolbar.

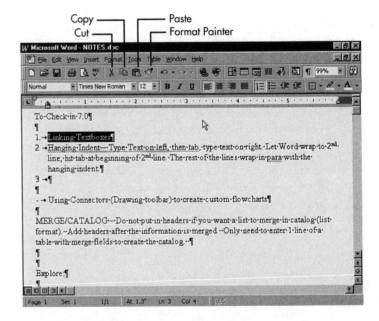

Cut

Cut removes anything that is selected and places it on the clipboard. It can be used as a method to delete selections, but it is different from using the Delete key. When you press the Delete key to get rid of a selection, it can only be retrieved using the Undo button. Cut is really a method for moving text rather than deleting it. Text is cut from one place and can be pasted in another.

7

To cut a selection:

1. Select the text.
2. Click the Cut button.

The selection is removed and placed on the clipboard.

Copy

Copy duplicates selected text. It is used when you don't want to get rid of the original selection, but you want to make a copy of it. Perhaps you are creating a series of forms that contain much of the same information, but they are not exactly alike. Copying the sections from one form to another saves a lot of repetitive typing.

To copy a selection:

1. Select the text.
2. Click the Copy button.

The original selection remains intact, and a duplicate is placed on the clipboard.

Paste

Paste takes anything that is cut or copied to the clipboard and places it at the insertion point. The Paste icon looks like a piece of paper coming off of a clipboard. It is, in fact, taking the information stored on the clipboard and placing it in the new location.

To paste a selection:

1. Position the cursor in the location where you want the contents of the clipboard to be placed.
2. Click the Paste button.

The clipboard is not empty when you paste from it. You can paste the same item multiple times.

JUST A MINUTE

> Whatever is stored on the clipboard stays there until you perform another Cut or Copy operation. As soon as you cut or copy something new, the clipboard dumps what was stored and replaces it with the new selection.

Most programs that were designed for use with Windows 95 have the Cut, Copy, and Paste functions. If, for instance, you create a picture in the Paint program, you can copy it to the clipboard, then paste it into your Word document. If you create a chart in Excel, you can paste it into a PowerPoint presentation. Text from a Word document can be pasted into any other

Office application. Cut, Copy, and Paste work as easily between applications as they do within a single application.

KEYBOARD SHORTCUT

Ctrl+X cuts a selection.
Ctrl+C copies a selection.
Ctrl+V pastes a selection.

You can also cut, copy, and paste from the Edit menu.

Copy and Paste Formatting

Experienced users have found that the Copy and Paste duo is also a valuable tool for copying formatting, such as fonts, indents, tabs, line spacing, and bullets and numbering. To copy a paragraph's formatting but not its contents:

1. Select the paragraph (including the paragraph marker).
2. Press Ctrl+Shift+C to copy a paragraph's formatting.
3. Select another paragraph that you want formatted in the same way.
4. Press Ctrl+Shift+V. The formatting is pasted from the copied selection. Only the formatting is copied, not the contents.

Copying Character Formatting

You might want the same character formatting (font, font size, and font style, and so on) applied to several areas in a document. If you don't want to copy the tabs, indentations, and other paragraph formatting, use this method to copy only character formatting:

1. Select text without selecting the paragraph marker at the end of the paragraph or line.
2. Press Ctrl+Shift+C to copy the character formatting.
3. Select another paragraph where the same formatting is desired.
4. Press Ctrl+Shift+V to paste the character formatting to this selection.

Copying Paragraph Formatting

There are other times when you don't want to pick up the character formatting but you want to apply the same paragraph formatting (tabs, indents, line spacing, etc.) to other paragraphs. To copy only paragraph formatting:

1. Select only the paragraph mark at the end of a paragraph that has formats you want to copy.
2. Click the Copy button on the toolbar.

3. Select the paragraph mark at the end of a paragraph where you want to apply the same formatting.

4. Click the Paste button. The paragraph mark contains all of the coding for paragraph formatting. Pasting one paragraph mark over another replaces the existing formatting.

You can also use the Format Painter button on the toolbar to copy and paste formatting:

1. Select a paragraph.

2. Click the Format Painter button. The mouse pointer becomes a paintbrush.

3. Move the paintbrush to another paragraph and click anywhere in the paragraph. The formatting from the first paragraph is applied.

The Format Painter can also be used to pick up only character or paragraph formatting in exactly the same way that the Ctrl key combinations do. Select text but not the paragraph mark to copy only character formatting. Select only the paragraph mark to copy the paragraph formatting without picking up the font characteristics.

Drag and Drop

Another way to move or copy text is with a technique called *drag-and-drop*. If you're working with large sections of text or moving text from one location to a place much further up or down in the document, Cut, Copy, and Paste are more efficient and reliable. If you just need to reposition one sentence ahead of another or to move a list item to another location, drag-and-drop is the quickest method.

 Drag-and-drop is when you use the mouse to grab a selection, "drag" it from one location, and "drop" it in another.

To drag-and-drop a selection:

1. Select text to be moved.

2. Position the mouse pointer in the selected text and click and hold down the left mouse button.

3. The mouse pointer will have a faint gray box with a vertical line that moves with it.

4. Move the vertical line (the drag-and-drop pointer) to the desired location.

5. Release the mouse button. The selection moves to the new location.

Figure 7.2 illustrates the use of drag-and-drop to rearrange the order of items in a shopping list. Cabbage is being moved down in the list with the other vegetables. As soon as the mouse is released, Cabbage will move above Turnips.

7

Figure 7.2.

Using drag-and-drop to reorder items in a list.

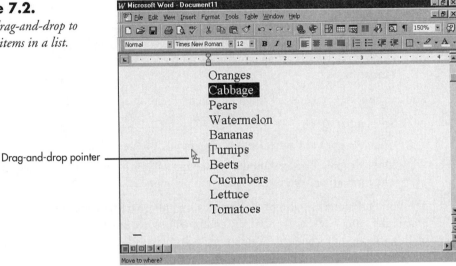

Drag-and-drop pointer ——————

Alt+Shift+up arrow moves a selected paragraph up one paragraph at a time.

Alt+Shift+down arrow moves a selected paragraph down one paragraph at a time.

TIME SAVER

Drag-and-drop can also be used to copy text. Use the same drag-and-drop technique but hold down the Ctrl key while dragging the selection. Release the mouse button first, then the Ctrl key. You will see a little plus sign with the drag-and-drop pointer, letting you know that you are copying the selection.

Cut, Copy, Paste, and drag-and-drop can also be used between two documents or two different applications. To use any of these options between Word documents, you can arrange the document windows easily by selecting Window | Arrange All as in Figure 7.3. Each document appears in its own window.

7

Figure 7.3.

Viewing all of the open documents.

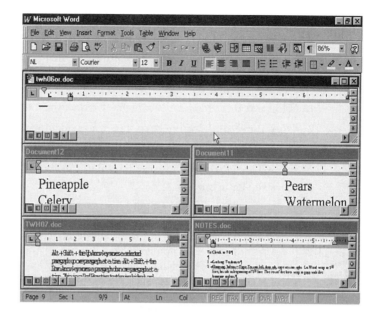

In Figure 7.4, drag-and-drop is being used to move the word Beets in Document11 to the shopping list in Document12. Copy, Cut, and Paste can also be used between documents if you have trouble holding on to the mouse pointer in the drag-and-drop process.

Figure 7.4.

Using drag-and-drop between two documents.

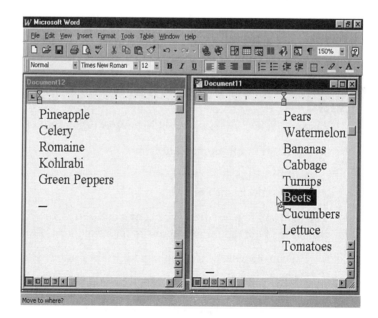

7

It is just as easy to work between two applications like Word and Excel when using Cut, Copy, and Paste or drag-and-drop. Information on combining Word and other applications is included in Hour 23, "Teaming Up Word with Other Office Applications."

To easily copy text between two documents:

1. Select text from the first document and click the Copy (or Cut) button.

2. Open the second document or start a new document. (If the document is already open, use the Window menu to switch between documents.)

3. Position the cursor where you want to insert the text.

4. Click the Paste button.

TIME SAVER

Another example of Microsoft's efforts to give more functionality to the right mouse button is the way it works with drag-and-drop. Select text, then click it with the right mouse button. Drag the selection to its new location and release the mouse button. A shortcut menu appears asking whether you want to move, copy, or link to the original selection. Select the one that fits what you're doing.

Find and Replace Functions

Find and Replace take on a new look in Word 97. Instead of having their own dialog boxes, Find and Replace are grouped together in tab format. If you use Find to search for a word, you can then replace the word with another word if you need to by switching to the Replace tab. There is no need to exit Find to get to Replace.

Find

There are at least three ways to initiate Word's Find function:

☐ Select Find from the Edit menu.

☐ Press Ctrl+F.

☐ Press Alt+E, then press F.

The Find and Replace dialog box comes up, as in Figure 7.5. Notice that the Replace tab is behind the Find tab for easy access to both functions. To find a word:

1. Type the word you're looking for in the Find what box.

2. Click Find Next. Word finds the first occurrence of the word. Click Find Next again if it is not the occurrence you want. Repeat the process until Word finds the occurrence of the word you're trying to locate.

3. Press the Esc key or click the Cancel button to exit the Find dialog box.

7

Figure 7.5.

Using Find to search a document.

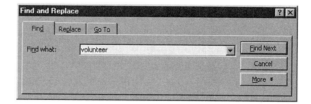

If you're trying to quickly find your way to a place in a document, Find is a great tool. Simply type a term that is found in that location in the Find what box. You might also want to see if you have overworked a word by using it too frequently. Use Find to move through the document to each occurrence of the word. If you're working with two versions of the same document, searching for something unique to one of them is an easy way to make sure you're using the right version.

TIME SAVER

Sometimes the Find and Replace dialog box is covering the word you searched for. If you position the mouse pointer in the title bar and click and hold down the left mouse button, you can move the dialog box out of the way. You can click in the document while the Find and Replace dialog box is open to make corrections to the document. After making changes, click the Find Next button in the Find and Replace dialog box to continue searching (you may need to click the button twice).

One of the helpful features in Word 97 is that you can continue a search after closing Find using the Select Browse Object feature. After you close the Find dialog box, the Previous and Next buttons on the scrollbar turn blue. Their functions change from PageUp and PageDown to Previous Find and Next Find.

The Previous/Next buttons continue to function as Find buttons until you click Select Browse Object and choose Browse by Page or another option.

Replace Text

The Replace function works with Find to locate text, and then replaces it with something else. It's not uncommon to type a long document and then find that one of the terms you used consistently is incorrect. Replace is a great way to find every place the term is used and correct them all at once. Say you used the term `Windows 97` instead of `Office 97` in a document explaining Office 97's new features. Replace can help make the changes.

To replace every occurrence of Windows 97 with Office 97:

1. Select Edit | Replace or press Ctrl+H to open the Find and Replace dialog box (see Figure 7.6.).
2. Type `Windows 97` in the Find what box.

3. Type Office 97 in the Replace with box.

4. Click Replace All if you're absolutely certain you want to replace every instance of Windows 97 with Office 97. If you don't want to replace all occurrences because you want to use Windows 97 somewhere in the document, click Find Next.

   Word finds the first occurrence of Windows 97. If you want to replace it, click Replace. If you don't, click Find Next.

5. Repeat the process of finding and replacing until you get the message Word has finished searching the document.

6. Click Cancel or press the Esc key to exit the Find and Replace dialog box.

Figure 7.6.

Using Replace to correct errors.

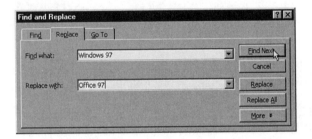

KEYBOARD SHORTCUT

Ctrl+H brings up the Replace tab in the Find and Replace dialog box.

Refining a Search

You can widen or narrow a search to include more or fewer forms of a word when using both Find and Replace. When Replace opens, as shown in Figure 7.6, you'll see a button in the lower-right corner that says More. Click More and an expanded Replace (or Find, if you select More from the Find tab) is available (see Figure 7.7).

To modify a search using the expanded Find or Replace, you can specify options such as Match case, which looks only for words with upper- and lowercase exactly as the word is typed in the Find what box. If you check Find whole words only, Word will find only whole words that match the word that is typed in the Find what box. It will not pick up plurals or other forms of the word. If you search for neighbor with this option selected, it will not find neighbors or neighborhood. The Sounds like option checks for words that sound the same but are spelled differently. If you search for sun, it will also find son.

You can dramatically expand a search by selecting Use wildcards. Wildcards are common symbols like the asterisk (*) and the question mark (?) where * or ? can stand for anything.

Figure 7.7.

There are many Replace (and Find) options.

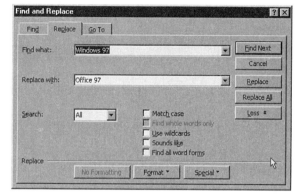

If you type Win* in the Find what box, Word looks for every word in the document that starts with Win. You might get words like:

- Windows
- Winslow
- winter (if Match case is not selected)
- winning

The question mark defines a single character rather than a set of letters. A wildcard search for t?n might bring up words like:

- ten
- tan
- tin
- ton

The Find all word forms option is a useful feature that finds all derivatives of a word (plurals, past tense, and so on). If, for example, you used the plural of a word, typing the root word finds the word and the plural form. You might, for example, want to replace the word car with the word automobile. With the Find all word forms option selected, you could also replace cars with automobiles at the same time.

This is a feature you need to be careful with and will probably want to use it on a case-by-case basis. Word even gives you a warning that a Replace All is not recommended for this option.

Replace Formatting

Click Format in the Replace tab, and the drop-down list shows all the formatting options that can be substituted using Replace. If you want to change a font that you used throughout a

7

document, this is an excellent way to make one pass through and change every place the font is used.

CAUTION

> Make sure that you don't have anything in either the Find what or Replace with boxes when replacing any kind of formatting. If you do, it replaces formatting only for these words.

To replace all Arial 12 point bold titles in a document:

1. Select Edit | Replace or press Ctrl+H to open the Replace dialog box.
2. Click the More button if the extended Replace selections are not visible.
3. Click in the Find what box.
4. Click Format for a drop-down list of formatting options that can be replaced.
5. Select Font.
6. Choose the font characteristics to be replaced: Font—Arial, Size—12 point, Style—Bold.
7. Click OK.
8. Click in the Replace with box, and again choose Font from the Format drop-down list.
9. Select a new font format such as Times New Roman, 14 point, Bold Italic, and click OK.

    Figure 7.8 shows the Replace screen. Notice that the fonts are listed under the Find what and Replace with boxes.

10. Click Replace All, or selectively replace each occurrence.

Replacing Special Characters and Elements

If you work with e-mail or receive other forms of electronic communication, you might get frustrated trying to copy the message to a document and manually delete all those carriage returns that break it up in short lines. It always takes twice as much paper to print and can't be shared as a readable document.

NEW TERM *E-mail* is short for electronic mail. E-mail messages are conveyed from one person's computer to another person's computer through computer networks. E-mail lines are usually shorter than normal lines.

Here's an idea for using one of Replace's Special options to get rid of all the extra carriage returns (paragraph marks) at the end of each line and let the text flow normally out to the margins.

7

Figure 7.8.

Replace can change fonts and other paragraph formatting.

Find this font ⌐

Replace with this font ⌐

The following steps are to preserve the places where paragraphs occur normally. A normal paragraph ends with a paragraph mark followed by another paragraph mark that creates the space between.

1. Click in the Find what box.
2. Select Paragraph Mark from the Format list (Word inserts ^p in the Find what box).
3. Select Paragraph Mark from the Format list again so that Word will insert a second ^p in the Find what box.
4. Type a character or combination that is not likely to be found anywhere in the document (such as ~ or *&*) in the Replace with box.
5. Click Replace All. All normal paragraph breaks have now been replaced with the special characters you typed.

The following steps are to get rid of all of the extra paragraph marks at the end of every line.

1. Click in the Find what box.
2. Select Paragraph Mark from the Format list (or type ^p in the box).
3. Click in the Replace with box and press the spacebar.
4. Click Replace All. (All of the remaining paragraph marks are replaced with spaces.)

The following steps are to bring back all of the natural paragraph breaks.

1. Click in the Find what box, and type the special characters.
2. Click in the Replace with box, and type ^p^p (the letter p must be lowercase).
3. Click Replace All (see Figure 7.9).

All the normal paragraphs that would have been eliminated when the paragraph marks were replaced were camouflaged as special characters while we got rid of the rest. The document is free of the annoying paragraph marks at the end of every line, and normal paragraphs are restored.

7

Figure 7.9.

Replace can eliminate extra paragraph marks in copies of e-mail messages.

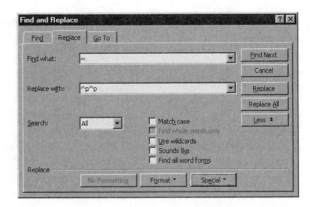

This technique also works when you get a document from a person who still uses the computer like a typewriter and presses the Enter key at the end of every line. Here's a quick list for this process:

☐ Find what: ^p^p

☐ Replace with: ~ and click Replace All

☐ Find what: ^p

☐ Replace with: space (press the spacebar once) and click Replace All

☐ Find what: ~

☐ Replace with: ^p^p and click Replace All

Experiment with Word's Replace function and you'll find many ways to use it for more than replacing text.

Summary

This hour shows how to cut, copy, and paste, or use drag-and-drop to move or copy text within a single document or between two documents.

Find lets you move quickly from one place to a specific word in your document. Replace lets you look for and replace one word with another—one word at a time or all occurrences of the word in a document at once. Replace also works to replace formatting, such as font styles and other special characters such as paragraph marks and page breaks.

Hour 8, "Setting Up the Page," features the how tos of setting up document margins, page numbers, headers, footers, and breaks.

Q&A

Q **I thought I was copying text and placing it in another location using the Ctrl+drag-and-drop method. Instead, it moved the text. What did I do wrong?**

A Always hold down the Ctrl key until after you release the mouse button. If you let up on the Ctrl key too soon, it moves rather than copies text.

Q **I have a hard time figuring out where to drop the box when I drag-and-drop something. Is there any easy way to know where it will land?**

A Ignore the box! Follow the vertical line; this is the real positioning tool. Put the vertical line exactly where you want to drop the text, then release the mouse button. The vertical line is just another mouse pointer.

Q **Find and Replace has another tab labeled GoTo. What does it do?**

A The primary function of GoTo is to quickly specify a page to jump to. Enter the page number in the box and click GoTo. It can be faster than using the scrollbar if you have a long document. Pressing Ctrl+G also brings up the GoTo dialog box.

Q **I tried to replace the paragraph marks in an e-mail message, but it didn't seem to work. I know I have paragraph marks. What could be wrong?**

A You may have inadvertently typed a space before or after the ^p in the Find what box. Be careful not to add any spaces before or after what you type in the boxes. Word recognizes the spaces as valid characters and looks for them. It may not find combinations in the document that include the paragraph mark and the space or spaces. Select everything in the box and press the Delete key, then try again.

7

Hour 8

Setting Up the Page

This hour looks at the intricacies of page setups. There are ways to automate some of the functions of building a document such as automatic page numbering, headers, and footers. All of the pages in a document will not necessarily have the same setup. It is important to understand how Word 97 deals with sections when some pages need to look different from others.

The highlights of this hour include

☐ How to set different margins for the first page than the pages that follow

☐ How to add page numbers

☐ What kinds of information can be added to headers and footers

☐ What the difference is between a page break and a section break

Margins

Margins create the picture frame of white space that surrounds a document. When you open a new document, there is already a frame around it. A page is normally 8½ inches wide and 11 inches high. If you look on the horizontal ruler, you'll see that it doesn't show 8½ inches. That's because Word assumes you'll want margins in every document. It creates a *default* margin for the sides, top, and bottom of the page.

NEW TERM   A *default* is a setting that was predefined by software developers as one that most users would select or one that optimizes the performance of the software. Defaults are automatically entered for many options to give users an idea of what the normal range of response should be. You can change many of Word's defaults.

There are three ways to set margins:

☐ Using File | Page Setup

☐ Using the rulers

☐ Using Print Preview

Setting Margins from File | Page Setup

Page Setup is the most common way to set margins. Word sets the default margins to 1 inch on the top and bottom and 1.25 inches on the sides. A lot of people like to have an even 1-inch margin on all sides. To change the margins:

1. Select File | Page Setup.

2. Click in the Left box, delete the current measurements (using the backspace or Delete key), and type 1 (Word adds the inch marks).

3. Click in the Right box, delete the current measurements, and type 1 (or use the down arrow to reduce the margin to 1 inch).

If you only want to change the margins for this document, click OK and you're done. If you want to have 1-inch margins for this and every new document, complete the following steps:

1. Click the Default button in the lower-left corner (see Figure 8.1).

Figure 8.1.

Using Page Setup to set default margins to 1 inch.

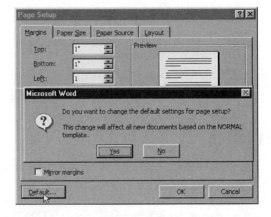

8

2. Click Yes when Word asks whether you want to change the default setting for Page Setup.

With the defaults changed, every new document you create has 1-inch margins on all sides unless you change them in Page Setup.

TIME SAVER

Instead of using the mouse, you can press the Tab key to move from one option to the next in a dialog box. Shift+Tab backs up one option at a time, in case you want to make a change.

Setting Margins from the Rulers

In Hour 6, "Formatting Paragraphs," you learned to use the horizontal ruler to set tabs and indents. The rulers are also a quick way to set margins, but it can take some practice to master the mouse technique.

Setting a margin from the rulers is much like setting an indent. It is a little trickier to position the mouse on the horizontal ruler at just the right spot. To set a left margin from the ruler:

1. Move the mouse slowly down from the First Line Indent button until you see a double-sided arrow with a Left Margin ToolTip (see Figure 8.2).

2. Click and drag the left indent to the right to increase the margin, or click and drag to the left to decrease the margin.

3. Release the mouse button to set the margin.

You can use the same technique to adjust the right margin. There is a thin gray line above the Right Indent button. This is the right margin line. Position the mouse above the Right Indent button on the ruler until you see the words Right Margin and the double-sided arrow, then drag the line to the right or left to adjust the margin.

Figure 8.2.

Setting the left margin from the ruler.

You can set the top and bottom margins from the vertical ruler as in Figure 8.3. If you don't see a ruler along the left edge of the screen, you are probably working in Normal view. Select Page Layout from the View menu (or use the Page Layout button above the Status bar). The vertical ruler is only visible in Page Layout view. To set a top margin for printing on a letterhead that needs about 2.5 inches at the top before text starts:

1. Position the mouse on the thin gray line between the darkened and white areas at the top of the ruler.

2. Click and drag the top margin line down until the darkened area (margin) reaches 2.5 at the top of the ruler.

3. Release the mouse button to set the margin.

As you move the margin, a line is displayed across the page that moves up or down as you move the top margin marker on the ruler. This provides an excellent visual to determine where your margin is at each location on the ruler.

Figure 8.3.

A dotted line across the page shows where the new margin will be.

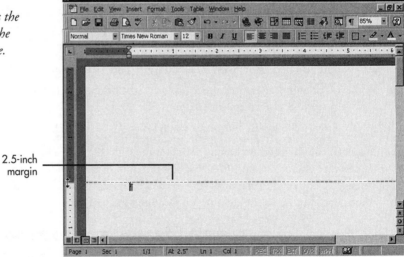

2.5-inch margin

JUST A MINUTE

There are many letterhead styles. Use a ruler to measure from the top of the page to a place below the header where text should begin. Use this measurement for the top margin. If there is text at the bottom of the letterhead, measure from the bottom of the page to a couple lines above the text to get a bottom margin measurement.

Once in a while you may grab a margin marker on a ruler and move it too quickly or you might find it difficult to set the margin to the exact measurement. You may want to use File | Page Setup to set the margins.

CAUTION

Printers won't allow you to print all the way to the edges of the paper. Many printers require at least a .3-inch margin on all sides. When you try to set a .2-inch margin, you get an error message as in Figure 8.4. If you click Fix It, the margin changes to the minimum required by the printer. If you ignore it, it leaves the margin at .2 inches, but your text may be cut off on that edge when it prints.

Figure 8.4.

Printers require a certain amount of margin space.

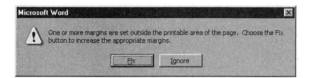

TIME SAVER

To bring up the Page Setup dialog box, double-click anywhere on the vertical ruler or in the dark area that indicates the margin space on the horizontal ruler.

Setting Margins from Print Preview

The third way to set margins is through Print Preview. Print Preview can be accessed in several ways:

☐ From File | Print Preview

☐ From the Print Preview button on the Standard toolbar

☐ By pressing Ctrl+F2

☐ By pressing Alt+F+V

Print Preview can display the whole page at once. The advantage to changing margins in this view is that you have a better picture of how all of the margins will look.

To set margins using Print Preview:

1. Click the Print Preview button, or select File | Print Preview.

2. Click the View Rulers button as in Figure 8.5 if the Rulers are not visible, and change the margins just as you would on the rulers in Page Layout view.

Figure 8.5.

Use Print Preview to change margins.

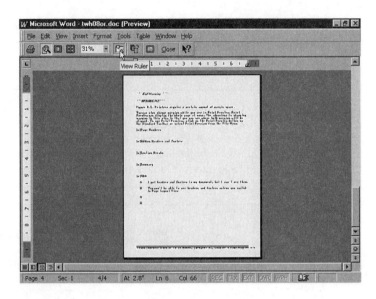

TIME SAVER

> You can also set tabs and indents on the ruler in Print Preview exactly as you do in Normal or Page Layout views.

Page Numbers

One of the tasks that Word can automate for you is adding page numbers to your documents. If you have a long document, you almost certainly want to add page numbers. It can get tedious, not to mention confusing, to type them on every page. Page numbers can be added through the Insert | Page Numbers menu or as part of a header or footer.

Figure 8.6 displays the Insert | Page Numbers dialog box. You have several options from which to choose:

☐ Position—Top of the page or Bottom of the page.

☐ Alignment—Left, Center, Right (less common are Inside and Outside, which relate to special publishing options).

☐ Show number on first page—Check this box if you want the page number to be visible on page 1. (Many documents do not display a number on the first page even though it will be counted as 1.)

8

Figure 8.6.

Selecting page number position and alignment.

Special publishing options for inside and outside alignment can be effective when printing on front and back or on *facing pages*. Check the Preview window to see what each option looks like before applying it.

NEW TERM *Facing pages* is a term used in publishing to refer to pages that are positioned side by side with elements on the right page in reverse order of the way they appear on the left page. An example is placing the page number in the lower-left corner of the left-hand page and in the lower-right corner of the right-hand page. This is the way most books are designed.

If you have a document that requires a different numbering style, you'll want to select Format from the Insert | Page Numbers dialog box. To change the numbering style to a capital letter style:

1. Select Insert | Page Numbers.
2. Select the desired position of the page number from the format box.
3. Select the desired alignment of the page from the alignment box.
4. Click Format.
5. Select A,B,C... from the drop-down list of number formats (see Figure 8.7).
6. Click OK to change the formats, then click OK again to save changes and exit the Page Numbers dialog box.

JUST A MINUTE

If you want the numbering to start with a letter other than A (perhaps you started lettering in a previous section with A, B, and C and want to start the next section where it left off) you can click Start At and enter D in the box to start with D in the second section.

Click Include Chapter Number and select a separator if you want to include these elements with the page number. To include chapter numbers, Word's heading styles must be used. You specify which heading level is used for the chapter numbers. For example, Heading 2 might be the style you have used for the chapter numbers.

If you want options other than the ones found in Page Numbers from the Insert menu, you'll want to explore the options for inserting page numbers from a header or footer.

Figure 8.7.

Choosing a page number format.

Adding Headers and Footers

Headers and footers offer lots of flexibility in the way page numbers and other document statistics can be displayed. If, for example, you want the word Page to appear with the page number, this addition can be made in a header or footer. To add a page number to a footer that displays as Page 1:

1. Select Header and Footer from the View menu. The Header and Footer toolbar will appear.

2. Click the Switch Between Header and Footer button to display the footer (see Figure 8.8).

Figure 8.8.

Using Header and Footer to add page numbers.

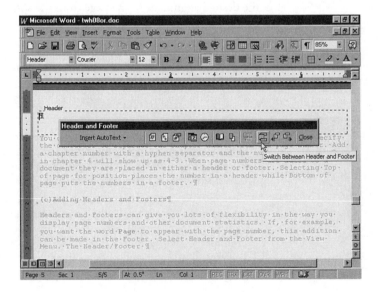

8

3. Tab twice to move to the right section of the footer.

4. Type the word Page, then press the spacebar.

5. Click the Insert Page Number button on the Header and Footer toolbar to insert automatic page numbering.

6. Click Close to close the header and footer panes.

If you inadvertently entered page numbers using Insert | Page Numbers and need to remove them, click the page number that shows in the footer (a four-sided arrow appears). Press the Delete key to remove the page numbers (see Figure 8.9).

Figure 8.9.

Removing numbers that were added using Page Numbers from the Insert menu.

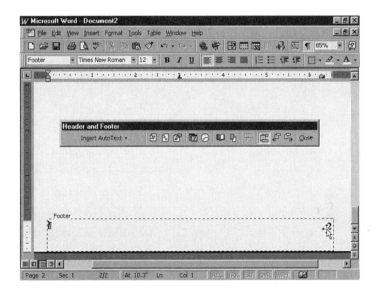

If you're in Page Layout view, double-click either the header or footer to quickly open it for editing. To close the header/footer, double-click anywhere in the document outside the header and footer.

There are three sections for every header and footer: a left section, center section, and right section. The Tab key moves between these sections. Elements you can add to a header or footer from the Header and Footer toolbar are

- ☐ Page numbers
- ☐ Total number of pages
- ☐ Date
- ☐ Time
- ☐ Special AutoText entries

You may have several entries in your AutoText collection, but Word has designed a few extra entries that come up when you click the AutoText button on the Header and Footer toolbar. These were designed specifically to be used with headers and footers and reports. Table 8.1 shows what will be displayed for each AutoText entry.

Table 8.1. AutoText entries in the Header and Footer toolbar.

AutoText item	Footer for page 1 will read
- PAGE -	- 1 -
Author, Page #, Date	James Martin Page 1 June 1, 1997
Confidential, Page #, Date	Confidential Page 1 June 1, 1997
Created by	Created by James Martin
Created on	Created on June 1, 1997 9:20 AM
Filename	Progress report.doc
Filename and path	D:\My Documents\Progress report.doc
Last printed	Last printed on March 14, 1997
Last saved by	Last saved by James Martin
Page X of Y	Page 1 of 12

How does Word know all of this information? Much of it is gathered from the document's properties. The next hour, "Managing Your Documents," explains document properties. Every computer keeps track of the date and time, so Word can ask the computer for those statistics.

8

TIME SAVER

> If Word enters dates in the header or footer in the M/D/YY format (6/1/97) and you prefer to have the dates spelled out completely, you can change Word's default. To change the date format:
>
> 1. Select Insert | Date and Time.
> 2. Click the picture of the date format you prefer under Available formats, then click the Default button.
> 3. Click Yes to confirm the change. Word uses this format for dates that are entered as fields, such as those in the header and footer.

If you have a two-page letter, you may want the second-page header and footer to be different from those of the first page. A report may have a different first page header and/or footer (or no header/footer) than the other pages. To set a different first page, click the Page Setup button on the Header and Footer toolbar and check the Different First Page box.

Breaks

Margins, page numbers, headers, and footers get more complicated when they need to be different in some parts of the document. An introduction to a book, a foreword, and a table of contents are examples of elements that don't fit the regular numbering system. You may want some of these items numbered with small Roman numerals (i, ii, iii). This is where section breaks can help.

Word can insert several kinds of breaks in a document. They each serve a different purpose. Table 8.2 describes the purpose of each kind of break.

Table 8.2. Kinds of breaks.

Break	Function
Page	Inserts a page break at the insertion point.
Column	Inserts a column break at the insertion point when working with columns (columns and column breaks are covered in Hour 19, "Jazzing Up Your Documents").
Section (Next page)	Inserts a section break and starts a new page.
Section (Continuous)	Inserts a section break and continues on the same page.
Section (Even page)	Inserts a section break and continues on the next evenly numbered page. If the break is inserted from another even-numbered page, a blank page is inserted between the sections.
Section (Odd page)	Inserts a section break and continues on the next odd-numbered page. If the break is inserted from another odd-numbered page, a blank page is inserted between the sections.

Figure 8.10 shows the different kinds of breaks that can be applied from the Insert |
Break menu.

Figure 8.10.

*Inserting a break in a
document.*

Page and Column Breaks

Sometimes you may just want a page break if the pages are numbered and formatted in the
same way. You might, for example, have a table that you don't want to split between pages.
To insert a page break before the table:

1. Position the cursor in the paragraph before the table.

2. Select Insert | Break.

3. Select Page break.

4. Click OK.

A manual page break is created. If you're working in columns, the same method can be used
to apply a manual column break. You would click Column break rather than Page break.

**KEYBOARD
SHORTCUT**

> Ctrl+Enter creates a page break. Ctrl+Shift+Enter creates a column break.

Section Breaks—Next Page

A section break can be used to create a break between pages or sections of the same page. To
add a section break:

1. Place the insertion point where the break should be.

2. Select Insert | Break.

3. Select Next page from the Section breaks options.

4. Click OK.

Each section can be formatted individually. The margins, headers, footers, and other elements can be different for each section. Using a Next page section break allows portrait and landscape sections within the same document. Portrait means that the document is lined up to print across the short width of the page while landscape prints across the long width. For regular typing paper, portrait prints across the 8½-inch side and landscape across the 11-inch side.

To set a page orientation to landscape:

1. Select File | Page Setup (or double-click the vertical ruler if you're in Page Layout view).
2. Click the Paper Size tab.
3. Select Landscape under Orientation.
4. Click OK.

You can mix portrait and landscape pages throughout a document as long as there is a Next page section break between each one. You can't print both ways on one page. The printer wouldn't know how to handle that assignment.

Although you can set page numbers to be different in each section, there may be times when you want the page numbering to continue from the first section to the next. To continue the same numbering sequence:

1. Position the cursor in the new section.
2. Select View | Header and Footer.
3. Click the Same as Previous button on the Header and Footer toolbar.
4. Click Close.

If you want the second section to start with a specific number, use the Format Page Number button on the Header and Footer toolbar. Click the Start at option and enter the page number you want the section to begin with. This is a useful feature if you are saving sections, such as chapters of a book, as separate files and want to number them consecutively. You can set the beginning page number for each file.

Section Breaks—Continuous

Choosing Continuous inserts a break but continues the next section on the same page. Figure 8.11 shows a document that has a heading in one section and the start of two columns of text in another section on the same page. The heading margins are .5 inches on the left and right, while the margins in the second section are 1 inch.

Figure 8.11.

Sections can be formatted differently on the same page.

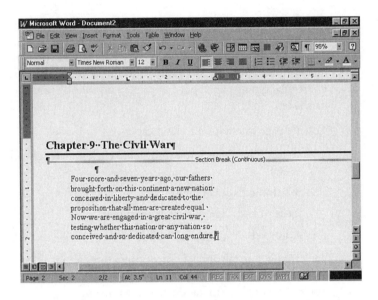

JUST A MINUTE

> If you want to have a heading on one page with columns underneath, as in the previous example, you must use a continuous section break.

Section Breaks—Even and Odd Page

Even page and odd page section breaks are seldom used unless you get into book publishing or other print medium where pages will be back-to-back and all of the chapters or sections start on either the even- or odd-numbered pages. Many times a book is laid out so that the chapters begin on the right-hand page, thus the first page of each section is an odd-numbered page.

Solving Page Break Problems

There are ways to get around some of the undesirable page splits that occur normally. It makes a document difficult to work with in the editing stages if there are manual page breaks in several locations. Even the smallest addition to a page can cause it to spill onto a new page. Manual page breaks cause separate pages with a line or two of text because the breaks won't allow text to wrap to the next page as it normally would have. There are two options that can help avoid some of these awkward page breaks: Keep lines together and Widow/Orphan control.

If a paragraph divides between pages and you want the entire paragraph on one page, try this:

1. Position the cursor anywhere in the paragraph.
2. Right-click to bring up the shortcut menu.

8

3. Select Paragraph.

4. Under the tab for Line and Page breaks, click Keep lines together (see Figure 8.12). Word does not split the paragraph between two pages.

The Widow/Orphan control prevents the problem of having a single line of a paragraph on a page by itself. The Widow/Orphan control looks at the first line of a paragraph (the orphan) and the last line of a paragraph (the widow). With Widow/Orphan control checked, it prevents either the widow or the orphan from being placed on a page by itself.

Figure 8.12.

Preventing awkward page breaks with Keep lines together and Widow/Orphan control.

Summary

Pages are framed by margins, which are part of the page setup. Another element of the page is its headers and footers, which automate processes such as adding page numbers and dates to every page of a document. Adding section breaks makes it possible to format some parts of the document differently from others.

Hour 9 looks at saving and printing documents and organizing them so that they can be found the next time they're needed.

Q&A

Q I tried to set the left and right margins from the ruler, but I couldn't find the double-sided arrows to change the margins.

A You need to be in Page Layout view to set margins from either of the rulers.

Q **I put headers and footers in my document, but I can't see them. Could I have deleted them by accident?**

A You won't be able to see headers and footers unless you switch to Page Layout view.

Q **I like to include a date in my headers but I prefer it to print the name of the month, the day, and the full year. Header/Footer only gives me the option for M/D/YY in numbers. Is there any way to change this?**

A Yes. Use Date and Time from the Insert menu. A list displays many choices for date and time formatting. Select the format you prefer. If this is the date style you use most often, click Default. If you say Yes to make the change, the next time you insert a date in a footer using the Date button, it will automatically use this format. Checking the Update automatically box will change the date each time you print the document. If you want the date to remain the same, leave the box unchecked.

Q **What would I use headers and footers for besides page numbers, titles, and dates?**

A A header or footer can contain anything you want to appear at the top or bottom of every page in the document. This could include a letterhead, a logo, borders and lines, and other graphics. Hour 19 includes ideas for using headers and footers creatively.

Real World Example

RW 2

Word in Real Time

Figure R2.1 shows the first page of a 10-page document that was double-spaced for a publication and now needs to be rearranged and formatted for use with a new audience. Some of the paragraphs will not be used in this version, and others will be shifted to different places. It needs a footer, page numbers, a title page, and section subtitles. The original file needs to remain intact.

Figure R2.1.
Modifying a report before distribution.

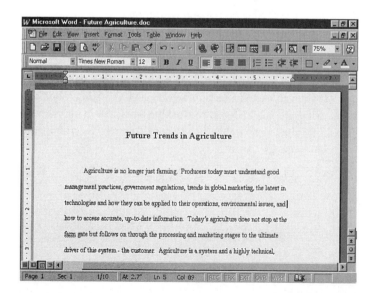

Step 1—Sketching the Document Plan

Grab paper and a pencil to sketch out the way you want a document to look before heading for the computer. Determine how many sections you will need and what kind of formatting will be applied to each section. Figure out whether you need headers and footers and what kinds of page numbering will be applied. This project requires three sections: a title page, an Executive Summary page, and the body of the report.

Section 1 (the title page) should have text centered vertically and horizontally. No header, footer, or page numbers are required.

Section 2 (the Executive Summary) needs a 1-inch margin on all sides, and a footer with the report title in the left section, the date in the center section, and the page number (in small Roman numeral style i, ii, iii).

Section 3 (the report) requires a 1.5-inch top margin and 1-inch margins on the other sides for page 1 and 1-inch margins on all sides for the pages that follow. The footer needs to remain the same as for section 2 with the exception that the page numbering needs to start with page 1 (in regular numbering style 1, 2, 3).

Step 2—Setting Up the Sections of the New Document

The document will require three separate sections. Set up the sections first. To start a new document and set up the sections:

1. Click New on the Standard toolbar.
2. Press Enter and select Insert | Break. Click Next page under Section breaks.
3. Press Enter again and add a second section break like the first.

You will see two sets of dotted lines across the page with the words Section Break (Next Page). If you can't see the section breaks, click the Show/Hide button on the Standard toolbar as in Figure R2.2. If you're working in Page Layout view, you will see the borders of the individual pages rather than the dotted lines. Continuous section breaks do appear as dotted lines in Page Layout view.

Figure R2.2.

Clicking Show/Hide to show the newly created section breaks.

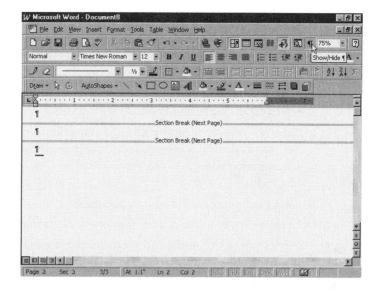

Step 3—Formatting the Sections

Margins, alignment, footers, and page numbers need to be formatted for each section as specified in the document plan.

Format Section 1 for the Title Page

To set up the first section:

1. Select the paragraph mark in section 1.
2. Click the Center button on the Formatting toolbar to center text that will be entered on the title page.
3. Select File | Page Setup and click the Layout tab.
4. Under Vertical alignment, select Center. This places the lines on the page an equal distance from the top and bottom margins.
5. Click OK.

Format Section 2 for the Executive Summary

The margins need to be set to 1 inch on all sides for section 2. Position the cursor in the second section and select File | Page Setup to set the margins.

To add a footer to section 2:

1. Select View | Header and Footer.
2. Enter text that should appear at the bottom of each page (for example, the title on the left, the date in the center, and the page number on the right). Note that text can be formatted in the footer just as document text is formatted using the Formatting toolbar.
3. Click the Insert Page Number button on the Header and Footer toolbar.
4. Click the Format Page Number button on the Header and Footer toolbar.
5. Select the i, ii, iii Number format and click Start at: i (see Figure R2.3). Otherwise, it will start numbering at ii because it considers the title page the first page.
6. Click OK.

Make sure that the footer does not have a label above it that says Same as previous. If it does, locate the Same as previous button on the Header/Footer Toolbar and click it to remove this option. The title page will be numbered if this option is selected.

CAUTION

> Sometimes you get a footer that you don't want in a previous section or one that follows. If you have turned off the Same as previous option, move to the footer that you want to remove, then highlight and delete its contents. It should not affect the headers and footers in other sections.

Figure R2.3.

Select the number format.

Page Number Format	? X
Number format:	i, ii, iii, ...
□ Include chapter number	
Chapter starts with style	Heading 1
Use separator:	(hyphen)
Examples: 1-1, 1-A	
Page numbering	
○ Continue from previous section	
⦿ Start at:	i
	OK Cancel

Format the Section for the Report

Section 3 will contain the report. It needs to be formatted with a footer like the one in section 2 with the title, date, and regular page numbers (1, 2, 3). To add a footer to section 3:

1. Position the cursor in section 3.
2. Select View | Header and Footer.
3. Click the Same as Previous button to make the text the same as the text in the Executive Summary footer.
4. Click the Format Page Numbers and select the 1, 2, 3 Number format and Start at: 1.

Step 4—Adding Text to the Report

Type the title page and Executive Summary text. The original document will provide the text for the report. Leave the new document open and open the original document. The text from the original will be copied into section 3 of the new document and manipulated. To do this:

1. Position the cursor anywhere in the original document and press Ctrl+A to select the entire document.
2. Click the Copy button on the Standard toolbar.
3. Select the Window menu and select the new document from the list of open documents at the bottom of the menu.
4. Position the cursor in section 3 and click the Paste button.

This section requires a 1.5-inch top margin for the first page and 1-inch top margins for the pages that follow. It is not a good idea to use a fourth section break to change the top margin for the second page of a section. Text and page numbers need to follow a normal flow throughout this section. Numbers can follow consecutively and additions or deletions to text will cause normal text wrapping between pages.

1. Select the title.
2. Select Format | Paragraph.
3. In the Indents and Spacing tab, type .5" in the Before box under Spacing. Word recognizes inches as well as point size for many such options.
4. Click OK.

This adds the extra .5 inch before the first paragraph that is needed for the first page margin.

The original document was double-spaced. To change it to 1.5 line spacing:

1. Select the whole document by pressing Ctrl+A or holding down the Ctrl key and clicking in the left margin.
2. Press Ctrl+5 to apply 1.5 line spacing, or select Format | Paragraph and select 1.5 lines from the drop-down list of line spacing options in the Indents and Spacing tab.

Highlight the title and increase the font size to 18 points using the Font size drop-down list on the Formatting toolbar.

Type in a subtitle such as the one in Figure R2.4 and format it as bold and italic. Highlight the subtitle and increase the font three point sizes by holding down the Ctrl key and pressing the right bracket (]s) three times (the keyboard shortcut for increasing font size).

Figure R2.4.

Adding and formatting a subtitle.

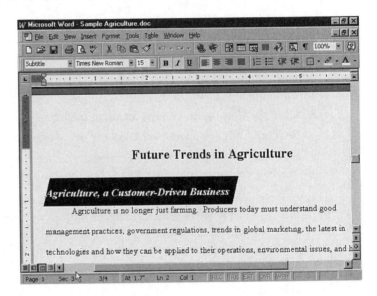

Select and delete paragraphs from the new document that will not be used. The remaining paragraphs can be rearranged using Cut and Paste or drag-and-drop.

Word has a function called Spike that works something like the clipboard, but the contents of the Spike are not replaced when new material is added as is done with the clipboard. It holds several items in the Spike until you empty its contents. To add an item to the Spike, select it and press Ctrl+F3.

This is a way to quickly move several nonadjacent paragraphs. In this report, two paragraphs from page 1, one paragraph from page 2, two paragraphs from page 3, and a paragraph from page 5 need to be moved to the end of the document. To use the Spike to accomplish this:

1. Select the two paragraphs from page 1 and press Ctrl+F3 to add them to the Spike.

2. Scroll down to page 2 and select the paragraph that needs to be moved. Press Ctrl+F3 to add it to the Spike.

3. Continue gathering the paragraphs from pages 3 and 5 in the document in the same fashion.

4. Position the cursor at the end of the document where the text is to be inserted and press Ctrl+Shift+F3 to empty the contents of the Spike (all six paragraphs) in this location.

With the addition of a few more headings, a little drag-and-drop, and the use of the Spike, the new report will take shape in no time.

PART

III

Personalizing Word

Hour

Hour 9

Managing Your Documents

This hour shows you how to organize, save, and print documents. Word 97 can help you avoid incidences of those files that fly off to never–never land—they take up space, but who knows where? Using the My Documents and Favorites folders can put a little order in the house; even the best-organized users occasionally misplace a file. Word has some great features to help find those strays.

The highlights of this hour include

- ☐ How files are stored on a drive
- ☐ What new features make it easier to organize and find files
- ☐ How to locate lost files
- ☐ How and when to save a document
- ☐ How to change printer settings

Saving Files

Files must be saved in order to be reused. If you have a file you want to use again, it needs to be saved. You can save a file to a hard drive, a floppy disk in a floppy drive, a network drive (if you're connected to a network), or a storage device such as a tape drive. There are several ways to save a file:

- [ ] Select Save from the File menu.
- [ ] Click the Save icon on the Standard toolbar.
- [ ] Press Ctrl+S.

When you save a file for the first time, the Save As dialog box comes up (see Figure 9.1). Word asks you to supply the following information:

- [ ] A name for the file (in the File name box)
- [ ] The type of file (in the Save as type box)
- [ ] A place to save the file (in the Save in box)

Figure 9.1.

Word asks you to give the file a name.

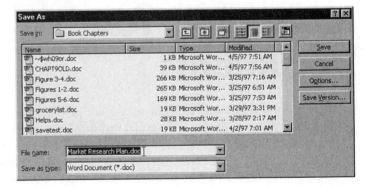

Once the file is saved and has a name, Word does not open the Save As dialog box the next time you save it. If you make changes to the document, click the Save button, and Word automatically saves the file without bringing up a dialog box.

Each time you start a new document, Word gives the document a generic document name like Document1 or Document2 until you save it. These are temporary files that will be gone when you exit Word unless you save and name them.

You can work with several documents at the same time. Select Window from the Main menu to display a list of all the open documents (see Figure 9.2). You change which document is displayed in the typing screen by clicking one of the document names in the list. This list shows that there are three unsaved documents—Document2, Document3, and Document7.

Figure 9.2.

The Window menu shows the names of all saved and unsaved documents.

Open documents ──────

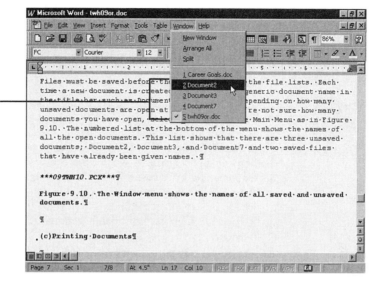

Having three unsaved documents open, as there are in Figure 9.2, should send up smoke signals. It's probably time to close or save some of the files. If you're working on a project that you can't afford to lose, save soon and save often!

It's a good idea to get in the habit of naming each new document immediately. Word's AutoRecover option is helpful, but it is less reliable for unnamed documents. If a storm causes a power outage and the computer goes down, chances are some things will be recovered, but not everything. Unsaved new documents are the most vulnerable.

Naming Files

If you have already started typing your document, Word will display the first line of text as a suggested filename. You can accept Word's suggestion or you can supply your own name for the file; simply start typing the name you want.

One of the beauties of using Windows 95 is that you can save files with long filenames. This is one of the features that comes from the Mac environment that PC users waited a long time for. Filenames used to be limited to eight characters with a three-character extension.

 An *extension* is the part of a filename that follows the period after the actual filename. The extension is the identifier that tells Word what program or type of program created the file. When you open a file of another type, Word's filters and converters look at the extension to figure out what kind of file it is. Word sees .pcx and recognizes it as a graphics file in PCX format.

You might suspect that a company's annual report for a given year would be called something like anrept93.doc. Now you can call it Annual Report for 1993. Word automatically adds the .doc extension for you. Filenames can be up to 255 characters, including spaces—that's probably more than you'll ever need.

CAUTION

> / \ ; : * ? " < > ¦
>
> These are the only characters that are not permitted when naming files or folders. (However, Word will permit the / and \ characters at the beginning of a filename; when these characters are added to the filename, the file is saved up one level from the current folder.) The tilde mark (~) is another character to avoid in naming files. Windows uses the tilde to indicate truncated filenames. Although you can use long filenames, it's good to keep them as brief as possible. Otherwise, file lists become unwieldy.

File Types

Word saves a file as a Word document unless you tell it to save the file as something else in the Save as type box. There may be times when you want to share a file with someone who doesn't use Word. The drop-down list in the Save as type box shows some of the other file types Word can save files in (see Figure 9.3). There are options to save in earlier versions of Word, Word for Macintosh, WordPerfect, and others.

Figure 9.3.

Saving a file for someone with a different word processor.

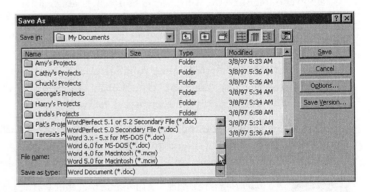

You might get a request for a file in *text* or *ASCII* format. Programs like Word and WordPerfect are sophisticated programs that have a lot of hidden information in a file. The information might tell the program to make text bold or to set an indention. Sometimes a file is needed that doesn't have any of the hidden programming code. That's when a text or ASCII file might be requested.

9

The important thing to remember is that if you get such a request, Word can handle it. Use Save As to save the file to any one of the text formats (text only, rich text format, and so on). You might steer clear of the Text with Line Breaks option unless someone specifically requests this format. It inserts a paragraph mark at the end of each line.

> *Text* and *ASCII* files are synonymous terms for a standard file type that includes the typed characters, spaces, punctuation, and other very basic elements such as ends of paragraphs. Some text file formats recognize tabs; others do not.

Text or ASCII files are stripped of hidden program codes, making them readable in any standard word-processing program as well as in some other types of programs. Converters are not needed to read or share these files between different programs. The down side is that the formatting is usually lost, as are any graphics or other objects that were inserted in the file.

You may sometimes need to make a copy of the file you're working on for someone else. You might want to save the document to a floppy disk. Instead of using the Save option, select Save As from the File menu. In the Save As dialog box, click in the Look in box and select the floppy drive that houses the disk. You can either keep the same filename or give it a different name.

Backups

Important files should always be backed up. *Backup* refers to creating a second copy in case something happens to the original. Backups should be saved somewhere other than the place where the original is saved. For example, if a file and its backup are both stored on the hard drive and something happens to the hard drive, both copies are gone. You can use floppy disks or a number of other storage devices to store backups.

People often don't heed the warning to make backups until they've lost critical files. Ask yourself, "What do I have to lose?" The answer determines the urgency and frequency of your backups. You might want to set up a regular time for backups; for example, you might want to back up every Friday afternoon. There are many software programs to help automate the process of backing up files.

Many offices are now connected to network drives where files are saved. These files are usually automatically backed up by the network administrator. If you need to recover a file that was stored on a network drive, your network administrator may be able to help.

Giving Files a Home

In addition to asking for a filename and file type, Word asks you where you want to store the file. You need to give it a permanent home if you want to use it again. Click the Save in box, and you'll see all the different places you can save a file.

If you want to save in one of the subfolders that is not displayed, click the folder name where the subfolder is located, and a list of all the subfolders in that folder appears. Selecting the subfolder name does not mean that you are in that folder. You must double-click the subfolder name to save a file in that subfolder. Look at the name in the Save in box to make sure that you are in the subfolder. Name the file as discussed previously and click Save.

The available save locations you have depend on the kinds of drives on your system. Some options that might be available to you include

☐ Hard drive

☐ Disk in a floppy disk drive

☐ Disk in a storage device such as a Zip drive

☐ Network drive (if you are connected to a network)

Organizing Files

Files can be stored in folders to keep them better organized. It helps to have some sort of file organization in mind before you start saving lots of files. Word 97 has several features that can make storing and retrieving files easier, but this is one place where structured types and free spirits probably disagree most.

Some people work better from stacks of papers out on their desks. They know exactly where everything is. Others have to have every piece of paper filed neatly away in a file drawer. Then there are folks who have stacks everywhere and don't know where anything is. That's the scenario to avoid when storing your Word documents.

The Folder System

Another idea to find its way to PCs from the Mac is the use of pictures or icons to tell you where files are stored. Prior to Windows, you had to know exactly where a file was and had to type its exact location and name to use it.

The first versions of Windows helped out by giving us at least a listing of file locations and names to choose from. Windows 95 went a step further by displaying locations as folders. The folders contain files and/or other folders, as shown in Figure 9.4.

Figure 9.4.

Folder icons represent containers for files and other folders.

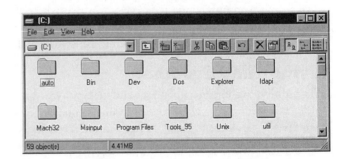

The files inside the folders are displayed as icons. The icons have different pictures depending on the programs they were created with. Figure 9.5 shows files created by the four main Office applications. The flying W denotes a Word file, the X denotes an Excel file, the small video screen denotes a PowerPoint file, and the key denotes an Access file.

Figure 9.5.

File icons show what programs were used to create the files.

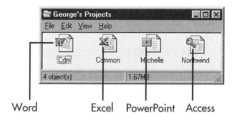

Folders can be created to hold files that fit into certain categories. Maybe you want to create folders for major projects you work on. Perhaps there are several people who use the same computer and you need to separate each individual's files, as shown in Figure 9.6. Whatever your system of organization, Word can adapt to your style. There are also a couple of built-in tools that you can use.

Figure 9.6.

Folders can be set up for individuals who work at the same computer.

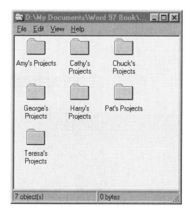

Create a Folder from File | Save As

One of the processes that used to slow down work was having to stop what you were doing to create a new folder. You had to get out of Word and go to File Manager, or exit Windows to a DOS prompt to create a folder (called a subdirectory in those days). It's now a simple task you can perform while you're in Word:

1. Select File | Save As.
2. Locate the drive and folder where you want the new subfolder.

3. Click the Create New Folder icon.

4. In the New Folder dialog box, type a name for the folder, and then click OK. If you're saving a new file at the same time you're creating the folder to put it in, double-click the new folder so that the Save in box displays the folder name.

5. Type a name for the file in the File name box and Click Save. If you're not saving a file, click Cancel.

The My Documents Folder

Windows creates a folder called My Documents for you. Whether you use it is up to you, but it is a design feature to help organize files. There are a couple of reasons for this feature:

☐ People didn't know where their files were saved. They just used the Save function and let Word put it wherever it wanted. They couldn't find files again after they were saved without a lot of searching.

☐ Document files were being saved in the same place as program files (the ones the programs need in order to run). When people deleted files to free up hard disk space, they often accidentally deleted program files.

☐ People do more job and computer sharing these days. It helps to know there is one standard location among computers in the office where documents can be found.

☐ Windows sets a default in Word to tell it to look first in the My Documents folder for files (see Figure 9.7)—saving files there makes them easy to find.

Figure 9.7.

Word looks first in the My Documents folder for files.

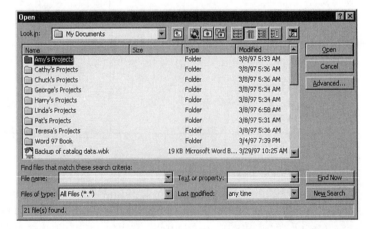

If you don't want to store your files in the My Documents folder, Word lets you choose where it looks first for files. Hour 11, "Customizing Word to the Way You Work," tells how to change this option. You can store all your files in My Documents if you like. Put the Excel, Access, Word, and PowerPoint files in the same place.

Each Office 97 program looks for files that were created by that program and displays them in the Open dialog box file list. PowerPoint, for example, creates files with a .ppt extension. When you start PowerPoint and select File | Open, you only see the PowerPoint files in the file list. Word creates files with a .doc extension. When you open a file in Word, you only see the files with a .doc extension unless you choose another file type (or select All Files) from the Files of type list (see Figure 9.8). You can always create subfolders in My Documents if you want to further categorize your documents.

Figure 9.8.
Word displays only Word (.doc) files unless you select another file type.

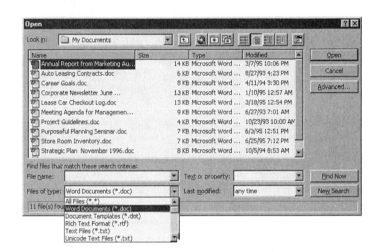

The Favorites Folder

A great Word 97 feature is the Favorites folder. Favorites is a little different from My Documents; it offers a way to create shortcuts to get to the files rather than a place to save the files themselves. A shortcut is simply a pointer to a file that is stored in another location. It is not the actual file. To add a shortcut to Favorites:

1. Select File | Open or click the Open button from the Standard toolbar.
2. Locate the file you want to add to Favorites by clicking the Look in box and finding the drive and folder name where the file is stored.
3. Select the filename from the file list.
4. Click the Add to Favorites button (see Figure 9.9). You can add to Favorites a shortcut to the file or to the entire folder where the file is stored.
5. Click OK.

Figure 9.9.
Adding files to the Favorites folder.

Look in Favorites ⌐ ⌐ Add to Favorites

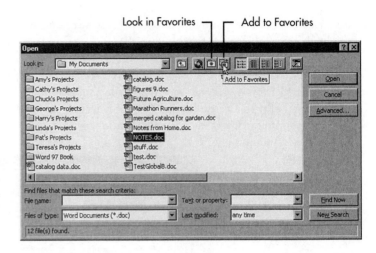

The next time you need to use the file you saved to Favorites:

1. Select File | Open or click the Open button on the Standard toolbar.
2. Click the Look in Favorites button.
3. Double-click the file's shortcut. Word goes to where the file is stored and opens it.

Finding Documents

No matter how well organized your files and folders are, you probably misplace a file from time to time. Word has tools to help find those occasional strays.

Finding Files—Open Document

There are many ways to find files from the Open dialog box. Sometimes it helps to see files sorted in a certain way. You can sort the file list by simply clicking one of the column headings above the file list (Name, Size, Type, or Modified). For example, you can click Name to sort the list alphabetically, or click Modified to sort the list by date, as shown in Figure 9.10.

If you don't see these buttons above the file list, it's because you are viewing the file list in Detail view. There are four ways to view files in the Open dialog box, and Detail is the only one that allows sorting.

☐ *List* displays files as small icons.

☐ *Details* displays filenames with their statistics: Name, Size, Type, and Modified.

☐ *Properties* displays document properties. Some of the properties are added by the computer (filename, date last saved, and so on), and some can be added by the user from File | Properties.

☐ *Preview* displays the first page of each file, as shown in Figure 9.11.

Figure 9.10.

Sorting the file list by the dates the files were last modified.

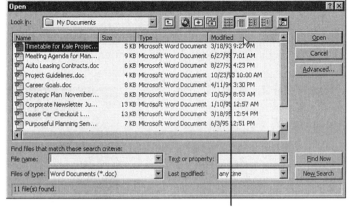

Last date modified

Figure 9.11.

Using Preview mode to display the first page of the document.

List   Details Properties   Preview

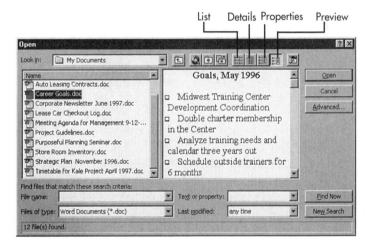

Viewing files in one of these ways can be your ticket to finding that misplaced file, but if that doesn't do it, try the following:

1. Select File | Open.

2. Click in the box that says Text or property.

3. Type a word that is contained in the document you're searching for. If there is something that only this file would contain, that's the best term to use. If not, try to find something that would only be found in a few files.

4. Click Find Now. Word looks through the folder selected in the Look in box for any file containing this text. The file list displays only the names of the files that include this text.

You can add summary information to your documents to make this kind of search more effective. Figure 9.12 shows the kind of information you can enter for a document from File | Properties. Entering unique file identifiers in areas like the Category and Keywords boxes can be very helpful when you need to find a file or a group of files.

Figure 9.12.

Using document proper-ties to identify files.

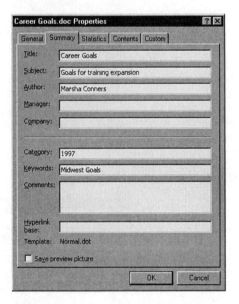

Type a couple of words that are unique to this document in the Keywords box. Keywords can be used as indicators to find the file. If you've ever used a computer search system in a library, you've worked with a keyword search. Enter a keyword, and the search system runs through millions of entries to find books and other resources that have been indexed with that keyword. When you enter keywords, you are building that kind of search system into your Word program.

Finding a file from its properties works exactly like finding text included in the file. Word asks for text or property in the Open dialog box. It also searches Properties (such as keywords) you entered in the summary for files that match.

TIME SAVER

A search using text or property also brings up documents that include the text in the filename. This is because the filename is one of the pieces of information the computer enters in the document's properties that you find listed under Files | Properties in the General tab.

9

The more you narrow a search, the quicker Word finds a file. Select one of the options such as Yesterday, This Week, or This Month from the Last Modified drop-down list for files that were created recently. Resubmit the new request by clicking Find Now. If no files are found, the Advanced Find function can widen the search.

Advanced Find

If the file is not in the folder in the Look in box, you may need to look further. Advanced Find can locate files that are stored anywhere on a drive that you have access to. To use Advanced Find

1. Click the Advanced button in the Open dialog box.

2. Select the drive to search from the drop-down Look in list (see Figure 9.13).

3. Select what you search for in the Property box (for example, text or property, filename, or keyword). The more you can narrow the places Word has to look, the faster the search.

4. Select a condition such as "includes words" or "ends with phrase." Conditions differ depending on the Property box selection.

5. Type what you want Word to search for in the Value box. In Figure 9.13, Word is asks to search for all files that include the word Marketing in either the documents or their properties.

6. Click the Add to List button to add your search criteria to the current list of criteria at the top of the box.

7. Repeat steps 3–6 to add more criteria if desired. The more criteria, the better the returns.

Figure 9.13.

Advanced Find expands Word's capability to find files.

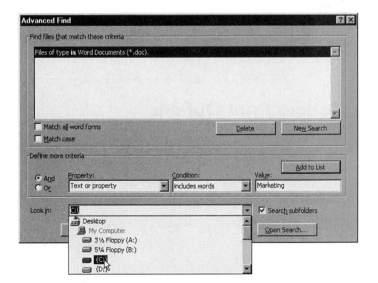

8. Check the box beside Search Subfolders to look for files in all the folders and subfolders for that drive.

9. Click Find Now, and Word brings up a list of files that fit the description.

Step-Up

Many earlier versions of Word's file search feature (Find File) were so slow that people only used it as a last resort. Word's file search is much faster now—you'll be pleasantly surprised. You get almost instant results unless you're searching huge network drives.

Printing Documents

Printing out a copy of a file is usually the primary purpose for creating it in the first place. The quickest way to send a document to the printer is to click the Printer icon on the Standard toolbar. Word asks no questions; it just sends the document off to print.

Print Preview

If you're printing the document for the first time, you might want to use Print Preview to view the file as it's going to print before putting it on paper. To view a document in Print Preview:

1. Click Print Preview on the Standard toolbar or select Print Preview from the File menu (see Figure 9.14).

2. Click the Multiple Pages button to see a thumbnail sketch of up to six pages at once.

3. Click the Printer icon to print from Print Preview if everything looks good.

4. Click the Close button or press the Esc key to exit Print Preview.

Setting Print Options

Sometimes you want to give Word a little guidance about what you want to print. You might not want to print every page of a document, or you might want several copies and don't want to have to press the Print button multiple times. These are times when you want to work through the Print dialog box shown in Figure 9.15. Table 9.1 explains the various print options.

9

Figure 9.14.

View a document with Print Preview before printing.

Print —

Close —

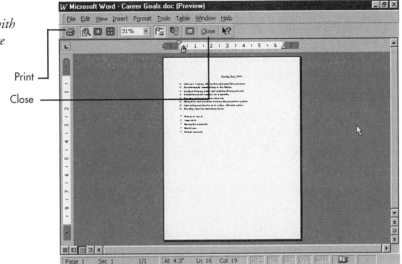

Figure 9.15.

Selecting printing options.

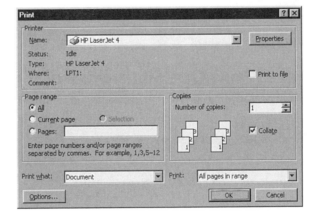

KEYBOARD SHORTCUT

Ctrl+P is a shortcut to the Print dialog box.

Table 9.1. Common printing options.

Print option	What it does
Name	Allows you to select from the drop-down list of available printers
Page range (All)	Prints all pages in the document
Page range (Current page)	Prints the page the cursor is on
Page range (Pages)	Prints specific pages or a range of pages
Copies	Prints the number of copies specified
Collate	Prints the pages in order (uncheck to print all copies of one page first, then all copies of the next page, and so on)
Print	Prints all pages, odd pages, or even pages

CAUTION

If you choose Collate, it takes much longer to print. If you have to get something out in a hurry, uncheck the Collate box.

Other Print Options from Page Setup

Some of the print options are part of the page setup. To set page setup options that apply to printing:

1. Select File | Page Setup.
2. In the Paper Size tab, select either Portrait or Landscape under Orientation.
3. In the Paper Source tab, select the paper tray you want to print from, as shown in Figure 9.16.
4. Click OK.

If you have two paper trays or an envelope feeder, they appear among the options. What you see under First page and Other pages is specific to your printer. Select the location you want the document to print from.

If you keep plain paper in one tray and letterhead in another, you may want to send the first page of a letter from the letterhead tray and the rest of the pages from the other tray. Select the appropriate trays for First page and Other pages.

Almost every printer lets you insert the sheets one at a time and initiate the print process from the printer rather than have all of the pages come out automatically. This is accomplished through the Manual Feed option. Check your printer manual to find out how this works for your printer. When you're using expensive forms such as mailing labels, you may want the tight control over the print process that Manual Feed offers.

Figure 9.16.

Selecting the paper source from Page Setup.

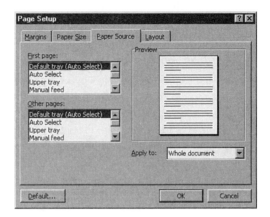

TIME SAVER

If you need to quickly print a file, you don't have to open it:

1. Select File | Open.
2. Locate the filename.
3. Right-click the filename.
4. Select Print from the shortcut menu. Word prints the file without opening it.

Summary

This hour explores how to save files for later use. Saving files in locations where they can be found is easily handled with the My Documents and Favorites folders. If you lose a file, Word has multiple ways to find it. Entering document properties can help index files to make them easier to find. Properties and Advanced Find features are powerful search tools to find files quickly.

Once created, documents are usually destined for print. Word's print options allow you to specify which pages and how many copies to print.

Q&A

Q **If it's so easy to find my files from the Favorites folder, shouldn't I make shortcuts to all my files there?**

A If you do, you'll soon be looking through long lists of files. It would be better to limit Favorites to those you use most often if you want to locate them quickly.

Q **I want to save a file for someone who has a word-processing package that isn't listed in the Save as type options. Is there some way I can save a file in formats other than those listed?**

A The first step is to find out whether the other word-processing package has options to accept files in different formats. It may be that the program can accept Word files or at least an earlier version of Word. It may not read Word files, but it might recognize WordPerfect files. You can always save as one of the file types the other word-processing package will read.

If all else fails, save the document in one of the text formats. Every word processing package can handle a text file. If graphics or other elements are important to the document that won't transfer in text format, there are programs on the market that will transfer files to and from almost any format. Explore all the other options before making the investment, though.

Hour **10**

It's All in the Way You View It

This hour is about the many options you see on the View menu, along with Print Preview. Some views are tied to a particular Word function such as outlining; others are simply a matter of personal preference in the way people like to view the Word screen. You can do some things in certain views that you can't do in others. Learning how and when to use each view is the focus for this hour.

The highlights of this hour include

☐ What elements are standard in most views

☐ How Normal and Page Layout views are different

☐ What kinds of tasks you do in each view

☐ What Print Preview can do for you

Word Views

Word has several view options that serve specific purposes and display different elements onscreen. Hour 3, "Getting Around in Word," discusses many of the screen elements, such as menus, toolbars, and scrollbars. Some views display elements that others do not. Because of the way each view is designed, some tasks are more easily accomplished in one view than another. Hour 11, "Customizing Word to the Way You Work," details some of the options you might want to change for each view.

There are two ways to change a document view. One is by selecting View Options on the View menu. The other is by using the View buttons on the left end of the horizontal scrollbar (see Figure 10.1). The View buttons provide quick access to Normal, Online Layout, Page Layout, and Outline views. Master Document view and Full Screen view are only available from the View menu. Print Preview can be accessed from the Print Preview button on the Standard toolbar or from the File menu.

Figure 10.1.

Use the View buttons to change views.

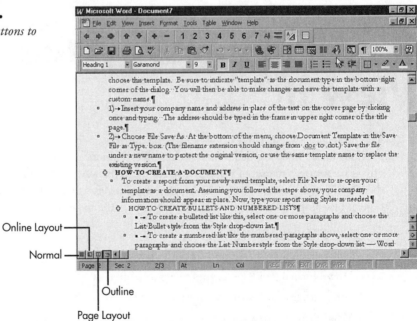

The Status Bar—The Key to Most Views

One of the key elements in every view except Full Screen view is the status bar that appears along the bottom of the screen. It lets you know exactly where you are in a document and what's going on. You can control some of Word's functions from the status bar.

10

Location Statistics

The statistics along the left half of the status bar give the current position of the cursor. From left to right, the status bar shows these position locators (see Figure 10.2):

☐ Page number—Page 2

☐ Section number—Sec 1 (If you create section breaks as discussed in Hour 8, "Setting Up the Page," each section will be numbered.)

☐ Current page of the total pages—2/14

☐ Distance from the top of the page—At 5.7"

☐ Number of lines from the top of the page—Ln 16

☐ Number of columns (characters) from the left margin—Col 18

Double-click any of the location statistics on the status bar for quick access to the GoTo option.

Figure 10.2.

The Status bar shows where you are and what's happening.

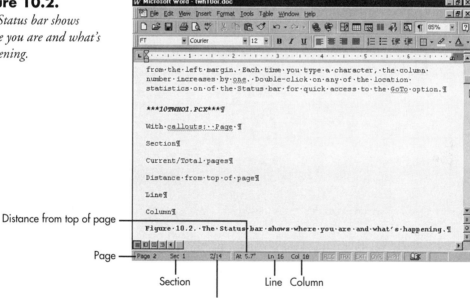

Distance from top of page

Page

Section

Line Column

Current/Total pages

Activate Word Options from the Status Bar

On the other half of the status bar are several buttons that are usually grayed out. If the buttons are grayed out, they are turned off. Double-click a button to turn it on. The button text turns black when the feature is on. Table 10.1 shows what these options are.

Table 10.1. Status bar buttons.

Button name	What the button does
REC	Record macro—starts the macro Recorder (see Hour 16, "Automating Tasks," to find out how to use macros).
TRK	Track changes—one of Word's editing tools used when more than one person needs to edit a document (see Hour 21, "Bookshelf and Word's Editing Tools," for more details).
EXT	Extend selection—turns on the Extend mode. Works with the F8 key to select different amounts of text.
OVR	Overtype—activates Overtype mode, which replaces rather than inserts text from the cursor forward.
WPH	WordPerfect help—activates the WordPerfect help screen. Click an option to see both the WordPerfect and Word equivalents for that action (see Figure 10.3).

Figure 10.3.

Help for WordPerfect users.

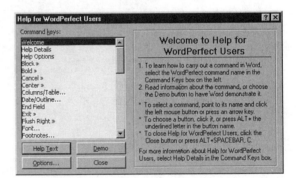

Step-Up

Earlier versions of Word used the Insert key as a toggle between Overtype and Insert modes. A toggle is like an on/off switch. The Insert key turned Overtype on or off in previous versions, but this feature was disabled in 97 because it was too easy to accidentally turn Overtype on.

Spelling and Grammar Status

To the right of the WPH button, you may see an icon that shows a pencil moving over the pages of a book. This indicates that the spelling check, grammar check, or both are turned on. When you stop typing, the pencil stops and there will be a checkmark or an X at the corner

10

of the book. The X means that Word found errors; the check says you're an excellent speller and grammarian and no errors were found. To fix a mistake, double-click the Spelling and Grammar Status icon to locate the error in the document. You have to double-click the Spelling and Grammar Status icon for each mistake; it doesn't automatically continue to the next one.

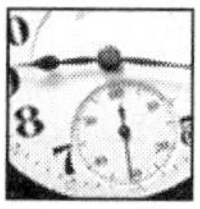

TIME SAVER

> If you're typing a long document, you won't want to stop for every error that the Spelling and Grammar Status checker finds. Wait until you've finished typing the entire document before running the spelling and grammar checks. Hour 21explains these features.

Print Status

One of the best-kept secrets about Word and other Windows applications is that you can stop a print job from the status bar if you catch it quickly. Trying to remember how to get through the Start menu to stop a print job usually means it's too late by the time you get there.

If you wanted to print one page of a long document, but instead you clicked the printer icon and sent the whole document to print, double-click the icon to cancel the print job. A small printer icon replaces the Spelling and Grammar Status icon on the status bar (see Figure 10.4.).

Figure 10.4.
Cancel printing from the status bar.

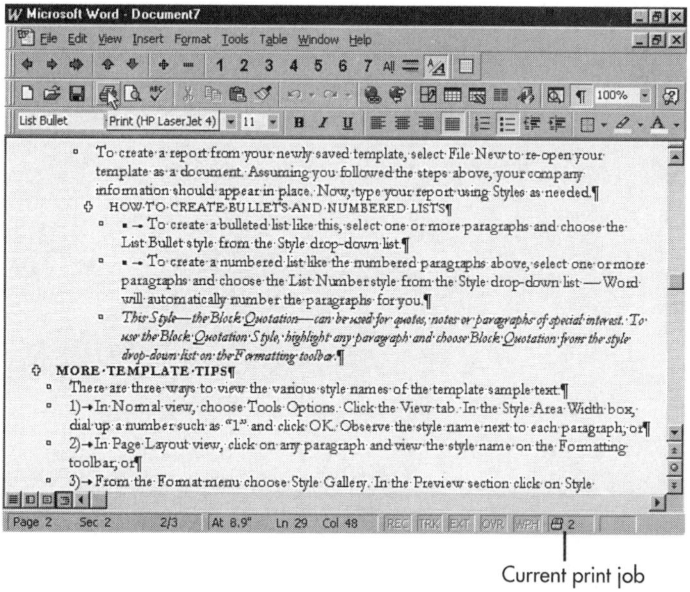

Normal View—A Good View for Typing

Normal view is the view that lets you work without frills, extra functions, or encumbrances that prevent you from getting your work done. It is the view to use when you want to do a lot of serious typing in a hurry. You won't see the edges of the paper. Instead of showing the divisions between sections and pages, a dotted line appears across the page to show where the breaks occur.

Graphics and other objects can't be displayed in Normal view. When you insert a picture or an object in Normal view, Word automatically changes the view to Page Layout. If you open a file that includes any graphic object, that object won't appear onscreen in Normal view.

There are very few options that you can specify in Normal view. Word optimizes the settings in this view to make it easy to work with. Usually, when you select Normal view from the View menu, Word sets the Zoom control on the Standard toolbar to an appropriate size to display the full line of typing. If it doesn't, you can adjust the Zoom control so that it does (see Figure 10.5). Select one of the preset magnifications or type any number between 10 and 500. Page Width adjusts the magnification to show everything between the left and right margins on the viewing screen.

Figure 10.5.

Adjusting the Zoom control to fit text in the viewing screen.

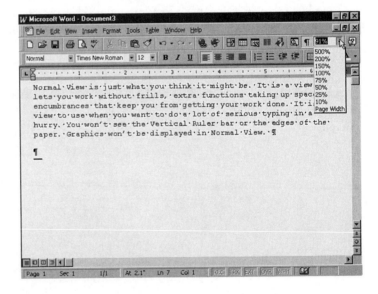

10

Page Layout View—A Good View for Graphics

Page Layout view is similar to Normal view except that it can display the following items, which are not visible in Normal view:

- ☐ The edges of the pages
- ☐ Physical breaks between pages
- ☐ Physical breaks between sections
- ☐ Columns
- ☐ The vertical ruler
- ☐ Headers and footers
- ☐ Graphics
- ☐ WordArt
- ☐ Objects inserted from other sources

Some people prefer to work in Page Layout all the time. Unless you are inserting graphic objects, Page Layout view is not much slower than Normal view, and it gives you an accurate picture of the way the pages will print (see Figure 10.6).

Figure 10.6.

Viewing a document in Page Layout.

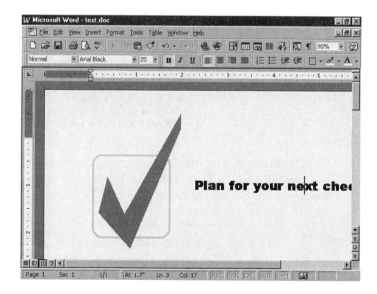

Full Screen View

Unlike the other view options, which are clustered at the top of the View menu, Full Screen view is near the bottom. Full Screen view is a combination of the benefits of Normal view (which has few screen distractions) and Page Layout view (which shows how the document will print). Full Screen view offers no screen elements except the Full Screen Close box seen in Figure 10.7. You can do a lot of straight typing without the screen clutter.

If you are in Page Layout view before you switch to Full Screen, the elements that are visible in Page Layout, such as graphics and page boundaries, are visible. If you switch to Full Screen from Normal view, only the elements that can be seen in Normal view are displayed. What you see in Full Screen depends on what view you were in previously.

Figure 10.7.

Use Full Screen view for an uncluttered typing page.

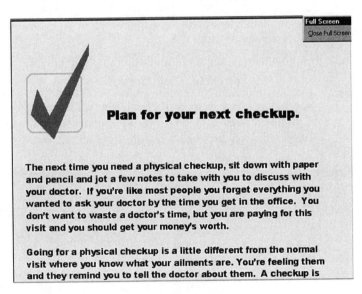

Move the mouse pointer to the top edge of the screen, and a miniature Main menu appears. You have full access to all menu functions, but the toolbars are unavailable. Click the Close button or press the Esc key to exit Full Screen view.

TIME SAVER

If you use the Office toolbar, the Main menu will be partially covered by it in Full Screen view. Using the Alt+hotkey combinations (such as Alt+F+S to save a file) can be very helpful for accessing the menus in Full Screen view.

10

Online View

Online view goes hand in hand with Word 97's Web publishing and online documentation features. Online documents are defined in Hour 1, "Word 97—A Multipurpose Tool," if you need a refresher. You can create an online document in another view. To see what it looks like when it is online, switch to Online view. Online view is different from other views in these ways:

- ☐ The ruler, the View icons, and the horizontal scrollbar are not visible.
- ☐ Custom backgrounds can be applied in Online view (Format | Backgrounds).

Custom backgrounds are applied to online documents to make them more visually appealing when they are viewed on a computer. Hour 24, "Working with the Web," discusses backgrounds and how to apply them to online documents.

JUST A MINUTE

If you use Format | Background in another view, Word automatically changes to Online view. This is the only view where backgrounds are visible.

Use Online view with or without the Document Map. Click the Document Map button on the Standard toolbar to turn it on or off. With major topic headings listed to the left of the document window, Document Map is an excellent tool for navigating through online documents (see Figure 10.8). Only topic or chapter headings that have been formatted with Word's Heading or Outline styles will appear as headings in the Document Map. If none of the heading styles have been applied, Word tries to figure out which items are headings (items that are in bold, for example). Document Map usually does a poor job of picking out main headings unless you apply the heading styles. Hour 12, "A Matter of Style," discusses styles and how they work.

Outline View

Using Word's Outline feature allows you to build an organizational framework for any document. It can display (but is not limited to displaying) what you think of as a traditional outline. The Outline view can also be used to organize a document into major headings with subheadings before you tackle the job of filling in text.

You can create a document in Outline view or take an existing document and view it as an outline. You may have occasions to do both. The Outline view is probably a tool you'll use to create the framework for a document, but it can also display an existing document in outline form. Outline view, like Online view, relies on heading styles to build points and subpoints. If you have a document without heading styles applied, Outline view has no real advantage. You don't see headings and subheadings.

Figure 10.8.
Navigating in Online view with Document Map.

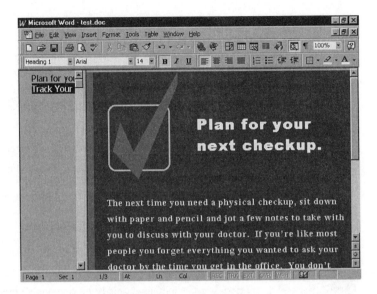

When you view an existing document in Outline view, you may or may not see the headings and subheadings as you think they will appear. Outline looks at a document for the heading styles to create an outline. In a document that has no special styles applied to it, the drop-down style list on the Formatting toolbar displays Word's heading styles, as shown in Figure 10.9.

Figure 10.9.
Word's Normal heading styles are used to create an outline.

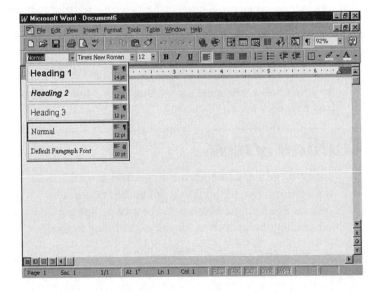

10

Outline looks for paragraphs that have been formatted with the Heading 1, 2, and 3 styles. These are assigned to the first three levels of an outline. Word also checks for bulleted and numbered lists, indents, and other formatting to try to create an outline from an existing document. A plus sign beside and a gray line beneath a paragraph mean that there are subheadings under this heading (see Figure 10.10) that can't be seen. Hold the mouse over the plus sign until a four-sided arrow appears. Double-click, and the subheadings are visible. Double-click again, and the subheadings are hidden.

Figure 10.10.

A plus sign indicates that there are subheadings under a heading.

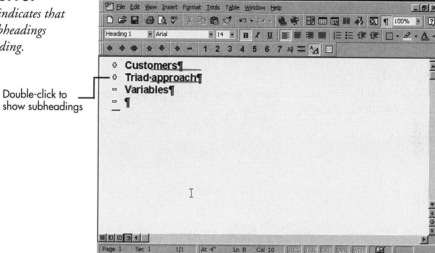

The Outlining toolbar is visible only in Outline and Master Document views. Buttons on the toolbar allow you to:

- ☐ Reorder sections of the outline
- ☐ Change the heading levels for paragraphs (promote and demote)
- ☐ View only certain heading levels (collapse, expand, or select the heading level numbers)

Hour 13, "Word's Outlining Features," tells how these options work in Outline view.

Master Document View

Master Document view is a feature designed to combine several subdocuments as one unit or to create a unified document from an existing document or outline. Individual book chapters could be subdocuments in a master document. Formatting, headers and footers, and page numbering can be applied to the master document to make it consistent throughout.

Master Document view looks very similar to Outline view. If a master document is composed of several subdocuments, the subdocuments are the first-level headings. You can use the Outlining toolbar just as you would in Outline view to rearrange documents or headings in a different order. An additional toolbar appears in Master Document view for working with subdocuments.

Clicking the Collapse Subdocuments button allows you to see only the names of the subdocuments (or files) in the master document, as shown in Figure 10.11. The button then changes to an Expand Subdocuments button. When you click Expand Subdocuments, the full text of all subdocuments can be seen.

Figure 10.11.

Viewing subdocuments in Master Document view.

Expand Subdocuments

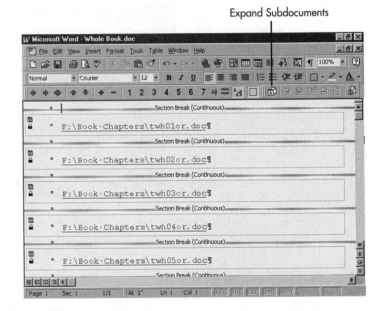

Print Preview

Print Preview is the one view that is not in the View menu. Instead, it is part of the File menu because it works closely with Print. Print Preview used to be nothing more than a way to view a full page of text before printing it. Now, however, Print Preview has many of the same options that the other views have. You can do any of the following from Print Preview:

- ☐ Use the ruler to set tabs, indents, and margins
- ☐ Use the scrollbar to navigate up and down in the document
- ☐ Print a document
- ☐ Edit a document

10

TIME SAVER

To edit a document in Print Preview, make sure that the Magnifier tool is turned off. When the Magnifier tool is turned on, the cursor becomes a Zoom tool to move in for a closer view of the document or move back out to a preview screen (see Figure 10.12). If you are going to edit text in Print Preview, increase the magnification in the Zoom control box to make text large enough to read.

Figure 10.12.
Turn off the Magnifier tool to edit text in Print Preview.

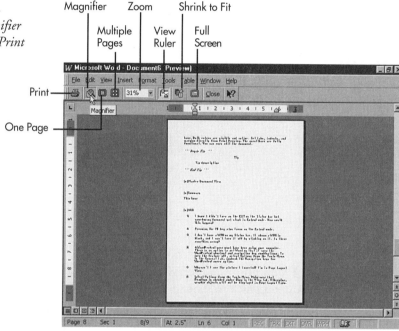

Click the Multiple Pages button to preview several pages at once. This is a good way to see whether page breaks occur where you want them. Click the One Page button to return to a single page view.

View Ruler

As soon as you click somewhere on the preview page, the rulers usually appear. If they don't, click the View Ruler button. This is a great way to eyeball margins and adjust them. Click and drag a margin along the ruler. A dotted line the full length of the page moves as you increase or decrease a margin. Desktop publishers like to shove margins around in this view.

Shrink to Fit

Shrink to Fit is a useful feature that can help decrease the number of pages by one. If you have a letter that you want on one page but a couple of lines have spilled onto a second page, click the Shrink to Fit button. Word tries to decrease the margins and font sizes to get everything on one page. It displays a message if it can't do the job. If it's only a couple of lines or a short paragraph, Word can usually make the adjustments without compromising the formatting.

Although students would probably appreciate an Expand to Fit feature in Word for all those term papers, they'll have to bump up the line spacing, increase the font size, and inch in the margins for now. This may be something for the next version of Word.

Summary

This hour covers Word 97's view features. Normal view is a good all-around typing view. Page Layout view shows the pages exactly as they will print. Online view displays the screen as it appears on the Internet or as an online help document. Outline view displays a document with normal style headings as an outline. Master Document view shows the organization of a master document in outline form. Subdocuments included in a master document appear as headings. Full Screen view is devoid of most screen elements, providing a way to see more of the document at once. Print Preview provides a full-page sketch of the way a document will appear in print.

Q&A

Q I know I didn't turn on the EXT option on the status bar, but somehow my document got stuck in Extend mode. How could this happen?

A Pressing the F8 key also turns on the Extend mode. Instances have been documented in Word 97 where Extend turns on mysteriously without having been enabled from the status bar or from the F8 key. If this happens, you may need to exit Word to clear up the problem.

Q I don't have a WPH button on the status bar. It shows a WPN button in black, and I can't turn it off by clicking it. Is there something wrong?

A A WordPerfect user may have been using your computer. There is an option to tell Word to use the WordPerfect shortcut and navigation key combinations. To turn the feature off, select Options from the Tools menu. In the General tab, uncheck the Navigation keys for WordPerfect users option.

Q Why can't I see the picture I inserted? I'm in Page Layout view.

A Select Options from the Tools menu. Make sure that Drawings is checked under Show in the View tab. Otherwise, graphic objects are not displayed in Page Layout view.

10

Q **I'm in Outline view, but the Outlining toolbar isn't showing up. How can I activate it?**

A Select Toolbars from the View menu, and click Outlining to display the Outlining toolbar.

Q **Sometimes I use narrow left and right margins, and I have to arrow across the page or use the scrollbar to see the text. I can set the Zoom control to a smaller number, but it makes text hard to read. Is there any way to see all the text without shrinking the view?**

A Yes, but only in Normal or Outline view. This doesn't work in Page Layout view. Select Options from the Tools menu. Check the Wrap to window option in the View tab.

10

Hour 11

Customizing Word to the Way You Work

This hour shows how to set up Word and the Word toolbars specifically for you and the way you like to work. It's like choosing whether to work in Normal view or Page Layout view—some prefer one way; others prefer another. Some of the options you choose may depend on the kinds of projects you do. There are enough options to fill a book, but this hour describes the ones that users are most apt to want and need.

The highlights of this hour include

☐ What options you can change

☐ Which options you shouldn't change

☐ How to add icons to toolbars

☐ How to create your own toolbars

Setting Options

Options on the Tools menu is a good place to begin when you want to start customizing your settings in Word. Each tab in the Options dialog contains related settings. This hour discusses some of the popular ones that users frequently want or need to change.

The View Tab

Selections in the View tab apply to only one view, such as Normal or Page Layout. The view you are in when you set these options determines which ones will be changed. You can tell which view settings you're changing by looking at the centered heading at the top of the View tab.

Figure 11.1 shows the options for Normal view. Compare these to the options in Figure 11.2 for Page Layout view. Normal view is the view used most for typing, so there are options that deal with text. Page Layout view displays graphic elements, so there are options for viewing graphics and other objects that are not in the Normal view options.

Figure 11.1.

View options for Normal view.

Current view

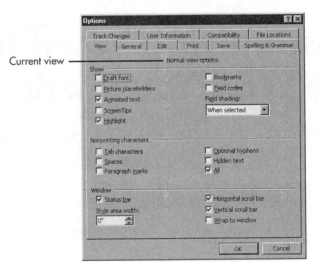

Normal View Options

You must be in a document that is in Normal view to set the Normal view options. If you have questions about what an option does, click the question mark in the upper-right corner of the Options dialog box title bar. The mouse pointer turns to the What's This pointer discussed in Hour 4, "Help?! There's Lots of It in Word 97." Click an option to bring up a screen tip that describes the function of that option.

11

Figure 11.2.

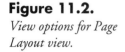

View options for Page Layout view.

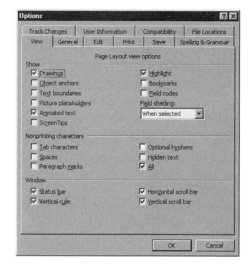

Draft Font

Draft font is a selection to speed up typing. Draft font displays a generic font that does not show character formatting, such as bold, or differences in font sizes. Special character formatting shows up as underlined text. Because Word can cut down on what it has to display graphically, typing is faster when this option is checked.

Picture Placeholders

Word 97 has many new graphic capabilities and they complicate the way picture placeholders work. If you used picture placeholders in earlier versions of Word, you would see a box rather than the graphic if you opted to display placeholders and not the graphics. This was a way to speed up work in a document that had several graphics inserted. If you uncheck Drawing Objects and check Picture Placeholders in Word 97, you won't see any indication of graphics that are inserted in the usual way when viewing the document.

Hour 17, "Working with Graphics," explains some of these new developments. For now, you may want to remember that picture placeholders don't work exactly like they did in previous versions.

Screen Tips

Displaying screen tips works with the Insert | Comment feature that allows document reviewers to place their comments in a pop-up box that the author can read, rather than in the document itself. When the Screen Tips option is selected, the reviewer's comments appear in a pop-up box when the reader positions the mouse over the comments that appear in the document as the reviewer's initials.

Nonprinting Characters

One of the buttons on the Standard toolbar is the Show/Hide button. This button allows you to either clear the typing screen of symbols (nonprinting characters) such as the paragraph marks, spaces, and tabs, or to change the view so that these symbols are displayed. You may prefer to type without seeing the nonprinting characters, or perhaps there are certain nonprinting characters you would like to see but others you'd prefer to hide. If you like the all or nothing options you get with the Show/Hide button on the Standard toolbar, leave this option set to All.

If you'd like Word to display only specific nonprinting characters:

1. Uncheck the All box.
2. Check all the nonprinting characters you want displayed.
3. Uncheck any nonprinting character options that may already be checked that you don't want displayed.
4. Click OK.

With these options set, the Show/Hide button on the Standard toolbar shows all nonprinting characters in the Show mode. Only the nonprinting characters you selected are displayed in the Hide mode.

For the typist who enters an extra space here and there, viewing spaces is a good idea. Some fonts make it harder to see these spaces than others. If you want to see only spaces, uncheck all of the nonprinting characters boxes except spaces.

Style Area Width

After you've covered styles in Hour 12, "A Matter of Style," you may want to see what new styles you've applied to the paragraphs in your document. Increase the number in the Style area width box. This creates a column at the left margin that displays the names of the styles applied to each paragraph, as shown in Figure 11.3. To remove the style area, set the Style area width back to 0 inches.

Scrollbars

You can turn off one or both of the scrollbars (vertical and horizontal) by unchecking these options. If you turn off the horizontal scrollbar, the View buttons that are part of the horizontal scrollbar are also hidden.

Page Layout View Options

To set the options for Page Layout view, change the current document to Page Layout view.

Drawings

To speed up working with a document that has several graphics, turn off the Drawings option by unchecking the box. This hides all the graphics in the document. Again, picture placeholders won't show frames to let you know where the graphics are if the pictures have been inserted normally.

11

Figure 11.3.

Add a style area column from the View tab.

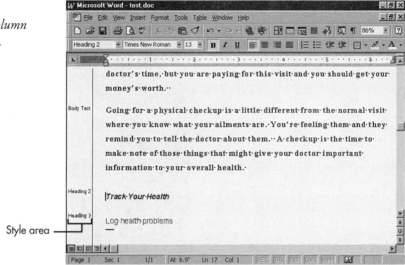

Style area ——

It's a little difficult to work in this mode because you can't be sure where the graphics are unless you switch to Print Preview or set the option back to show drawings. A better solution is to leave Page Layout set to display drawings and switch to Normal view for fast maneuvering.

TIME SAVER

Both Normal and Page Layout views have an option to view highlights. Highlight is a new feature that appears as a button on the Formatting toolbar and looks like a marking pen with a yellow line under it. It acts like a marking pen, too. Click the Highlight button and drag the highlighter pen across any text you want to highlight. You can view the colored highlights if you have Highlight checked in the View tab.

The General Tab

The General tab has all-purpose options that don't really fit into specific categories like Print, Save, or View.

The Blue Screen

Bring back the blue screen! Since the earliest days of Word, people got used to a blue typing screen with white text. WordPerfect users may also be used to the blue screen. With the advent of the first Word for Windows, the default turned to a white screen and black letters. If you've been looking for the old blue screen, it's here in the General tab. Check Blue background, white text as in Figure 11.4.

Figure 11.4.

Back to the days of the blue screen.

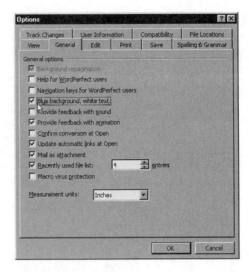

Recently Used File List

A lot of people don't realize that the File menu contains a list of files that were recently opened (see Figure 11.5). A file can be opened from this list by clicking it. If you want to increase the number of files Word displays on the File menu, increase the number in the box beside the Recently used file list option. Word can display up to nine filenames, but the File menu is too short to display all nine. An arrow at the bottom of the menu will take you to the listings that didn't fit.

Figure 11.5.

Opening a recently used file from the File menu.

Recently used file list ⎯⎯

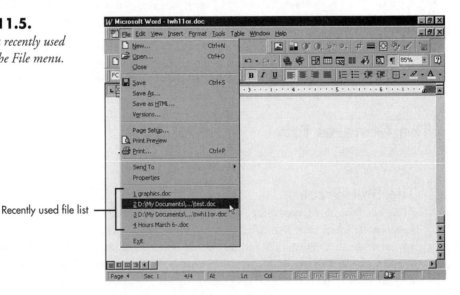

Macro Virus Protection

Checking the Macro virus protection option will configure Word to warn you when you open files that contain macros or other customized items such as toolbars and menus. This does not mean that they contain viruses, but there is a potential for viruses when these items are shared. You have the option of opening the document without the macros or other potentially harmful customizations.

Update Automatic Links at Open

This option allows you to update any links contained in a document to the most recent versions as the document is opened. For example, you may have a link to an Excel chart in your Word document. If the Excel chart changes, the most current modifications will be displayed when you open the Word file that contains a link to the chart.

The Edit Tab

Figure 11.6 shows the Edit options. These options have to do with typing and selecting text.

Figure 11.6.

Use the Edit tab to change typing and selection options.

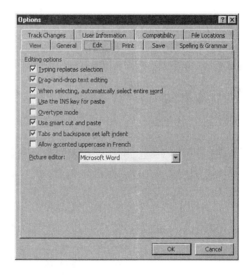

Typing Replaces Selection

If you select a section of text and then start typing, Word usually replaces whatever is selected with the text you type. To change this option, uncheck the Typing replaces selection box. Text is inserted in front of the selection when this feature is turned off.

Drag-and-Drop Text Editing

You can turn off drag-and-drop. When you do, the mouse is used as a selection tool rather than a tool to move or copy text. If you are slow on the draw with the mouse and find yourself dragging text around and moving it when you don't intend to, you might want to turn off drag-and-drop. Uncheck the Drag-and-drop text editing option to disable this function. If you find that drag-and-drop is not working and you want it to, this is the place to enable that function.

Use the Insert Key to Paste

Some people use Copy and Paste between Windows and DOS applications and are accustomed to using the Insert key to paste from the clipboard. If you check the Use the INS key for paste option, the Insert key operates as a Paste key in Word.

Tabs and Backspace Set Left Indent

Many people don't realize it, but Word automatically creates an indent when you press the Tab key if the Tabs and backspace set left indent option is enabled. Word's IntelliSense thinks you want to create a first line indent when you begin a new paragraph with a tab and automatically converts the tab to a first line indent. Tab twice, and it works like pressing the Increase Indent button on the Standard toolbar twice. You can't see the tab marker if you have the Show/Hide button set to show nonprinting characters because Word converted it to an indent.

Likewise, the Backspace key will decrease the left indent with this option set. If you're working in a document where you don't want Word to assume that the first tabs in a paragraph are indents, uncheck this option.

The Print Tab

You may refer to the Print options often to handle specific assignments (see Figure 11.7).

Figure 11.7.

Changing Word's printing options.

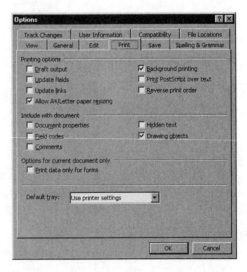

Update Fields

A date that was entered as a field in a footer is supposed to be updated every time you print the document. If it's not giving you the correct date when it prints, this is probably a sign that the Update fields option is not checked. Any fields that contain variables that change are not updated unless this is checked. The information in fields may change. To make sure that you have the current information, check the Update fields option.

Update Links

Update links works like Update fields. There may be a link in the Word document to an Excel chart. Linking means that the current program reaches out to another location for information to include. If that information has changed since the document was last used, you probably want the new information included. Check Update links to tell Word to use the most recent edition of the linked file.

Document Properties

Check Document properties under the Include with document options if you'd like a copy of the information you enter in the file's properties to print when you print the document. This is a bit of overkill when files are so easy to find in Word 97. It's hardly necessary to create a hard copy reference.

Print Comments or Hidden Text

You might need to print a document with comments or hidden text. Comments are editorial notes that are added to a document and are not normally printed. Hidden text is also something you would not usually want included in the printed document. You might, however, need something like a blind copy of a letter. Format the blind copy information as hidden text. Print the letter for the recipient, then select File | Print. Click the Options button to bring up the Print Options dialog box and check hidden text before printing the blind copy. Don't forget to turn the hidden text option off before the next print job.

To format text as hidden:

1. Select the area of text to hide.
2. Select Font from the Format menu (or right-click and select Font from the shortcut menu).
3. Click Hidden text under the Effects options.
4. Click OK.

The Save Tab

This is where you can tell Word how and when to save files, to create backups for every file you create, and to set passwords for files that need to be secured.

Always Create Backup Copy

The Save tab sets several options worth noting (see Figure 11.8). If you want to make sure that you always have a second (backup) copy of your work, check Always create backup copy. Word creates a backup file that will be one version prior to the one currently saved—it only works for files that have been named and saved. This is a way of insuring that there is a backup if the original file is corrupted or accidentally deleted. You may not have all of the current updates in the backup file, but you will probably have most of them.

Figure 11.8.

Save! Save! Save! options.

When Word creates a backup copy for a file, it gives it the same name as the original file but calls it "Backup copy of…" and adds a .wbk (Word backup) extension to the filename. Earlier versions of Word used the .bak extension for backups.

Allow Fast Saves

Allow fast saves is an option to steer clear of for now. It has been known to cause some problems, especially when working with a document that is a different file type, such as another version of Word. Fast Save appends anything new that was added since the last save instead of resaving the whole document. That's why it runs faster, but it may be unreliable. It also bloats the file size because of the way it saves (appending instead of overwriting).

JUST A MINUTE

If you have the Always create backup copy option selected, you cannot select Allow fast saves.

11

Embed TrueType Fonts

Embed TrueType fonts can be an important option if you are sharing a file with someone who doesn't have the same fonts you do. Embedding the fonts actually attaches the fonts to the file. They must be TrueType fonts, however. To find out whether a font is a TrueType font, check the drop-down font list on the Formatting toolbar. Fonts that are TrueType have a shadowed T symbol beside them. Embedding the fonts makes the file much larger.

NEW TERM *TrueType* fonts were a creation of Apple Computer and later Microsoft to accomplish two things: first, What You See Is What You Get (WYSIWYG) technology to display fonts onscreen just as they will print, and second, scaleable fonts. TrueType fonts can literally create any size character that will fit on the specified page size.

Embed TrueType Fonts with Characters in Use Only

If you select Embed TrueType fonts, you also have an option to embed characters in use only. This means it only attaches the particular sizes and styles of the fonts used in the document rather than every possible rendition of the fonts. If the person receiving the file will have to manipulate font sizes and styles, you shouldn't use this option; select Embed TrueType fonts by itself. It makes a huge difference in file size, though. If the other person won't be changing the fonts, it's a good idea to use Embed characters in use only. A test trial showed a one-page file saved with embedded fonts was 142KB. The same file saved with the addition of Embed characters in use was only 13KB. A sizable difference!

Allow Background Saves

Allow background saves lets you keep right on typing while Word does its autosaving and backing up. This is a great help when you're working on long documents. Without this option, you have to sit and wait every time the backup copy or AutoRecover saves.

AutoRecover

When you select Save AutoRecover, you can specify how often Word saves to temporary files that can be recovered in case of a power outage or a computer problem. If this is set to 30 minutes, it means that you won't lose more than your last 30 minutes of work. This is also an important option for unsaved documents. If your computer shuts down abnormally for some reason, Word will bring back many of your unsaved documents with names like `Document1 Recovered`, as well as your named documents. Don't rely on these options as your primary backup, though, or you'll be courting disaster.

TIME SAVER

You may want to set your AutoRecover to 10 minutes. Since this option works automatically, it rarely disturbs your work flow. Besides, you will have a greater sense of security knowing you won't lose much if disaster strikes.

Password Security

File sharing options apply only to the current document. If you need to make a document secure, you can set a password that will be required to open the file. To set a password:

1. Type a password in the Password to open box.

   You will see a series of asterisks as you type in the password. This is a form of security so that others won't see the password as it is entered.

2. Click OK.

3. Word asks you to type the password again for verification.

Share the password with only those who should have access to the file. You can set different levels of security for a document, as shown in Table 11.1.

Table 11.1. File security levels.

Security level	File sharing options to set
Read/Write	Don't set passwords or check the Read-only option. Anyone is free to open and change the file.
Read Only	Enter a password in the Password to open box and check the Read-only recommended box.
Selective Read/Write	Set passwords for both Password to open and Password to modify. Check the Read-only recommended box. Share the Password to open with those who are permitted only to read the file. Share both passwords with those who are allowed to both read and modify the file (see Figure 11.9).

Figure 11.9.

Requiring passwords to open or modify a file.

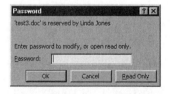

JUST A MINUTE

Checking the Read-only option by itself is ineffectual. When anyone tries to open the file, Word gives a message saying that the document should be opened as read-only unless changes need to be made. It then asks if you want to open it as read-only. Click Yes, and the file will be read-only. If you click No, the file opens and can be freely edited.

11

CAUTION

Anyone who knows the passwords can remove them by deleting them from the Save options. You may want to consider this when sharing the passwords. You might also want to write the passwords down in a secure place just in case you forget them. If you forget what they are and no one else knows, you can't open the file!

Spelling and Grammar

Hour 21, "Bookshelf and Word's Editing Tools," explains some of the features you may want to turn on or off in the Spelling & Grammar tab. You can turn the automatic spelling and grammar checkers on or off from this tab. There may be certain words like the ones that contain uppercase or numbers that you want the spelling checker to ignore. If so, check the Ignore words in uppercase and Ignore words with numbers options.

The Grammar check option has a nice feature to specify the writing style of the document so that it accepts grammar that is appropriate to the type of document. What is acceptable in casual writing may not be appropriate for technical writing. The drop-down list of options contains entries for Casual, Standard, Formal, Technical, and Custom. If you click the Settings button beside the Writing style box, you can select or deselect many of the types of grammatical errors Word checks for.

Track Changes

Track Changes is used when more than one person uses and edits a file. You can specify color coding and identification, such as underline, that will be used for each person who works with the document. There are options for identifying how inserted text, deleted text, changed formatting, and changed lines will be displayed after edits are made.

The User Information Tab

When you enter summary information in the document properties (File | Properties), does someone else's name show up as the author? User Information allows you to change this information. Any time Word enters summary information, a return address for envelopes, or initials for reviewer's comments, it looks at the information recorded in the User Information (see Figure 11.10).

The Compatibility Tab

In the Compatibility tab are options that let you customize some of Word's functions the way you're used to having them operate with other programs, such as WordPerfect or earlier versions of Word. There's a long list of things you can change to make Word more compatible with your work style.

11

Figure 11.10.

*Change User Informa-
tion to your name and
address.*

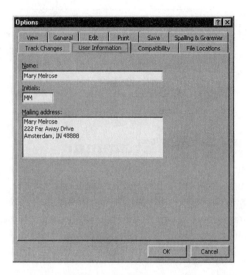

The Font Substitution button allows you to open a document that contains fonts that you do not have on your system. The Missing document font box contains all of the font names used in the document that are not on your system. Select a font in the Missing document font box, then click the Font substitution box to select one of the fonts on your system that closely approximates this font. Do this for each of the missing fonts. Word doesn't really replace the fonts; instead, it changes the way they display and print.

The Recommended options for list lets you specify options for a specific word-processing application. Occasionally, Word has to guess what file type you are importing and may not guess correctly. By selecting the correct file type from the drop-down list (for example, WordPerfect 5.*x*), you can specify how Word will translate the open document. The list of options at the bottom will change depending on the program you select in the Recommended options for list. Select those that apply to the current document and uncheck the rest.

The File Locations Tab

The last of the Options tabs is File Locations. You can tell Word where you want it to look for files if you don't want to keep your files in the My Documents folder. You might already have all your files saved in a directory called `c:\Word Files`, and that's where you want Word to look first for files. To change this option in the File Locations tab:

1. Select Documents from the File types list.
2. Click the Modify button.
3. Select the location where your files are stored (see Figure 11.11).
4. Click OK, then click OK again.

11

Figure 11.11.
Look somewhere other than My Documents for files.

You will probably never need to change any of the other File Locations options; they are part of the primary installation. In fact, you may find that things don't work correctly if you do change them.

Customizing Toolbars

One of the first Word for Windows versions included the Envelope icon on the Standard toolbar. It caught everyone's attention, and it became a habit to use the button every time you wanted to print a single envelope. Along came the next version of Word, and the Envelope icon was gone!

Microsoft tries to pack so much into each new version that some of the buttons have to go to make way for buttons for the new features. It's encouraging to know that there are ways to get familiar buttons back. There used to be a few extra spaces on the Standard and Formatting toolbars to add buttons like the Envelope, but the toolbars are now full of buttons for all the new features.

You may want to create your own toolbar and add buttons for commands you use often. To create a new toolbar and add the Envelope button to it:

1. Select Customize from View|Toolbars.
2. Click the Toolbars tab.
3. Select New.
4. Enter a name for the toolbar. Word gives the file a generic name, like Custom 1, unless you change it. If Custom 1 works for you, you can keep this name.
5. Select Normal.dot from the Make toolbar available to drop-down list to make the toolbar available in every document, as shown in Figure 11.12. Or, select the current document name if you want to use the toolbar only with that particular document.
6. Click OK.

Figure 11.12.

Creating a new toolbar.

A new toolbar is created and will be displayed as a small box in the Customize screen. Click the new toolbar's title bar and drag it off to the typing screen. The next step involves adding the Envelope button to the new toolbar.

1. Click the Commands tab.
2. Select Tools from the Categories list.
3. Envelopes and Labels is an option in the Tools menu. If an option is on one of the existing menus, it is grouped with the commands under that category. Scroll down in the Commands list to find Envelopes and Labels.
4. Click and drag the envelope icon up to the new toolbar and release the mouse button (see Figure 11.13).

Figure 11.13.

Placing the Envelopes and Labels button on the new toolbar.

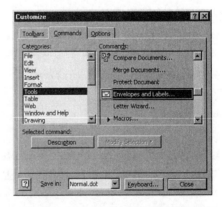

As soon as you release the mouse button, the Envelope icon is added to the new toolbar.

If you add a button that doesn't display an icon beside it in the list, Word creates a button with the command name on it. For example, if you drag the Tools Calculate command

11

(another of the commands listed under the Tools category) to the new toolbar, the button displays the words Tools Calculate. To change a text button to a picture button:

1. Click the Modify Selection button.
2. Select Default style from the menu.
3. Click the Modify Selection button.
4. Select from the icons listed under Change Button Image, as shown in Figure 11.14.
5. The Calculator icon is a good choice to replace the words Tools Calculate. Click the Calculator icon.
6. Click the Close button.

Figure 11.14.

Select a picture icon instead of using a text button.

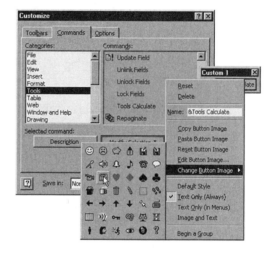

To remove an icon from a toolbar:

1. Select View | Toolbars | Customize.
2. Click and drag the button off the toolbar to any place on the typing screen. The icon is removed from the toolbar. Figure 11.15 shows the Tools Calculate icon being removed from the Custom toolbar.
3. Click Close.

CAUTION

The quickest way to make enemies is to remove some of the standard icons from the Formatting and Standard toolbars. People expect to have these functions available when they sit down to use Word. If you are the only one who uses your computer, then purge away. If not, be very careful about which buttons you remove.

Figure 11.15.

Removing a toolbar button.

TIME SAVER

If you've made changes to a toolbar and can't remember what it was like before you started tinkering with it, you can reset the toolbar to the original settings. Select View | Toolbars | Customize. Select the toolbar name and click the Reset button. Word will ask whether you want to make the changes to Normal.dot. Click Yes, then click Close.

Summary

This hour acts as a guided tour of some of Word's capabilities to suit every work style. View, Print, Save, and other options can be changed from Tools | Options. You can create your own toolbars and add toolbar buttons for any of Word's commands.

Hour 12, "A Matter of Style," introduces using, creating, and applying styles.

Q&A

Q I selected the Use the INS key for paste option from the Edit options, then I decided I didn't like it. When I turned this feature off, the INS key became the toggle for Overtype like it was in earlier versions of Word. How can I reset the INS key to not function as an Overtype toggle?

A To remove the Overtype toggle from the Insert key, exit Word. It doesn't save this option. This seems to be a glitch in the program. The Insert key should be back to normal the next time you start Word. For people who got used to the Overtype

11

option and liked it, this is one way to get it back temporarily. To make it permanent, assign Overtype to the Insert key as a keyboard shortcut by doing the following:

1. Select Customize from the Tools menu.

2. Click Keyboard from the Commands tab.

3. Under Categories, scroll down to All Commands and select it.

4. Select Overtype from the Commands list.

5. Click in the Press New Shortcut Key box and press the Insert key. (Word displays the letters *Ins* in the box.)

6. Click Assign, then click Close.

Q I created a toolbar that I'd like to place up with the other toolbars, but it opens in a separate box by itself. How can I make it like the others?

A Double-click the toolbar's title bar to place it with the other toolbars (dock it). If you don't like where Word docks it, grab the light-colored vertical bars at the left edge of the toolbar (the Move bars) to move it to another location on the screen. To place the toolbar back in a separate box (called a floating toolbar), double-click the Move bars.

Q I put a toolbar icon on one of the toolbars that didn't have a picture beside it in the Commands list. It put the words on the icon. I wanted to change it to a picture icon, but the Change Button Image was grayed out when I tried to modify the icon. Where did I go wrong?

A You ran into the exception to the rule. This procedure won't work if the command shows an arrow at the right edge of the command name. This is like the menu options that include other options. The Change Button Image is not available for these items.

PART
III

Hour 12

A Matter of Style

This hour shows how to use and modify the abundant styles and templates in Word 97. Styles are created to change the look of the way text displays. Font and paragraph formatting are the primary ingredients in styles. Templates take advantage of styles by creating a sample document with custom styles and text or graphics already in place.

You will discover in this hour that you can easily create your own styles or build templates from existing documents. Learn how to use Format Painter to copy styles from one paragraph to other paragraphs.

The highlights of this hour include

- ☐ What the difference is between a style and a template
- ☐ How to modify an existing style
- ☐ How to create new styles and template
- ☐ What the Style Gallery is and how to use it
- ☐ How to use the Format Painter to copy styles

Styles versus Templates

There are two ingredients in a style:

- ☐ Font formatting
    - ☐ name
    - ☐ style
    - ☐ size
    - ☐ color
    - ☐ special effects
    - ☐ character spacing
    - ☐ animation
- ☐ Paragraph formatting
    - ☐ paragraph alignment
    - ☐ spacing and indents
    - ☐ bullets and numbering
    - ☐ outline heading levels

Step-Up

Borders and shading used to be a part of the paragraph formatting and would affect the entire paragraph. Word 97 allows you to select text and apply borders and shading just to the selection. If applied to a selection rather than an entire paragraph, borders and shading become part of the font formatting. This is a great new addition to Word.

One of the biggest confusions is the difference between a style and a template. A *style* is a group of characteristics that apply to a paragraph. A *template* is a sample document that can include many different styles, individualized toolbars and macros, page layout definitions, and graphics (such as a company logo). A template can also include user-defined AutoText entries, custom menus, and shortcut keys that apply specifically to that template only.

Part of the reason for the confusion is that Word has a primary style called Normal style. Technically, Normal style is one of the styles in the Normal template called `Normal.dot`. All templates have a `.dot` extension. You may often hear people refer to the Normal template as Normal style. Styles are not saved individually as files with their own names, but templates are. A lot of things are included in the Normal template other than styles, including the Word options you learned to set in the previous hour.

12

When you select New from the File menu, tabbed options show different templates that have been created for special purposes, such as letters and faxes. These "sample" documents provide the framework to begin creating a new document. A set of styles was used to create each of these templates.

Figure 12.1 shows the Contemporary Memo template. There are graphic elements onscreen and a setup for the headings and major items you would want in a memo. These templates were created with instructions in the area where you type the body of your message. There are areas in square brackets ([]) that say *Click here*. When you click one of these areas, the area is selected, and you can type in the appropriate information. Whatever you type replaces the Click here box.

Figure 12.1.

The Contemporary Memo template.

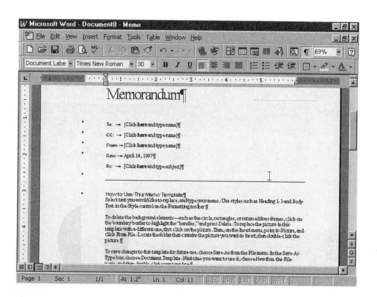

Viewing Styles

If you use Normal view and select the View option to show a style area as discussed in the last hour, you see that each paragraph has a style listed beside it as in Figure 12.2. There are several different styles in this one short template. You can also tell what style is applied to a paragraph by clicking in the paragraph and checking the style name in the style box on the Formatting toolbar.

To find out what formatting is applied to a paragraph

1. Select the What's This? option from the Help menu.
2. Click a paragraph; a screen tip appears that shows the paragraph and font formats applied to that paragraph (see Figure 12.3).

Figure 12.2.

Styles used in the Contemporary Memo template.

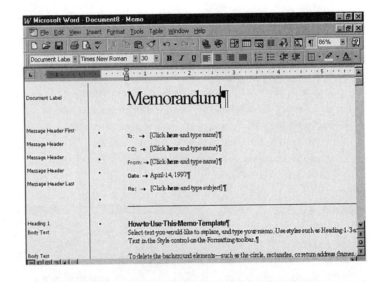

Figure 12.3.

Click a paragraph to invoke a screen tip about paragraph and font formats.

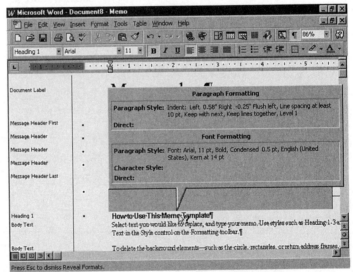

Applying Styles from the Formatting Toolbar

Using the Formatting toolbar is the easiest way to apply styles. The style box at the far left has a drop-down list that shows all of the styles that are currently available. Figure 12.4 shows the styles available in the Normal template.

12

Figure 12.4.

*The styles preview list
shows the current styles.*

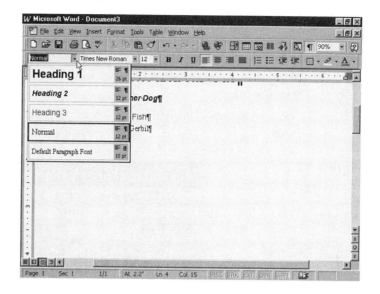

Every new document created using the New button on the Standard toolbar uses the Normal template to set paragraph and font formatting. The standard styles in the Normal template are important in that they form the foundation for building most documents and have heading styles recognized by outlines, master documents, and online documents. There are only a few styles in the Normal template, but you can create others to add to your repertoire, as you will learn later in this hour.

To apply one of the styles from the style box on the Formatting toolbar

1. Select the paragraph you want to format.
2. Click the down arrow beside the style box to bring up the styles preview list.
3. Click one of the style names.

The style is applied to the selected paragraph.

Style Gallery

A great way to apply a group of styles is to use Style Gallery from the Format menu. Style Gallery is a series of templates from which styles can be applied to other documents. If you look at the list in Style Gallery, you'll notice that they match the names of the templates in the tabbed sections in File | New.

At the bottom right of the Style Gallery dialog box are different options for displaying selected styles in the preview window:

☐ *Document* shows how the styles would affect the current document. (If you're just starting a new document and haven't typed anything yet, the preview window will be blank.)

☐ *Example* shows the template itself (the one that would come up if you opened it from File|New).

☐ *Style samples* shows sample paragraphs with the styles in the selected template (see Figure 12.5).

Figure 12.5.

Previewing style samples.

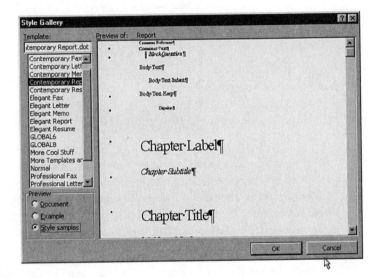

If you find a template in the list with styles you want to apply to your document, click OK. Word applies the new styles to anything you already have typed into the document. The new styles are then available from the drop-down list of styles in the style box.

CAUTION

If you have applied styles using Style Gallery, you cannot undo the changes. Your only recourse is to close the file without saving it in order to bring back the file with the original styles.

The difference between applying styles this way and using one of the preformatted document templates from File|New is that Word does not set up a sample document for you. It applies the formats only to existing text and makes the styles available while you're working in this document.

This means that you can apply the set of styles from Contemporary Fax or another template to any other document without the text or graphics that are a part of the template.

Modifying Styles

You can change any of the standard styles or those in Word's templates. There may be font or paragraph formatting changes that you make regularly to a style that you can adjust by permanently changing the style formatting.

Changing Your Default Font

One style that people often change is the default font. There might be users who like the 10-point font size that Word installs as the default, but the standard letter and document font is usually a 12-point font. The easiest way to change the default font is by selecting Format | Font. To do this

1. Select Format | Font.

2. Choose the font, font style, and size that you want to use for your default font.

3. Click the Default button in the lower-left corner as in Figure 12.6. Word will ask whether you want to change the default font. Click Yes.

Figure 12.6.

Changing the default font.

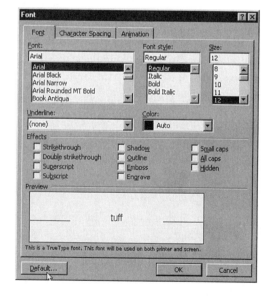

Modifying Styles Using the Style Box

If you want to redefine an existing style, it is easy to do so using the style box. To modify a style:

1. Select a paragraph that is formatted with the style that you want to change (such as Heading 2).

2. Change the font and/or paragraph formatting to the way you want the style to be.

3. Click once in the style box and type the *exact* name of the style (in this case, Heading 2). If you don't type the name exactly, Word creates a new style with the name you type in the style box.

4. Press the Enter key. Word knows that you want to do something with the existing Heading 2 style. The dialog box in Figure 12.7 appears.

5. Check the Update the style to reflect recent changes checkbox. To make the change permanent for this style, check the Automatically update the style from now on option.

6. Click OK.

Figure 12.7.

Modifying an existing style from the style box.

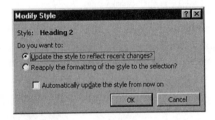

You can also modify styles using Format | Style. It involves a few more steps than using the style box method. To use Format | Style to modify a style

1. Select a paragraph formatted in the style you want to modify.

2. Select Format | Style. The style for the selected paragraph should appear highlighted in the styles list.

3. Click the Modify button.

4. Click the Format button to bring up a list of formatting options that can be changed.

5. Select an option from the list (Font, Paragraph, Tabs, Border, Language, Frame, or Numbering).

6. Make the desired changes in the dialog box and click OK.

7. Repeat steps 5 and 6 to make changes to other options that you want to modify in the style.

8. Click the Add to template option if you want the changes to the style permanently applied to the template so that all new documents based on this template include the modified style.

9. Click the Automatically update option if you want the style modified everywhere in the current document.

10. Click OK.

12

11. Click Apply to apply the modified style to selected text, save the style changes, and close the dialog box, or click Close to save the style changes and close the dialog box without applying the modified style to selected text.

Format Painter

There are many ways to copy the formatting from one paragraph to another, but the easiest way is with Format Painter on the Standard toolbar. Format Painter looks like a paintbrush, and the analogy is supposed to relate to dipping the paintbrush into a bucket to pick up paint and then spreading the paint on a surface. In this case, Format Painter picks up formatting from one selection and spreads or paints it to another selection. To use Format Painter

1. Select a paragraph that has formatting you would like to copy to another paragraph.
2. Click the Format Painter icon (the mouse pointer changes to a paintbrush).
3. Click anywhere in the paragraph to which you'd like to apply the formatting.

Format Painter paints the new paragraph with the characteristics it picked up from the first paragraph.

If you want to apply the same formatting to several paragraphs, double-click the Format Painter after you've selected the formatting you want to copy. Double-clicking leaves the formatting in the paintbrush until you click the Format Painter again to turn it off. You can apply the same formatting to as many paragraphs as you want without having to copy it to the paintbrush each time.

TIME SAVER

If you have manually applied styles using Format | Font or Format | Paragraph, immediately select another paragraph to which you want to reapply the same formatting, and press the F4 key or Ctrl+Y. These shortcut keys allow you to repeat your last action. The shortcut keys are not always successful in repeating the actions of Format Painter, however. Results are not always consistent. The F4 key or Ctrl+Y can do much more than repeat formatting; they can repeat almost any action.

Adding and Saving Styles

Now that you know how to use Word's styles from the Formatting toolbar and Style Gallery, you might want to create your own styles. This used to be one of the more complicated word-processing tasks. With Word 97, it's a simple matter.

You may have special projects such as invitations for which you want to apply specific font and paragraph formatting. By creating and saving styles, you eliminate the repetitive steps of selecting text and going through the font and paragraph formatting each time you create a new invitation. Perhaps you are required to fill in forms and the fonts have to be a certain size to fit in the spaces, or you may need a specified number of decimal-aligned tabs. Create styles for these formats and apply them over and over. It's a great way to automate some of the processes that might otherwise take a lot of manual formatting.

To create a new style

1. Format a paragraph with the font and paragraph characteristics you want to include in the style.
2. Select the paragraph.
3. Click in the style box (the current style name will be highlighted).
4. Type a name for the style such as Big Bold! as in Figure 12.8.
5. Press the Enter key.

A new style is created and added to the drop-down styles preview list.

Figure 12.8.

Creating a new style.

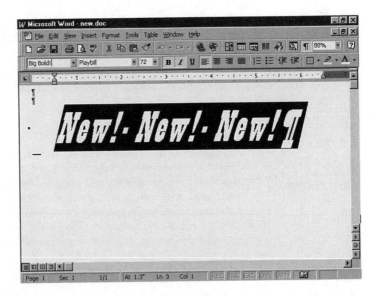

Style Organizer

When you create a new style, it is available only while you're working on the current document unless you add it to another template or document. To add a style to the Normal template

12

1. Select the paragraph that is formatted with the new style.
2. Select Style from the Format menu.
3. Click the Organizer button (see Figure 12.9).

Figure 12.9.

*Selecting the Organizer
to add a style to the
Normal template.*

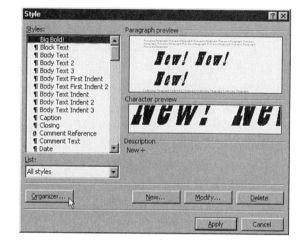

Style Organizer brings up the styles in the current document in the left window and the styles in Normal.dot in the right window. To copy a style to Normal.dot:

1. Select the style you want to add to the Normal template from the styles list.
2. Click the Copy button (see Figure 12.10). The style you selected is added to the style list under Normal.dot.
3. Click the Close button to complete the process.

Figure 12.10.

*Copying the Big Bold!
style to the Normal
template.*

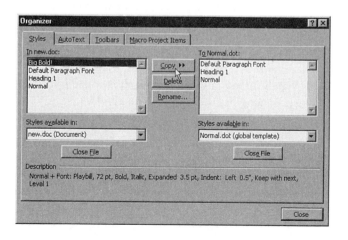

12

After a new style is added to the Normal template, it is available from the style box in every new document that is created using the New button on the Standard toolbar. This process works to copy any style from one template to another.

Copying Styles from a Template

There may be styles in some of the built-in templates that you'd like to add to the standard styles. For example, you might like a couple of the heading formats used in the Professional Report template to be available when you're working in every document. Use Organizer to add them to Normal.dot from the template:

1. Select Format | Style.
2. Click the Organizer button.
3. Click the Close File button on the left. The button changes to an Open File button.
4. Click the Open File button.
5. The Open dialog box opens in the Templates folder.
6. Double-click the folder that contains the template from which you want to copy a style.
7. Double-click the template name to display a list of styles in that template.
8. Select the style(s) you want to copy. Note the following tip on selecting more than one item from a list.

TIME SAVER

There are several ways to select items from many kinds of lists in Windows applications. Holding down the Ctrl key and clicking individual items is a method to select items in a list that are nonadjacent. Holding down the Shift key and clicking the first and last items in a list selects both of these items and everything in between. You can also click an item and hold down the mouse button, then move it up or down to select a group of adjacent items.

9. Click the Copy button, and the selected styles are copied to window on the right under Normal.dot (see Figure 12.11).

Copying Styles Between Documents

If you develop a document with specialized styles, these styles can be applied to another document. Styles can be applied from documents as well as templates. To copy styles from one document to another

1. Select Format | Styles.
2. Click the Organizer button in the Styles dialog box.

12

Figure 12.11.

Copying styles to the Normal template.

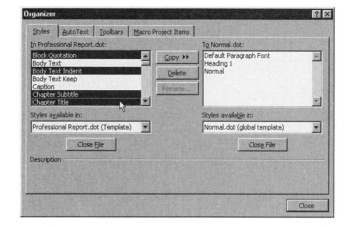

3. Click the Close File buttons for both the left and right windows (the current document and Normal.dot). The style boxes are cleared, and the buttons both say Open File.

4. Click the Open File button under the left window.

5. Click the Look in box to find the location of the document with the styles you want to copy. (The Up One Level button backs you out of the Templates folder. Continue to click the Up One Level button until you see the folder where your files are stored.)

6. Select Word Documents in the Files of type box (see Figure 12.12).

Figure 12.12.

Selecting a document from which to copy styles.

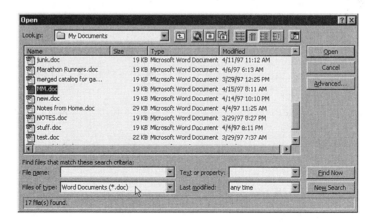

7. Locate the correct file and double-click it.

8. Repeat steps 3–7 using the Close button under the right window to select the document you want to add the styles to.

9. Select the styles from the document in the left window to be copied to the document in the right window. (Click a single style name, Ctrl + click several noncontiguous style names, or Shift + click the first and last style names for a contiguous selection.)

AutoFormat

One of the fastest ways to apply styles and do some document cleanup at the same time is to use another of Word's Auto features called AutoFormat. AutoFormat is a powerful feature that looks at an existing document and figures out how it can help standardize the document formatting.

Figure 12.13 is the dialog that appears when you select AutoFormat from the Format menu. There are options to format a general document, a letter, or an e-mail message. Using AutoFormat from the Format menu is a chance to have AutoFormat make a single pass through a document and fix all kinds of things.

Figure 12.13.

Using AutoFormat to apply styles and clean up a document.

You have two choices with AutoFormat:

☐ AutoFormat now—AutoFormat doesn't ask questions, it just goes ahead and reformats the document.

☐ AutoFormat and review—Asks your permission each time it proposes to make a change.

You have more control with AutoFormat and review, but it takes a lot more time. You can specify certain options before you run a document through AutoFormat to preselect some options you do or do not want AutoFormat to change. To set AutoFormat options

1. Select Format | AutoFormat.

2. Click the Options button.

12

3. Check the options you want AutoFormat to do for you. Uncheck the ones you don't want (see Figure 12.14).

Figure 12.14.

Changing AutoFormat options.

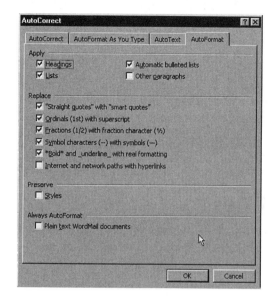

4. Click OK, and then click OK again to start AutoFormat.

If you look at the kinds of options that are included in AutoFormat, you'll realize that it is already hard at work in the background while you're typing. You've probably noticed that it automatically numbers or bullets successive lines once you've started a list. These are the kinds of options that also show up in the AutoFormat As You Type tab. It applies heading styles or automatically removes extra paragraph marks.

AutoFormat can

☐ Replace straight quotes with smart quotes (the ones that curve in toward text).

☐ Format ordinal numbers with superscript (2nd becomes 2nd).

☐ Make real-looking fractions (1/2 becomes $\frac{1}{2}$).

☐ Change hyphens to en and em dashes.

☐ Format text between two asterisks as bold and text between two underscores as emphasized text (for example, *Keep Up the Good Work* should appear as **Keep Up the Good Work**, and _Keep Up the Good Work_ changes to *Keep Up the Good Work*).

☐ Change Internet addresses to hyperlinks with the Internet and network paths with hyperlinks option. (This option is discussed in Hour 24, "Working with the Web.")

Superscript and *subscript* are font effects. Superscript raises letters and makes them smaller. Subscript lowers letters and makes them smaller. These character formats are important for numerical and scientific equations.

 En dash and *em dash* are named from the typographical en and em measurements. An em was typically the size of a capital M and an en was half the size of an em. An en dash is the type used as a separator in ranges of dates such as 1995–1997. Em dashes (the longer variety dashes) are used to set off afterthoughts or explanatory notes.

If you worked hard on your document and you defined styles the way you wanted them, be sure to check the Preserve Styles box so that AutoFormat won't change them.

If you want to further modify the document after running AutoFormat, choose one of the templates from the Style Gallery and apply the styles to the document.

Summary

This hour introduces styles in their many forms. New styles can be easily created using the style box on the Formatting toolbar. Normal style is not technically a style, but a template that includes many things other than font and paragraph formatting.

You can add styles to the Normal (Global) template through the Style Organizer. Styles can be copied from one document to another document as well as to a template.

AutoFormat can automatically apply styles and perform a quick check for other formatting changes it can make, such as deleting extra paragraph marks. Using the AutoFormat As You Type option is a way to let AutoFormat make formatting changes while you're working.

Hour 13, "Word's Outlining Features," shows how to use Word 97's outline feature. Outlines help you organize your thoughts and documents so that they follow a logical sequence.

Q&A

Q Is there any way to change right and left margins with styles so that they default to 1 inch rather than 1.25 inches?

A It can be done, but not through the Styles options. Use Page Setup from the File menu. Set the right and left margins to 1 inch, and then click the Default button. Word asks whether you're sure you want to change the defaults for page setup. It tells you that this affects all new documents based on the Normal template. Click Yes. New documents you start will have 1-inch margins.

12

Q **I copied the styles from one document to another, but the next time I used the file the styles didn't show up in the Styles Preview list. Don't they stay with the file?**

A If you exit the file that you copied the styles to without saving the changes, the styles you copied are not saved with the file.

Q **I was working with a file in which I was entering dates without the year (for example, 1/2), and I didn't want Word to convert them to fractions. I turned off the AutoFormat feature that replaces fractions, but it still converts them. What can I do to turn this off?**

A There are two places to check to make sure that Word won't automatically correct some of these options. Look at both the AutoFormat and the AutoFormat As You Type tabs. The feature must be turned off in both places. You can also click the Undo button (or press Ctrl+Z) to reverse an AutoFormat action.

12

RW **3**

Word in Real Time

Creating a Custom Template

Templates are created to lay out as much of the formatting and content for a document as possible so that these steps don't have to be repeated for each new document. You can modify any existing templates by opening the templates themselves and making changes to them. For instance, there are templates that display a company logo. You could open the template and replace the existing logo with your own.

To change a template, it must be opened as a template. When you select New from the File menu to start a new document and select one of Word's templates, you have the option of opening it as a document or as a template (see Figure R3.1).

When you open the template, any changes you make to it become part of the template. After the template is redesigned the way you want it, open it as a document each time thereafter to preserve the elements that you want to remain the same. The template becomes the pattern for new documents.

Figure R3.1.

Opening a template to change it.

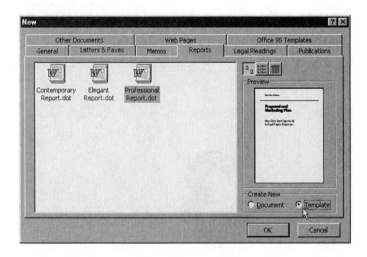

Before you begin creating a template, make a list of all the things you do manually in a document before you ever type text. In this sample template, you'll create a two-page letter. The following elements are added to the template:

☐ Space at the top of page 1 to allow for letterhead printing

☐ Page 1 set up to print on letterhead

☐ A field to print the current date each time the letter is printed

☐ A custom header for page 2

☐ Fill-in fields for the inside address information

☐ A signature block with a scanned (electronic) signature

Step 1—Setting Up Page and Print Options for Letterhead

Page 1 needs to be set up to print on letterhead. Press Enter twice to insert two extra paragraphs in the document. The first paragraph will be formatted to place the additional space at the top of the letter for letterhead. The other paragraphs will retain normal paragraph formatting that can be carried forward. To add extra space at the top of page 1:

1. Measure the letterhead to figure out how much extra space is needed to print page 1 on letterhead.

2. Select the first paragraph marker, and select Format | Paragraph from the menu.

3. In the Spacing before box, type the amount of space required before the first line of text. You can specify inches if you type in the inch marking (as in 2.5").

4. Click OK.

Many newer printers are designed with two paper trays so that one can be filled with plain paper and the other with letterhead. This example explains how to select two different paper trays in the same document. If your letterhead is in a tray called the upper tray and the plain paper is in a tray called the lower tray, use the following process to specify which page to print from each tray:

1. Select File | Page Setup.

2. In the Paper Source tab, select Upper tray from the First page options because letterhead is stored there for this printer. Your printer may have different options depending on your printer type.

3. Select Lower tray from the Other pages options because this is where the blank paper is stored. Again, your printer may be different. All the pages after page 1 will print from this tray.

4. Click OK.

Figure R3.2.

Setting up page 1.

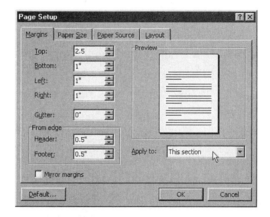

Step 2—Inserting a Date Field

A date field can be added to the first line of the document. The field will be automatically updated to the current date each time you print. To add a date field:

1. Position the cursor on the first line of the letter.

2. Select Date and Time from the Insert menu.

3. Select the format you prefer. Make sure the Update Automatically box is checked so that the date will be current each time you use the template.

4. Click OK.

Step 3—Adding a Header to Page 2

Many people add a header to the second page of a letter that references the date and the person's name. The first step is to add a page break so that there are two pages.

If you can't see the paragraph marks in the document, click the Show/Hide button on the Standard toolbar. Position the cursor in front of the third paragraph mark and insert a page break by pressing Ctrl+Enter or selecting Insert | Break from the menu and choosing Page break from the Insert options. To set up the header to include the date and page number:

1. Position the cursor on page 2.

2. Select Header and Footer from the View menu.

3. Insert a blank line for the first line of the header (you'll use this line later).

4. On the second line, type Page and add a space, and then click the Insert Page Number button on the Header and Footer toolbar. Click the Format Page Number button and type 2 in the Start at box.

5. Tab twice to move to the right section of the header. Insert the date by selecting Date and Time from the Insert menu and clicking one of the date formats.

6. Select File | Page Setup from the menu and click the Layout tab.

7. Under Headers and Footers, check the Different first page box. With this option checked, the header will not appear on the first page.

8. Click OK.

Click the Close button on the Header and Footer toolbar or double-click anywhere in the typing screen to return to the document.

Step 4—Adding Fill-in Fields

Fill-in fields are a handy invention that allow you to enter certain information when you print the document. This works well when you have a form letter that requires only an inside address and salutation change. To add the fill-in fields:

1. Position the cursor in the document where the first line of address will go.

2. Select Insert | Field.

3. Click Mail Merge in the Categories list.

4. Select Fill-in from the Field names list.

5. The text in the Field codes box changes to FILLIN.

6. After the word FILLIN, enclose in quotes the question you want Word to ask for the first line of the inside address (for example, "Who is this letter to?") as in Figure R3.3.

Figure R3.3.

Adding a question to a
Fill-in field.

7. Click OK, and a sample dialog box shows you what the question box will look like. Click OK.

8. Position the cursor on the next line.

9. Repeat steps 2–7, but use an appropriate question such as "What is the first line of address?" for the second fill-in question.

10. Insert a fill-in field for each line of address, entering a question for each line.

11. Start the first line of the body of the letter with Dear, add a space, then insert another fill-in field for salutation.

Figure R3.4 shows what the document looks like when the fill-in field codes are showing. If you can't see the fill-in fields in the document, press Alt+F9. This is an on/off toggle for viewing or hiding field codes. You can also select the paragraphs that have field codes you want to display, and right-click to bring up the shortcut menu. Select Toggle Field Codes to display or hide the field codes.

One last fill-in needs to be added to the document. Use the first blank line that was created in the header to add the name of the person you're sending the letter to. To add this last fill-in field:

1. Display the field codes if they are not showing (Alt + F9).

2. Select the line that says FILLIN "Who is this letter to?" *MERGEFORMAT.

3. Click the Copy button on the Standard toolbar or press Ctrl+C.

4. Select View | Header Footer.

5. Select the first line of the header, and click the Paste button or press Ctrl+V.

Word adds the same information to the header that is displayed in the first line of the inside address (the addressee's name) when the document is printed.

Figure R3.4.

Displaying the fill-in field codes.

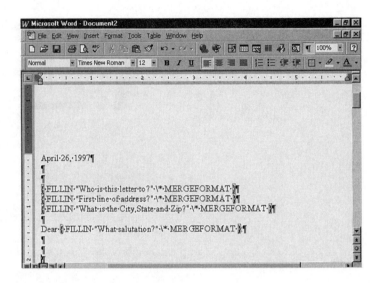

Step 5—Adding a Signature Block to the Second Page

A signature block is the standard closure for a letter. It contains the complimentary close (for example, Sincerely or Respectfully Yours), four blank lines to allow for the written signature, the typed signature, and the sender's job title if applicable. After the job title, the typist's initials and notations for enclosures can be included.

It is a simple process to insert a scanned (electronic) signature in a signature block to save hours of hand signing (we all know that Robert H. Treller does not sign all those Publishers Clearinghouse mailings). A good printer can render an electronic signature so well that the reader won't recognize that a computer generated it.

If you don't have access to a scanner, there are usually people around who do. Many copy shops rent computers on an hourly basis that includes the use of a scanner. It will take you about five minutes to scan your signature (ten, if you have to learn the scanning software).

On a clean piece of paper with a good pen, write your signature two or three times, then scan the page. The scanning software allows you to select a portion of the page to save to a file. Examine the signatures and choose the one that looks the best. Save that portion of the page to a file. The scanned image is saved as a picture that you can insert in any document.

To insert a signature block with an electronic signature:

1. Position the cursor on page 2.

2. Press Enter a couple of times to allow for the body of the message on page 2.

3. Type your normal signature block. Leave only one line between the complimentary close and the typed signature.

4. Position the cursor in the line after the complimentary close.

5. Select Insert | Picture | From File.

6. Locate the scanned signature graphic file and double-click it. The graphic will probably be too large for the signature block.

7. Click the picture of the signature and note that several small squares surround the picture. These are called positioning handles.

8. Grab the positioning handle in the lower-right corner; this displays a double-headed diagonal arrow (see Figure R3.5).

Figure R3.5.

Use the positioning handle to resize the signature.

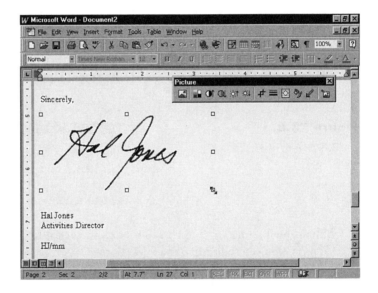

9. Move the mouse up and to the left to make the picture small enough to fit nicely into the signature block.

10. Remove any blank lines between the scanned signature and the typed signature.

Hour 17, "Working with Graphics," covers the insertion and manipulation of graphics in greater detail.

Saving the Template

You have the framework for a two-page letter that you can use often. You know how to save a document. To save this document as a template, do the following:

1. Select File | Save As.

2. In the Save as type box, select Document template. Word finds the Templates folder and displays the template subfolders in the file list.

3. Double-click the Letters folder.

4. Enter a name for the file in the File name box (for example, `two-page letter with signature`).

5. Click Save.

The next time you want to use the letter, select File | New and the Two-Page Letter with Signature template will be listed in the Letters tab. Type the body of the letter, and the letter is ready to print.

Step 7—Printing the Letter

When you click the Print button on the Standard toolbar, you get a series of boxes with the fill-in questions (see Figure R3.6). These are the questions you typed in for the fill-in fields. If the question boxes don't come up, select Tools | Options and check Update Fields in the Print tab options.

Figure R3.6.

Answering the fill-in questions.

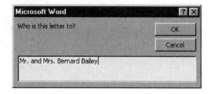

Enter the information in each fill-in box and click OK. Word prints the letter with the information you supplied in the fill-in boxes.

TIME SAVER

If you send the same letter to many people, you can include the text of the letter itself in the template before you save it. If there are only certain words that you change in the document, add fill-in fields where you want to personalize information.

Templates can be used in lots of ways. Examine the kinds of documents you create and those few items you modify when you reuse them. Try to figure out whether a template might be in order for some of the documents you create repetitively.

As you created the template, there was no mention of font or paragraph formatting. This was to show how different a template is from individual styles. You can include styles in a template, but a template is much more than a group of styles. It is a recipe you use over and over that has similar ingredients—like the basic cookie dough recipe where you add raisins one time, chocolate chips the next, and oatmeal the next to make it different.

PART
IV

Word the Workhorse

Hour

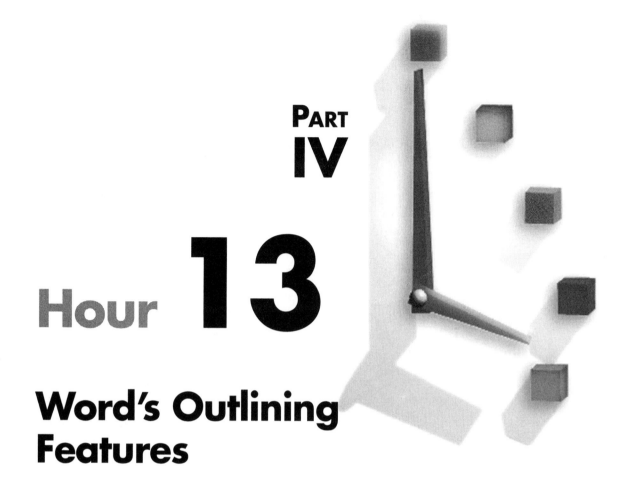

Hour 13

Word's Outlining Features

by Ruel T. Hernandez

Word 97 has wonderful outlining features to help you write term papers, reports, and other documents that you need for school, work, and fun (and outlines are great for writing books like this one)! With the outlining features, you make outlines of whatever you are writing. Outlines are like preliminary sketches of what you want to write. You can think of an outline as the skeleton of the topics and items you want to cover in your writing. An outline can help you organize your thoughts before you actually start writing. Once you have an outline, you can fill in the details.

The highlights of this hour include

- ☐ A discussion of the Outline view
- ☐ Instructions for using the Outlining toolbar

Working in Outline View

The Outline view in Word 97 is easy to use. At the bottom of the screen on the left end of the horizontal scrollbar, you'll see four tiny buttons. The first button is for Normal view, the second is for Online Layout view, the third is for Page Layout view, and the fourth is Outline view. You can also access these view selections from the main menu bar at the top of your Word 97 screen by clicking the View menu selection—you will see the same four view options plus the Master Document view. In Hour 10, "It's All in the Way You View It," I discussed all of the view options, but, needless to say, this chapter discusses the Outline view in a little more detail.

If you are doing normal everyday writing and you want to do some outlining, you will find yourself switching between Normal view (for regular text writing) and Outline view. Click between the two, and you should see the text in your document switch between the two views. Figures 13.1 and 13.2 show the differences between Outline and Normal view.

Figure 13.1.

Outline view shifts your document into an outline format.

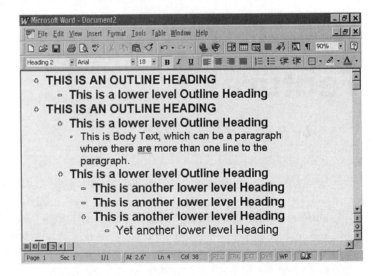

The Outline view shifts some of your text to the right, and plus signs and dashes may show up on the left side of your document. (The next section covers how to "collapse" some of the outline headings that you see in Outline view.) An Outlining toolbar shows up at the top of your Word 97 screen below the menu bar, the Standard toolbar, and the Formatting toolbar. The Outlining toolbar typically shows up as the third toolbar onscreen and replaces the ruler bar.

You know how to activate and switch between Normal view and Outline view, but how do you use the outlining features? To use the outlining features, you have to go to the Outlining toolbar.

13

Figure 13.2.

Normal view shifts your document back in a "normal" mode where you can write your document.

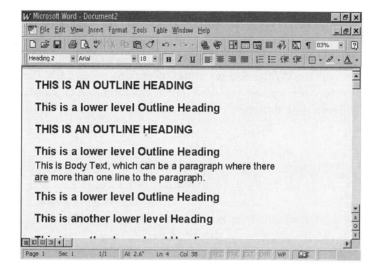

The Outlining Toolbar

The Outlining toolbar is very easy to use. Let's take a look at the buttons on the Outlining toolbar.

Figure 13.3.

The Outlining toolbar is below the menu bar, the Standard toolbar, and the Formatting toolbar.

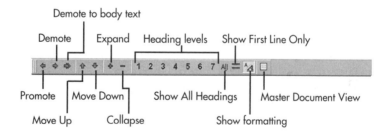

KEYBOARD SHORTCUT

There are a few shortcut keystrokes you can use in writing your outline: Tab and Shift+Tab. Instead of clicking the Demote button on the Outlining toolbar, press the Tab key on your keyboard to demote a branch on your outline. This is useful if you want to keep your hands on the keyboard. You can press the Tab key prior to typing any text for a lower (demoted) branch. Instead of typing your text and then clicking the Demote button, press Enter to start a new line, press the Tab key to demote the line to a lower branch, and then type your text. You can also press Shift+Tab to promote a branch of your outline instead of clicking the Promote button on the Outlining toolbar.

13

Promoting, Demoting, and Demoting to Body Text

The first three buttons on the Outlining toolbar are the Promote, Demote, and Demote Body Text buttons. To understand their functions, let's take a look at how an outline is put together in Word 97. An outline consists of headings, where each heading may have subheadings, and each subheading may have more subheadings, and so on. For instance, an outline might look like the following:

+   Heading level 1
   +   Heading level 2
      +   Heading level 3
         +   Heading level 4
            -   Discussion under this subtopic
         -   Heading level 4 with Body Text
      +   Heading level 3
   +   Heading level 2
      +   Heading level 3
         +   Heading level 4
            +   Heading level 5
               +   Heading level 6
                  + Heading level 7

The plus signs (+) indicate that there are subheadings or body text under a heading. The minus signs (-) indicate that there are no subheadings or body text under a heading. The period (.) signs indicate that the text is body text instead of a heading/subheading. Body text is the regular text of your document. The headings and subheadings designate the different parts of the body text in your document.

For instance, say you want to make an outline that looks like the following:

+   Outline about Pets
   +   Household Pets
      - Cats
      - Birds
      - Dogs
      - Care and Feeding

To make this outline in Word, do the following:

1. Open a new document.

2. Switch from Normal view to Outline view (click the Outline View button on the horizontal scrollbar at the bottom-left of your Word screen).

3. Type your first line, Outline about Pets, and then press Enter.

4. Type the second line, Household Pets, click the Demote button on the Outlining toolbar, and then press Enter.

5. Type Cats on the next line, click the Demote button, and then press Enter.

6. Type Birds on the next line and then press Enter.

7. Type Dogs on the next line and then press Enter.

8. Type Care and Feeding on the next line and then press Enter.

You should have an outline similar to the one shown in Figure 13.4 (the text font size may be smaller on your actual screen).

When you promote a heading, you are moving that heading to a higher heading level where heading level 1 is the top level. For instance, if you want to move a heading at level 3 to level 1, you would place your cursor on that heading and click the Promote button. Demoting a branch or a heading works the same way except that you are moving the heading to a lower level. Now this "moving" between different levels is a little different from "moving" text around in the document. You are not actually moving text to a different section of the outline. You are just changing the level of the heading.

Figure 13.4.

Use the Outlining toolbar to make this outline about pets.

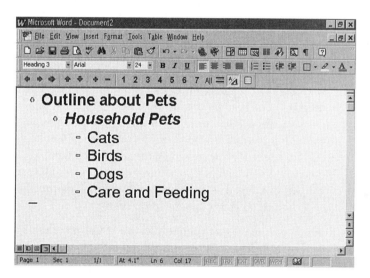

What if you find that the subheading for Care and Feeding in the previous example should be a higher heading level by itself? You can place your cursor on the Care and Feeding heading and promote it by clicking the Promote button. Your outline should then look like Figure 13.5.

```
+       Outline about Pets
    +       Household Pets
        -   Cats
        -   Birds
        -   Dogs
    + Care and Feeding
```

13

Figure 13.5.

The Care and Feeding heading was promoted to a higher level in the outline.

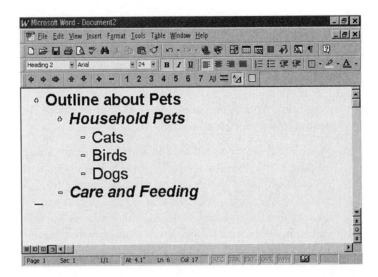

Likewise, if you find that the Care and Feeding heading should be placed back as a subtopic under the Household Pets heading, you would place your cursor on the Care and Feeding heading and click the Demote button to move that heading back to the lower heading level.

It's really that easy to promote and demote a heading. You might find that you don't want the text to be a heading after all, but rather, text in a heading. In this case, you can also select Demote to Body Text, which is where, instead of writing a new heading, you are writing body text. After typing a heading, you can press your Enter key, click the Demote to Body Text button, and type your paragraph text as you normally would. Note that for the body text, there is a dot instead of a plus or minus sign. It would be at this point that you might find yourself switching back to Normal view by clicking the Normal view button at the bottom of the screen on the horizontal scrollbar.

You may want to draft your outline first in Outline view, then switch to Normal view. You could then type your text in Normal view. When you switch back to Outline view, you would find that your paragraph text under a heading would be at the body text level.

Expanding and Collapsing the Outline

The next two buttons are the Expand (+) and Collapse (-) buttons. In Outline view, place your cursor on a heading and then click the Expand/Collapse buttons to see the subheadings under that heading. Each click expands or collapses the outline headings one level at a time.

Moving Headings Up and Down Through an Outline

Okay, you know how to promote, demote, and demote to body text. But what about moving headings and text around an outline? This is simple: Use the Move Up and Move Down buttons on the Outlining toolbar.

To move a heading, place your cursor on the heading, and click the Move Up or Move Down button to move the heading up or down through the outline.

If you want to move everything under a heading, select the heading and everything under the heading (the subheadings, the text, and so on). Start clicking the Move Up or Move Down button to move the blocked heading/subheadings/text to wherever you want.

JUST A MINUTE

> You can also move headings and body text by selecting and then dragging and dropping the headings and body text from one part of the outline to another part of the outline. Similarly, you can cut and paste parts of your outline. However, for those of you who are not comfortable with dragging and dropping text (you might accidentally drop the selected headings and body text in the wrong place), you may want to use the Move Up and Move Down buttons instead.

Heading Number Buttons

The 1 through 7 heading number buttons are like Collapse/Expand buttons that let you collapse and expand your outline to the outline heading level that you specify. If you click the 1 button, you will collapse your outline to the level-1 headings. If you click the 7 button, you will expand your outline to level-7 headings.

Show All Headings, First Line Only, and Formatting Buttons

The next three buttons are the Show All Headings button, the Show First Line Only button, and the Show Formatting button. As with the other Outlining toolbar buttons, these buttons are easy to understand and use.

Click the Show All Headings button to show all headings regardless of heading level as well as all body text. If you click the Show All Headings button again, you collapse the outline.

If you want to see only the first line of each heading, click the Show First Line Only button. Click the button again to see all the lines of each heading.

If you click the Show All Formatting button, you can hide and show the special formatting (such as bold formatting, and so on) you have for text in your outline.

13

Numbering Your Outline Headings

Okay, you now know the basics of promoting, demoting, and writing body text for your outline. You know how to switch back and forth between Normal and Outline view. But how do you number the headings of your outline? You can let Word number the headings automatically for you, and you can delete and change the heading numbers as well.

In Outline view, choose Edit | Select All, select Format | Bullets and Numbering, then click the Outline Numbered tab. This should display a Bullets and Numbering panel similar to the one shown in Figure 13.6.

Figure 13.6.

You can select different outline numbering formats for your outline.

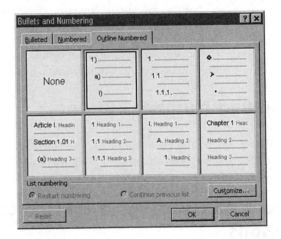

Select the numbering style you wish to use and click OK. You should then see your headings numbered. If you move or promote/demote a heading, the numbering changes.

If you make a new heading, but do not want that heading to be numbered, simply delete the number that is automatically inserted by Word 97 from the Outline Numbered tab of the Bullets and Numbering dialog box. Simply place your cursor on the heading that is to be unnumbered, then click None. You may want to set your numbering before you start writing the main text for your document. For those who are wondering whether paragraphs and other body text will be numbered, they are not supposed to be. However, if they are numbered, the numbers should disappear when you demote the paragraphs and other body text by clicking the Demote to Body Text button. The backspace key also deletes the numbers, but you should make sure the paragraph is demoted to text so there are no numbers.

You can select different numbering styles for different parts of your outline. Similarly, you can select only certain portions of your outline for numbering. Instead of selecting the entire outline, you would just select those parts of the outline that you want numbered, select Format | Bullets and Numbering, and then select the numbering style you want. Make sure the Restart Numbering option is selected.

Seeing Heading Styles in Normal View and Changing a Paragraph's Outline Level

One nice feature you will want to know about is how you can see the outline levels for parts of your document when you are in Normal view. To do this, select Tools | Options and then click the View tab. Toward the bottom in the Windows section, set the Style Area Width to .6 or .7 inches (or larger or smaller depending on how much information you want to see), and then click OK. After you have done that, when you are in Normal view you will see a Style Area column on the left side of the screen, which shows you the style of various parts of your document. To remove the column with the style information, click Tools | Options, and repeat the previous steps, setting the Style Area Width to 0.

Summary

You have learned in this chapter that using the outlining features of Word 97 is very easy. You can now switch between Normal view and Outline view. You learned how to promote, demote, and demote to body text certain parts of your outline. You also learned how to move parts of your outline around by using the Move Up and Move Down buttons. You can easily expand and collapse an outline. You also know how to show all or parts of an online. You can set up a Styles column in Normal view, and can set paragraphs to an outline level so you can see them while in Outline view when all the paragraphs are collapsed from view. Now that you know how to use outlines in Word 97, you will find yourself more organized and productive when you write your reports and other documents.

13

Q&A

Q **I don't like the fonts that I am getting in Outline view. Can I use different fonts when I am in Outline view, and will they be the same when I go back to Normal view?**

A Yes, you can. You can use the functions you use in Outline view as you would in Normal view. The fonts should stay the same when you switch back to Normal view.

Q **My Outlining toolbar disappeared. How do I get it back?**

A Click View | Toolbars | Outlining to turn the Outlining toolbar on or off.

Q **Can I print a document as an outline without printing the whole document?**

A Yes, you can print an outline. Switch to Outline view, collapse your outline so you only see the headings of your outline, and then print.

13

Hour 14

Working with Tables

This hour explains how tables are created, modified, and enhanced. Tables are one of the most powerful features in Word 97. Tables turn Word into a spreadsheet, a database, a calendar-creator, a Web designer, or a tool to create publications. New in Word 97 is the Draw Table feature, which lets you put your artistic touches on tables. The new Tables and Borders toolbar gives one-touch access to table creation and formatting.

The highlights of this hour include

- ☐ How to insert a table
- ☐ How to use the Tables and Borders toolbar
- ☐ What AutoFormat can do to enhance tables
- ☐ How to add columns of numbers in tables
- ☐ How to use tables creatively

Inserting a Table in a Document

There are several ways to insert tables in documents. Before you start, however, you may want to turn on the Tables and Borders toolbar. The Tables and Borders icon on the Standard toolbar activates the Tables and Borders toolbar (see Figure 14.1). Drag it either to the top or bottom of the screen to move it out of the typing area. You can also use the alternate method, which is to select Toolbars from the View menu and click Tables and Borders.

Figure 14.1.

The Tables and Borders toolbar.

The Insert Table Icon

The simplest way to insert a table is to click the Insert Table button on the Standard toolbar. Insert Table lets you build a grid for the table with the number of columns and rows you want.

When working with tables, the term *cell* is important. Cells are the individual squares that make up a table. A cell is often defined as the intersection of a column and a row. A row is a group of cells running across the page, while a column is a group of cells that go down the page. For example, Figure 14.2 shows a table being inserted from the Insert Table icon that has four rows and six columns. You can tell by the text under the picture (4×6 Table).

Figure 14.2.

Inserting a table from the Standard toolbar.

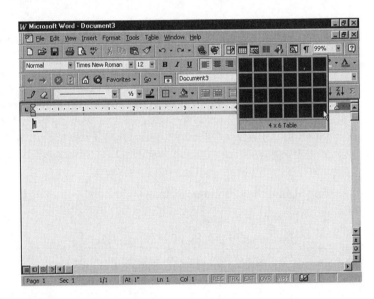

To insert a table using the Insert Table button on the Standard toolbar:

1. Position the cursor at the point in your document where you want to insert a table.
2. Click the Insert Table button.
3. Select the desired number of columns and rows by moving the mouse pointer across and down until you have a table the size you want it, then click.

14

One of the nice things about tables is that they are easily modified after you insert them. You can add rows, delete columns, change the sizes of columns or rows, or change the size of a single cell. Tables are as flexible as you need them to be.

Insert a Table from Menus

Inserting a table from the Table menu is a more precise way to lay out a table. Figure 14.3 displays the dialog box that comes up when you select Insert Table from the Table menu. You can specify the number of columns and rows, and set the column width to an exact size. The default column width says Auto, and this is what you get when you use the toolbar button for Insert Table. Word automatically sets the size of the columns to an optimal width to stretch from the left margin to the right margin. You can specify exact widths for the columns if you already know what size you want them.

Figure 14.3.

Inserting a table from the Table menu.

One of the buttons in the Insert Table dialog box shown in Figure 14.3 is AutoFormat. AutoFormat includes several predesigned table formats that can be applied. If you've worked with Excel's AutoFormats, these designs will look familiar. Figure 14.4 shows the dialog box that comes up when you click AutoFormat.

Figure 14.4.

Using AutoFormat to add a table design.

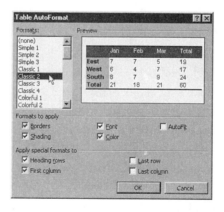

You can select which of the AutoFormat design elements you want to apply to the table. If you don't like the shading, uncheck the Shading box. If you don't like the font styles Word selected, uncheck Font. These options are probably less important when you're using

AutoFormat to create a new table than when you are applying AutoFormat to an existing table. You may have gone to a lot of trouble to use special fonts or borders and don't want them replaced by AutoFormat.

The Apply special formats to options add special formatting to heading rows and the first column because these are the sections you usually use for headings. Uncheck these options if you don't want them. You can also apply special formatting to the last row and last column. These are particularly useful when you need a row or column of totals to stand out in a document.

Select an AutoFormat design from the list and watch what happens in the preview window when you apply one of the options. The font may be accented, or a line drawn to separate either the row or column from the rest of the table. Select a design you like, set the options you want to include, and click OK.

If you have already created a table and want to apply one of the AutoFormats, click the AutoFormat button on the Tools and Borders toolbar. The same AutoFormat dialog box comes up that you saw in Figure 14.4. You can apply AutoFormat options to the existing table.

Draw Table

Draw Table is a new feature that the artist in you will appreciate. We typically think of tables as cold, calculated cells of equal size, like a spreadsheet full of numbers. Draw Table would probably not be appropriate for a spreadsheet-type table. It's too difficult to make the cells equal in size using Draw Table.

DrawTable is, however, a freeform drawing tool that lets you define an outside border for the table and then draw lines inside the border for individual rows and columns. To create a table using Draw Table:

1. Activate Draw Table from the Table menu or from the Draw Table icon on the Tables and Borders toolbar (the one that looks like a pencil drawing a single line).

   If you're in another view, Word switches to Page Layout because Draw Table is a graphic tool. The mouse pointer turns to a pencil.

2. Click and hold down the mouse button on the page where you want your table. The pencil will have a square attached to it.

3. Drag the pencil down and to the right to create a box that will be the outline for your table (see Figure 14.5).

4. When it is sized about the way you want it, release the mouse button.

14

Figure 14.5.

Use Draw Table to get creative with tables.

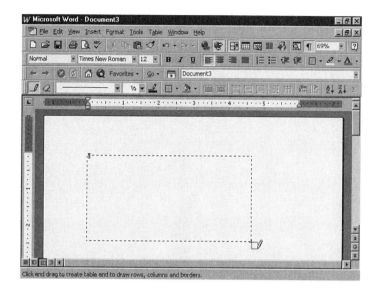

To insert a new column or a row:

1. Click the Draw Table icon if it is not already turned on (if it's turned on, it looks pushed in and lighted); the mouse pointer will still look like a pencil.

2. Click the top border of the table and start moving down with the pencil. The pencil knows where you're headed and creates a column.

3. Click the left border of the table and start moving the pencil to the right. The pencil creates a row.

As long as the Draw Table button is turned on, you can continue to draw columns and rows until you have the table looking the way you want it. You can start drawing lines from any existing edge or cell border. One of the real pluses is being able to draw a column that only goes as far as a certain row, or a row that only reaches to a particular column as in Figure 14.6. There's a lot of creative freedom in using Draw Table.

Adding Rows and Columns to a Table

You can easily add more rows or columns to any table, whether it was created with the Insert Table button or with Draw Table. First, you need to know how to select portions of a table. Table 14.1 shows the selection methods for tables.

14

Figure 14.6.

Fine-tune rows and columns with Draw Table.

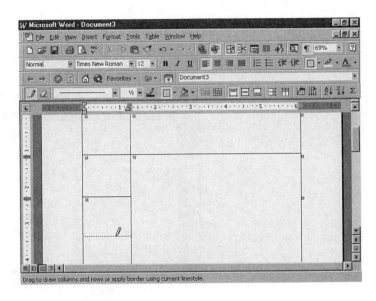

Table 14.1. Selecting parts of a table.

Selection	Selection method
A cell	Position the mouse pointer in the cell in a location where the pointer is displayed as an arrow pointing up and to the right, then click.
A row	Click in the left margin next to the row (with the arrow pointing to the right), or click anywhere in the row, and select Table|Select Row.
A column	Position the mouse pointer above the column until it turns to a dark arrow pointing down, then click (see Figure 14.7), or click in any cell in the column and select Table|Select Column.
The entire table	Position the cursor anywhere in the table and press Alt + (numeric keypad) 5 (the Num Lock key must be turned off when using this key combination to select a table). Or, click in the table and select Table|Select Table.

If you're already working in a table, the Insert Table button on the Standard toolbar changes to either an Insert Rows or Insert Columns button. If you have a row selected, the icon is used to insert rows. If you have a column selected, the icon changes to Insert Columns.

With a row selected, click the Insert Rows button to insert a row above the selected row. Keep clicking the Insert Rows button to insert more rows. With a column selected, click the Insert Columns button to insert a column to the left of the selection.

14

Figure 14.7.

Selecting a column.

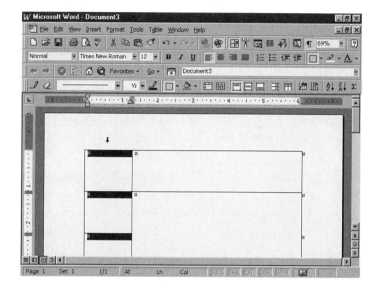

To insert a row at the end of a table, press the Tab key in the last cell of the table. To insert another column at the right edge of a table, position the mouse above the table just past the last column until you see the black arrow that points down. Click the mouse button, then click the Insert Columns button on the toolbar or select Insert Columns from the Table menu.

TIME SAVER

If you insert a table on the first line of a document and later decide you need text above the table, you can insert a regular paragraph above a table by placing the cursor in the first cell of the table and pressing Ctrl+Shift+Enter.

Entering Text into a Table

One of the reasons you don't need to have all rows established when you create a table is because Word automates the addition of rows as you type. To begin adding text to a table, position the cursor in the first cell of the table. Type everything you want in the cell. If you type more text than the cell can handle on one line, the text wraps to a second line in the cell and the cell height is enlarged to permit the extra lines. To move to the next cell in the row, press Tab. The Tab key is the primary key for getting around in tables. When you come to the last cell in a row, pressing the Tab key advances to the first cell in the next row. If there is no row following the last cell, a new row is automatically created. Table 14.2 lists some navigational keys you'll use in tables.

Table 14.2. Navigational keys for tables.

Keys	Function
Tab	Moves one cell to the right; starts a new row if pressed in the last cell of a table.
Shift+Tab	Moves one cell to the left, or to the last cell in the row above if the cursor is in the first cell of a row.
Down arrow	Moves to the cell below the current cell (if the cursor is in the last line of the cell).
Up arrow	Moves to the cell above the current cell (if the cursor is in the first line of the cell).
Alt+Page Down	Moves to the cell below the current cell from any line in the cell.
Alt+Page Up	Moves to the cell above the current cell from any line in the cell.

If you are at the end of an existing table and you press the Tab key in the last cell, a new row is inserted on the next line. As you can see, you need start only with a single row. Word adds the extra rows as you need them.

Aligning Table Text

You learned about aligning text in Hour 6, "Formatting Paragraphs." The same principles apply to text in tables. Text can be left-aligned, right-aligned, centered, or justified in cells.

> **Step-Up**
>
> One of the great enhancements to Word's Table feature is being able to align text vertically within a cell. You can align text at the top, bottom, or center of a cell. Move the mouse across the Tables and Borders toolbar and you'll find selections for Align Top, Center Vertically, and Align Bottom. There is also an icon to change the direction of text (Change Text Direction).

Figure 14.8 shows some of the different alignment options. The directional text feature adds the versatility for placing text that Excel has had for a long time. If your headings are too long to fit horizontally in a table, rotating text with the Change Text Direction button provides an easy solution.

14

Figure 14.8.

Table text alignment options.

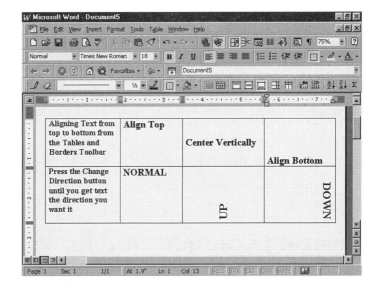

You might want text centered both vertically and horizontally in a cell and the direction of text changed to display vertically rather than horizontally. To do this:

1. Click in the table cell.
2. Click the Center button on the Formatting toolbar.
3. Click the Center Vertically button on the Tables and Borders toolbar.
4. Click the Change Text Direction button on the Tables and Borders toolbar as many times as needed to place text in the direction you want. Text will rotate between the normal, top-to-bottom, and bottom-to-top placement options as you click the button.

JUST A MINUTE

When you change the direction of the text to one of the vertical text options, the Alignment buttons change functions. For example, the Left Align button becomes the Align Top and the Align Top becomes the Left Align function. You'll notice that the toolbar icons flip directions for the alignment icons. This is because the text has a different orientation to the top and sides of the cell when it is rotated.

14

Using Tabs in Tables

The Tab key is used to get back and forth in a table, so it can't be used to set a real tab in a table cell. One of the primary reasons for needing a tab in a table is to set a decimal-aligned tab that lines up numbers on the decimal point. It is very hard to get lists of figures to look good without a decimal-aligned tab.

To insert a tab in a table, press Ctrl+Tab. You can also set tabs from the ruler or by selecting Format|Tabs. The easiest way to insert decimal-aligned tabs in a column is to

1. Type the text (numbers) in the column cells.
2. Select the column.
3. Select Format|Tabs.
4. Type in a number for the Tab stop position (for example, .5 inches). Click Decimal under Alignment.
5. Click Set, then click OK.

Word automatically inserts the tabs in every cell of the column. You won't even see the tab markers in the cells. Once a tab is set, you can move it on the ruler if it's not where you want it.

Resizing Columns and Rows

When you use the Insert Table button on the Standard toolbar to insert a table, the column and row sizes are preset to fit the width of the page. The columns are all the same size. You may want to alter the sizes so that they better fit the contents of the columns. For example, you may want a column containing names to be wider than a column that includes birthdays. Columns are easily resized. When you position the mouse pointer in the space between two columns on the ruler, a double-headed arrow appears with the message Move Table Column, as shown in Figure 14.9. Move the pointer right or left to resize the columns.

Figure 14.9.

Moving a column.

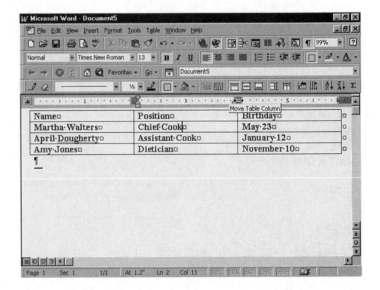

14

You can also move columns by positioning the mouse pointer on the line between two columns. The mouse pointer changes to a line with an arrow on either side. Click and drag the line in either direction to change column sizes. One of the problems with this method is that it's easy to grab a single cell and move the cell rather than the whole column. The column must be selected in order to move it. If a single cell is selected, only that cell will be resized.

There may be times when you actually want to move a single cell. This is particularly true when tables are used to create forms. Cells often need to be specific widths to accommodate the different kinds of information that must be entered in the form. They won't necessarily line up neatly in columns. To resize a single cell:

1. Select the cell (click in the cell with the mouse pointer pointing up and to the right).
2. Position the mouse on either the right or left border of the cell (the pointer changes to the line with an arrow on both sides).
3. Click and drag the border either to the left or to the right to resize it.

Distribute Rows and Columns Evenly

When you start dragging columns around, you are bound to get columns that don't look the way you want them. Perhaps you have two columns on the left side of the table that need to vary in width and four columns that need to be the same width. By the time you've dragged and adjusted columns, you may have altered the sizes of the four columns enough that they are not the same. The Tables and Borders toolbar has new tools to help correct these kinds of problems. To make the last four columns the same size:

1. Select the columns by positioning the mouse pointer above the first of the four columns until the dark arrow appears.
2. Click and drag the mouse pointer to the right to select all four columns.
3. Click the Distribute Columns Evenly button on the toolbar.

All four columns are proportioned equally to fit the amount of available space.

Distribute Rows Evenly works the same way for rows. Select the rows, then click the Distribute Rows Evenly button, and all of the rows will be of equal height. The capability to distribute rows and columns is a great Word 97 enhancement to the Table feature.

AutoFit

If you want to let Word figure out the size for columns, AutoFit is a handy feature. AutoFit looks at the text in the cells and adjusts the columns to accommodate the widest line of text

14

in the column. Text in the cells will wrap as needed to keep the columns within the page margins. If you want to use AutoFit for the whole table:

1. Select the table (Table | Select Table or Alt+5 on the keypad).
2. Select Table | Cell Height and Width.
3. Click AutoFit in the Column tab.

If you accidentally move a couple of single cells and they don't line up with the other cells in the columns, AutoFit will readjust the table cells to bring them back into nice straight columns. It resizes all of the columns in the process.

Split Cells and Merge Cells

Merging cells is useful when you want to center a title in the first row of a table as in Figure 14.10. The second row of the table is the only one that is formatted normally. The first row is three cells merged together to allow for the title.

Figure 14.10.

Merging and splitting cells.

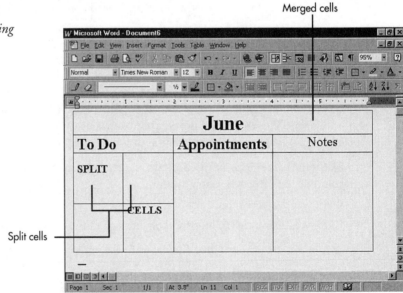

To merge cells:

1. Select the cells to be merged (combined).
2. Click the Merge Cells icon on the Tables and Borders toolbar, or select Merge Cells from the Table menu.
3. Click the Center button on the Standard toolbar (or press Ctrl+E) if you want to center text across the columns.

14

Splitting cells is just as easy. To create more cells within a single cell as in the first cell of the third row in Figure 14.10, select the cell and click the Split Cells button. A dialog box asks how many columns and rows you want the cell divided into. It actually creates another small table within a cell.

Deleting Rows or Columns

If you've tried using the Delete key to remove a row or column, you know it doesn't work. The Delete key removes the contents of the row or column, but leaves the cells. To delete a row, select it and choose Delete Rows from the Table menu. Similarly, delete a column by selecting it and choosing Delete Columns from the Table menu. To remove an entire table, select the table and then select Table|Delete Rows.

Sorting a Table

There are times when you will want to sort a table. If you enter the reservations for an event in a table as they are received, it may be a little hard to keep track unless the entries are ordered in some way. The table could be sorted alphabetically by the guests' last names to make it easier to reference.

You would normally include headings above the columns to indicate what information is in each column. The column headings for a reservation list might be Last Name, First Name, Phone, and Reservations.

Word tables are smarter than they used to be. A default is set to tell Word that the first row is a header row. When you sorted a table in earlier versions, it would sort the header row along with all the other rows unless you specified that the first row was the header row. Your headings always ended up in the middle of your table somewhere. Now you have to tell Word when you *don't* have a header row.

There are two ways to sort a table. The easiest is to select the column you want to sort by. In this example, the sort is by the last name, which is the first column. Click the Sort Ascending button on the Tables and Borders toolbar. The list is sorted alphabetically by last name. If you want to sort on one of the other columns, simply select another column and click the Sort Ascending button.

You can also sort in reverse order by clicking the Sort Descending button. When you're working with numeric data, this is often a preferred method for displaying facts and figures.

Businesses like to note their top salespeople and will want the big producers at the top of the list. To specify other Sort options, select Table|Sort. To sort on more than one column, specify the first sort from the selections in the Sort by drop-down list. Select a second sort from the Then by drop-down list. Figure 14.11 shows a sort by last name, then by first name. This is helpful when you're typing a phone listing or roster and need to have both parts of the name

14

sorted in the alphabetical listing. This is also where you can tell Word when you don't have a header row. Click the No header row radio button if there are no headings in your table.

Figure 14.11.

Sorting a table by first and last names.

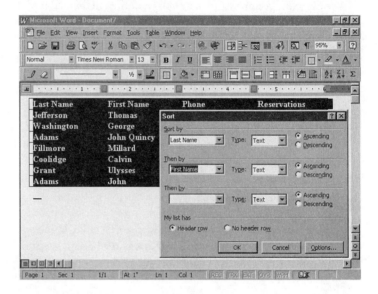

Sorting rearranges an entire table in a certain order. If you simply want to reorder a couple of rows in a table, you can use the same keyboard combination used to move text up and down. Alt+Shift+Up arrow or Down arrow moves a selected row up or down to promote or demote a row. For example, select a row and press the Alt+Shift+Up arrow to move the row ahead of the previous row.

Converting Text to a Table

Sometimes you have already typed text when you decide you want it in a table. Tables are really easier to work with than tabbed text to create manageable lists and columns of text. Text in a list is usually separated by tabs or commas, but it can be in almost any format for Word to divide it into a table. To convert text to a table:

1. Select the text you want to convert to a table.

2. Select Table|Convert Text to Table. The Convert Text to Table dialog box opens.

3. Word looks at the selected text and determines the number of columns it thinks are required. If this is incorrect, type the number of columns needed in the Number of columns box.

4. Choose one of the options for Separate text at (for example, if your text is separated by tabs, click the Tabs option).

5. Click OK.

14

If the text being converted to a table is separated by tabs or another separator, there should be only one separator between each item. Additional separators throw off the table conversion. The Undo button does work if things don't work quite right in the conversion process.

If your text is not separated by one of the standard options (paragraphs, tabs, or commas), you can specify any other character you separated text with, including a space. Type the character in the Other box. Figure 14.12 shows a simple list with a single space between each item and a table that was created from the same list by converting text to a table. A space was entered in the Other box by clicking in the box and pressing the spacebar. Word inserts a cell division wherever there is a separator (in this case, a space).

Figure 14.12.

Creating a table from text.

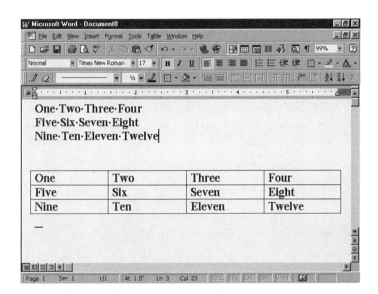

It is just as easy to turn a table into text. When you select a table, the option under Table is no longer Convert Text to Table. It becomes Convert Table to Text and gives the same options to replace cell divisions with text separators.

AutoSum

When you're working with figures in a table, it's nice to be able to add up columns of numbers without a calculator. AutoSum does the job in Word tables. Position the cursor in the cell below a column of numbers and click the AutoSum button to calculate the sum of the numbers above (see Figure 14.13).

14

Figure 14.13.

Calculating a column of numbers with AutoSum.

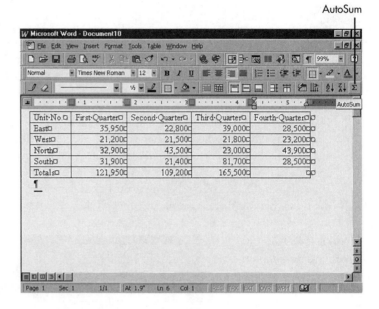

Unlike a spreadsheet program, Word does not automatically update the sums if you change numbers in the table. You will need to either use AutoSum again to repeat the calculations or right-click each of the sums and select Update field from the shortcut menu.

You can do other types of calculations using Table | Formula if you know a little about mathematical expressions and spreadsheet terminology. It's not complex, but you'll probably end up in a spreadsheet program if your figures need to be updated from time to time. Updating the fields or repeating AutoSum for each column is not only time-consuming, it can be inaccurate if you miss a column.

Cells in a table start numbering with A1 for the top-left cell—the first cell in the table. A1 is the first cell in the first column. The next cell in the row is B1, and so on. The next row starts with A2 and the numbering continues in this way. Figure 14.14 shows a table and indicates how cells are numbered. In this figure, the Formula function is being used to calculate bowling averages. To calculate an average such as the one in this table:

1. Position the cursor in the cell where you want the result to appear.
2. Select Table | Formula.

The Sum function appears in the Formula box. This is the most commonly used function, so it comes up as the suggested calculation.

1. In the Formula box, select and delete the Sum formula.
2. Type = (every formula begins with the equal sign) in the Formula box.

14

3. Select Average from the drop-down list under Paste (or type Average after the equal sign in the Formula box).

4. The range of cells must be specified for the calculation. In this example, A2:A4 is the range and the range is placed in parentheses. A2:A4 designates everything between and including cells A2 and A4.

5. Click OK to enter the calculation in cell A5.

The same method is used to calculate the average for the rest of the columns. For column 2, the cursor is placed in cell B5 and the average is calculated for cells B2:B4 and so forth.

Figure 14.14.

Calculating a bowling average.

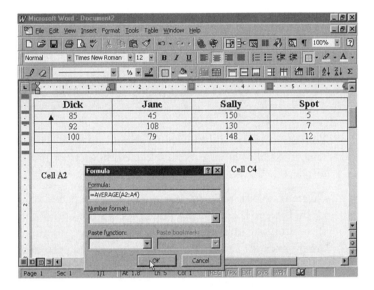

Tables as a Design Tool

Tables are not only a great tool for numbers and lists, but can be used in a variety of other ways. You might choose to do a newsletter in table format. Rather than use the standard columns, you can remove the borders so that no one knows that the publication was laid out as a table. To remove table borders:

1. Select the table.

2. Select Format | Borders.

3. Click None in the Borders tab.

You can also add or remove borders from the drop-down list of border options as shown in Figure 14.15. The last selection is grayed slightly and shows no dark lines. This is the selection for no border. The other icons are visually descriptive of the kinds of borders that can be selected.

Figure 14.15.

Using the border options to remove borders.

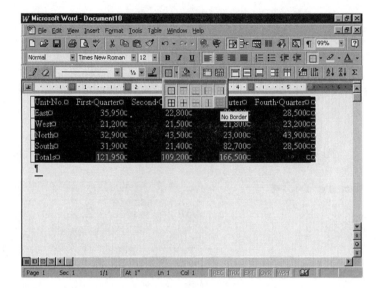

You may still see a faint gray border around the cells. These are the gridlines. To see what the table looks like without them, select Gridlines from the Table menu to turn the gridline display off.

Create a one-page newsletter using a table rather than standard columns. Be creative and use Draw Table to lay out sections of different sizes. One of the great new features is the eraser. If you want some of the lines to show but not others, use the eraser on the ones you don't want. Simply click the Eraser button and drag it over a portion of a line to make it disappear.

Figure 14.16 shows a newsletter that was created in a table (with the gridlines showing). Figure 14.17 shows the same newsletter without the gridlines visible. Only one line is really there—the one underneath the header; the others were gridlines. Gridlines don't print. They're only there so that you can see where you're working in a table. When borders are applied, the lines are dark and solid rather than faint gray and the gridlines will print.

In Figure 14.16, there is space added between the gridline and the text in the second cell of row two. To add the extra space that you normally want between columns of a newsletter:

1. Select the cell (or column if you want added space between two columns).
2. Select Format|Paragraph.
3. Type in a left indent (in Figure 14.16 there is a .3-inch left indent).
4. Click OK.

Indents can be used in table cells just as they are in paragraphs. You can also add graphics to a table. To insert a graphic in a table, it must be placed as an inline graphic. Details on inline graphics versus graphics that float above the text layer are discussed in Hour 17, "Working

14

with Graphics." Tables take on a whole new look when borders and shading are applied. Hour 19, "Jazzing Up Your Documents," shows how to apply borders and shading to tables and other documents.

Figure 14.16.

Creating a newsletter in a table.

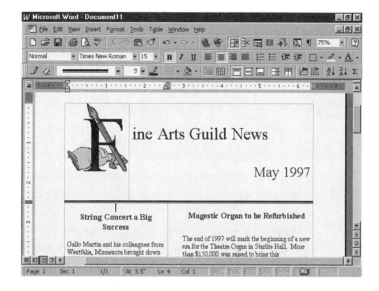

Figure 14.17.

The newsletter as it will print (without the gridlines).

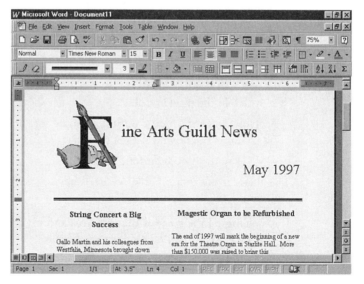

14

Use tables to create sidebars, calendars, menus, or any number of documents that require text to be placed in distinct areas on the page. You'll be surprised how much easier it is to work with tables than with tabs for text placement.

Summary

This hour highlights one of Word 97's greatest achievements. Tables can be sketched out with Draw Table. The options to rearrange text in tables are almost endless. One of the most significant additions to the new table features is being able to rotate text using the Change Text Direction tool. You can easily sort tables or convert tables to text—do the reverse to convert existing text to a table. Add up the columns of numbers in a table with AutoSum. Tables are feature-rich workhorses in Word 97.

Q&A

Q Is there a way to prevent a row that has more than one line of text from splitting between two pages?

A Yes. Select Table | Cell Height and Width. Uncheck the box that says Allow row to break across pages. It forces the row that would normally split between pages to move to the next page.

Q When I try to insert a table from the Insert Table icon, I can only get a table as large as five columns and four rows. Why can't I make a bigger table?

A If you click the Insert Table button, move the mouse pointer across and down, and click the last cell (lower right) to set the table size, the largest table you can create is one that is five columns by four rows. If you click the Insert Table button, click in the first cell (upper left), and move the mouse pointer across and down to set the table size, you can insert a table as large as eight columns by thirteen rows. If you want to create a table that is six columns by six rows:

1. Click the Insert Table button.
2. Click in the top-left cell.
3. Hold down the mouse button and drag the mouse to the right to select six columns and down to select six rows.
4. Release the mouse button.

The alternative is to use Table | Insert Table to specify the number of columns and rows.

Q I was changing the sizes of the columns and my table moved off the right edge of the paper. Why can't I see it to readjust it?

A You are probably in Page Layout view or another view that displays the page as it will print. Switch to Normal view and you can grab the right edge of the table and move it back. Bring it back to the right margin to be within the print range. You could also resize all the cells to bring them within the page margins by selecting Table | Cell Height and Width, select the Columns tab, and click AutoFit. This will, however, resize all the columns.

14

Q **I like being able to sort a table. Is there any way to sort a list of items that isn't in a table?**

A Yes. Select text you want to sort, then select Table | Sort. The same dialog box comes up that you see when you sort a table, but it says Sort Text at the top. Usually you sort by paragraph (which would be line-by-line for a list). Once in a while, you type a list with first name, then last name, and wish you'd typed the last name first so that you could get an alphabetical listing. To put the list in order by last name without retyping:

1. Select the list.
2. Select Table | Sort.
3. Select Word 2 (last name) in the drop-down list under Sort by.
4. Select Word 1 (first name) from the Then by list.

The list is sorted without requiring you to retype it!

14

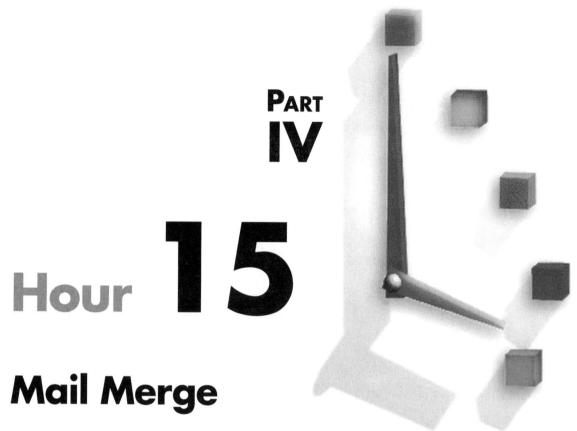

Hour 15

Mail Merge

This hour explains how and why you would use mail merge. Today's business environment is fast paced and communications need to be timely. Employees no longer have the time to type the same letter to twenty people, nor would they want to with the kinds of tools that are available.

Mail merge used to be so complicated that instead of using it, people would type the contents of the letter and then type over the name and address to send the same letter to a different person. That works fine if you only have to do this for one or two people, but if you want to send the letter to twenty people, typing over the name and address can be time consuming. You also have no record of who the letters were sent to. Mail merge was created to expedite this process.

The highlights of this hour include

- ☐ How to set up a mail merge for form letters
- ☐ How to create a list with mail merge
- ☐ How to use mail merge for mailing labels and envelopes
- ☐ What kinds of files you can use for data sources in Word

Why Use Mail Merge?

Mail merge is not just a tool for creating form letters, but that's its primary purpose. You get junk mail every day that someone created with mail merge. It is now possible for individuals to buy a CD-ROM or a series of CD-ROMs with the names and mailing addresses of practically everyone in the country. These CD-ROMs contain data that is collected and packaged so that others can use it. A vendor can purchase one of these packages and write a letter with codes that read the information from the CD-ROMs. Your name and address can be inserted in the letter using mail merge. You've probably received letters that use your first and last names in the salutation, such as *Dear David Smith*. Most people don't call you by your first and last names.

The reason the letters are written that way is because the data was created with only one name field. We talked briefly about fields in Hour 1, "Word 97—A Multipurpose Tool." Fields are the units used to hold certain pieces of information. The pricier data sources break down the information into more fields than the ones you can buy off the shelf in many stores. That's why some letters say, Dear David Smith and some say Dear David or Dear Mr. Smith—the first and last names are separate fields you can use individually.

Mail merge can also be used to create mailing labels. You might send an organizational newsletter to a hundred people once a month. If you had to type these same labels every month, you'd probably spend at least half a day just getting the labels ready. With mail merge, you can print out the 100 mailing labels in a matter of minutes.

Why use mail merge? It's a great time saver. After you see how mail-merge documents are set up, you'll discover that it's not the complicated process it used to be.

Main Documents and Data Sources— What's the Difference?

Mail merge has two major components. One is the main document and the other is the data source. The main document is the form letter, the mailing label form sheet, or another document that contains codes for information that comes from another file—the data source. The data source is the file that contains information such as names and addresses that will be combined with the main document to complete a merge process. You might compare it to a fill-in-the-blank form. The main document is the form. The data source contains the information that goes in the blanks.

Mail merge can be used to create a single letter that can be individualized for as many people as you wish. The main document is typed normally, but the recipient's name, address, and salutation are added to the document as fields (placeholders for information that comes from another source). By connecting the main document to a data source that contains the information for many individuals, the information that was entered as fields is replaced with the information from the data source. Field names in the data source *must* match the field names in the main document.

The term *merge* is descriptive of what happens in this whole process. The main document and the data source are merged, or combined, to create a final product such as a sheet of mailing labels or a batch of letters. This all happens because of the field codes in the main document that match the fields in the data source. During the merge process, the main document field codes are replaced with the contents of the fields in the data source.

Main Documents

Figure 15.1 shows a main document. It is a letter from a fictitious Widgets company, and has what looks likes some odd codes in it. If this looks like a foreign language, don't worry. You'll soon understand the language of merge. If you can't see the codes in a merge main document, press Alt+F9 to display the field codes. The Alt+F9 key combination toggles the field code display on or off.

Figure 15.1.

A main document with merge codes.

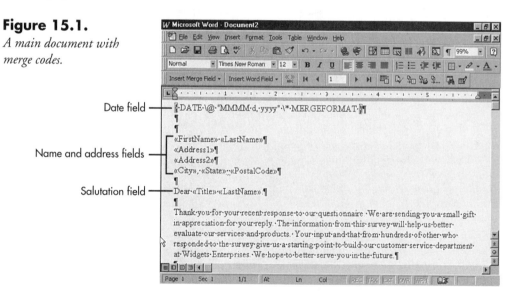

Date field — ·DATE·\@·"MMMM·d,·yyyy"·*·MERGEFORMAT·¶

Name and address fields — «FirstName»·«LastName»¶
«Address1»¶
«Address2»¶
«City»,·«State»···«PostalCode»¶

Salutation field — Dear·«Title»·«LastName»·¶

Line one contains the codes to insert the current date. Each time the letter prints, it prints the current date if this field is present. You learned a bit about inserting dates in the discussion on headers and footers in Hour 8, "Setting Up the Page." Select Insert | Date and Time from the menu, choose one of the available date formats, and check the Update automatically box. If you don't add the update automatically provision, the date will be inserted, but it will not be a field and will not change if you use the document again.

The lines following the date are the information fields for the name, address, and salutation. The body of the letter is already typed into the main document. The only thing that is needed is a source to bring in the names and addresses of the people the letter is to be mailed to. That's where the second component in mail merge comes in—the data source.

Data Sources

The data source can come from any one of a number of sources. It can be an Access database, an Excel spreadsheet, Microsoft's Address Book, or a data source that you create in Word. Figure 15.2 shows a typical data source created in Word and displayed in table form. The line at the top is called the header row, which was mentioned in Hour 14, "Working with Tables." In this case, the header row contains the field names (Title, Firstname, and so on).

The main document must have field codes that match the field names in the document source header row. In the merge process, the field codes in the main document, like the ones shown in Figure 15.1, read from the document source shown in Figure 15.2 to gather the information it needs to fill in the field codes.

Figure 15.2.

A data source in table view.

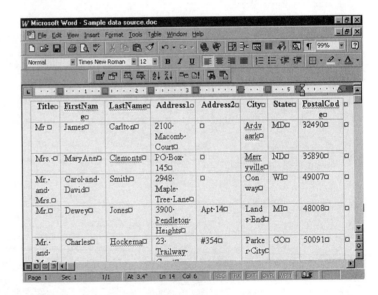

Creating a Simple Mail Merge

To set up a mail merge, two documents are needed—a main document and a data source. This example goes through the steps of a mail merge from start to finish. A new main document and a new data source are being created. You could also create a main document and use an existing data source such as an Access or a dBASE file to do a mail merge. A mail

15

merge always begins with the main document, and the merge itself (combining the main document and the data source) must take place within the main document.

Step 1—Setting Up the Main Document

The first step is to set up the main document. To do this:

1. Select Tools | Mail Merge. The Mail Merge Helper dialog box appears, as in Figure 15.3.

Figure 15.3.

Creating a mail-merge document from a new document.

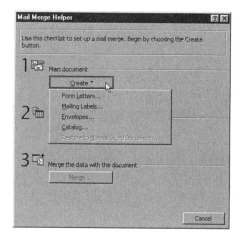

2. Select Form Letters from the Create drop-down list to create a form letter.

   A dialog box appears, asking whether you want to create the main document from the active window or from a new document.

3. Click New Document if you have another file open. (If you were in a document that you wanted to use for the mail-merge document, you would click Active Window.)

Step 2—Setting Up the Data Source

After the new main document is created, you are returned to the Mail Merge Helper dialog box. Step 2 is to set up the data source.

1. Click the drop-down Get Data list.
2. Select Create Data Source as shown in Figure 15.4.

Figure 15.4.

Selecting a data source—Create Data Source.

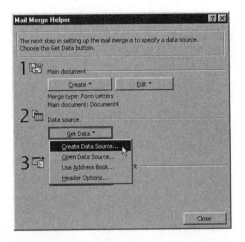

Step 3—Adding and Removing Fields from the Data Source

Word displays the Create Data Source dialog box, where you specify what the field names will be in your data source and your main document (see Figure 15.5). Word shows a list of suggested fields in the box of field names. If you don't like the ones Word has chosen, you can delete them and add your own.

Figure 15.5.

Selecting field names for the merge document.

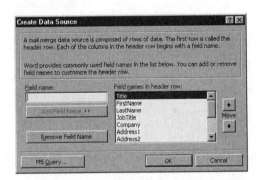

Delete field names that you don't want in your data source by selecting each field name individually and clicking the Remove Field Name button for each deletion. If, for example, you want to remove the Country, HomePhone, and WorkPhone fields:

1. Select Country from the Field names in header row list. Click Remove Field Name.

2. Select HomePhone from the list. Click Remove Field Name.

3. Select WorkPhone from the list. Click Remove Field Name.

15

These three field names are removed from the data source. To add a field, type a name in the Field name box and click Add Field Name.

TIME SAVER

> Adding a field for salutation offers more flexibility in the way you address people. You might have a mix of individuals in your data source. Some you would call by their first names, some you might address by nickname, and others you might address more formally by title and last name. There is no way to allow for these different types of salutations with the preset field names.

You can rearrange the order of the field names in the list by selecting a field name and clicking the move up or move down arrow buttons to move the item up or down in the list. You do not need to have fields in any specific order. They can be inserted in any order in the main document. One good reason to rearrange the order is to facilitate data entry. You will often work from a list that has the information in a specific order. It is much easier to enter the information in the data source if the fields are ordered in the same way that the information appears in the printed list you are working from.

Step 4—Naming and Saving the Data Source

After you delete, add, and move field names in the list, click OK. Word prompts you to give the data source document a name, as shown in Figure 15.6. This is sometimes a source of confusion for people. You are saving and naming the data source document at this point, *not* the main document.

Figure 15.6.

Naming the data source document.

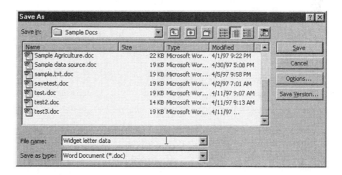

Step 5—Editing the Data Source

When you save the data source document, a dialog box opens asking whether you want to edit the data source or the main document. It really doesn't matter which you do first. You need to do both when you are creating the data source. Click Edit Data Source to fill in the information about the people the letter is to be sent to (see Figure 15.7).

Figure 15.7.

*Click Edit Data Source
to begin entering names
and addresses.*

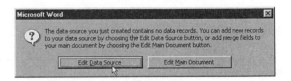

The Data Form dialog, shown in Figure 15.8, appears with boxes to enter information for each person. Working in the Data Form dialog is similar to working in a table. Press the Tab key to move from one field to the next. Press Shift+Tab to move up one field. After you enter the information in the last field of a record, press the Enter key or click the Add New button to begin a record for another person.

Figure 15.8.

*Entering information in
the Data Form dialog.*

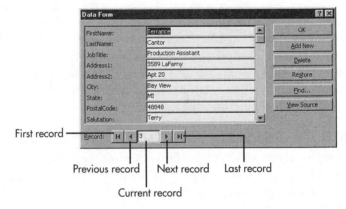

A *record* contains the collection of fields (individual pieces of information) that pertain to a single individual. In other types of data source documents, a record might contain related information for something other than individuals (for example, the names of items in a home inventory, or products in a catalog).

If you don't have information for a certain field, tab to the next field. You don't have to enter information in every field. For example, if you have an individual who has one line of address but not a second line, enter information in the Address1 line and skip the Address2 line. Word can handle blank lines and eliminate them from the document when you are in the printing stage. When you finish entering the information for every individual, click OK. You are returned to the main document.

15

CAUTION

> It is important to be consistent when you enter information in a data source. People often don't consider how the information will be combined with the main document when entering data. If, for example, you decide to shortcut the process and enter all of the name information (first and last name) in the first name field and then decide you want to include the first name in the salutation, it can't be done with the data as it has been entered. If you have two contacts at the same address, you might decide to use the first name field for one contact and last name for the other contact. Imagine the mess you'll have when you try to merge this information (Dear Firstname Lastname will translate to something like Dear Mary Smith Carl Walker).

15

Step 6—Adding Fields to the Main Document

Word needs to know where you want the information from the data source to be placed in the main document. The Mail Merge toolbar is visible when you are in a merge document. The Insert Merge Field button provides the information you need to insert the fields in the main document. To add fields to the main document:

1. Position the cursor in the document where you want to insert the first field.

2. Click the Insert Merge Field button to bring up the list of all the fields that are in the data source file.

3. Select the first field to insert (FirstName).

   If you need spaces or punctuation between fields, it must be entered in the main document. In this case, press the spacebar to insert a space after the FirstName field.

4. Click the Insert Merge Field button again to select the next field (LastName).

5. Press Enter to start a new line.

6. Click the Insert Merge Field button and insert the Address1 field. Press the Enter key to start a new line, then repeat the process for the rest of the address fields. Remember to add spaces, commas, or other punctuation that should appear in the document. The comma between city and state and the punctuation after the salutation are prime examples.

7. Add the salutation field in the appropriate location, as shown in Figure 15.9.

Figure 15.9.

Inserting the Salutation field in the main document.

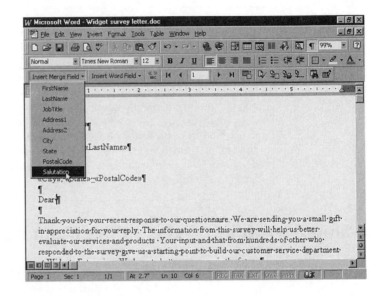

Step 7—Previewing Before Printing

After all the pertinent fields have been added to the main document, you're ready to determine whether everything is going to merge correctly before you print the letters. First, click the Check for Errors button on the Mail Merge toolbar. This feature checks to make sure there are no problems in either the main document or the data source that would prevent the document from printing properly. If there are problems, you can fix them before wasting paper.

To see what your letters will look after the letter is merged with the information from the data source, click the View Merged Data button (see Figure 15.10). Word displays the letter with the data included. Scroll through all the letters by clicking the Next Record button. You can navigate through the records using the buttons on the Mail Merge toolbar just as you do in the Data Form dialog. To move to a specific record, click in the Go To Record box and type in the record number. If things look good and you're ready to print, move to step 9 to print the letters. If not, go to step 8 to fix the problems.

Step 8—Fixing Errors Before Printing

If there are errors that need to be corrected before printing, check the main document and make any necessary changes. To make changes to the data source, click the Edit Data Source button on the right end of the Mail Merge toolbar. Edit Data Source opens the Data Form dialog, where you can make changes to the data.

15

Figure 15.10.

Viewing the merged letter.

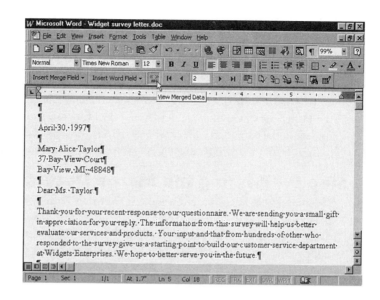

You may not have a problem with the data itself (the information you entered in the fields), but say you found errors or omissions in the field names themselves. To modify or add another field:

1. Click the View Source button in the Data Form dialog.

2. Click the Manage Fields button on the Mail Merge toolbar.

   The Manage Fields dialog box comes up. You can add or remove fields just as you did when you first set up the fields. You can also rename one of the existing fields as in Figure 15.11. The PostalCode field is renamed Zip.

Figure 15.11.

Changing a field name.

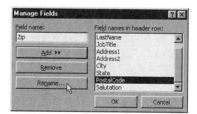

3. Click Rename to change the field name.

4. Click OK.

Return to the main document by clicking the Mail Merge Main Document button on the Mail Merge toolbar. This takes you to the main document.

The field names in the data source must match the field names in the main document. If you change the name of a field in the data source, you must remove the old field from the main document and insert the new field. In this case, you need to select the PostalCode field in the main document and press the Delete key to remove it.

When you click the Insert Merge Field button on the Mail Merge toolbar, you no longer see the PostalCode field name. Insert Merge Field includes only the names of fields that are present in the data source. Because PostalCode was changed to Zip, you now see Zip in the list. Insert Zip in the document where PostalCode was removed.

Step 9—Printing the Merge Documents

If you're satisfied that the letters look the way they should, you're ready to print. It's a good policy to print a sample before printing all the records. If you have 100 records in your data source, you don't want to print all 100 and then find out that something isn't working quite right. What you see onscreen may not always match what prints. To print the a test letter:

1. Click the Mail Merge button on the Mail Merge toolbar, and the Merge dialog box opens (see Figure 15.12).

Figure 15.12.

Print a sample first.

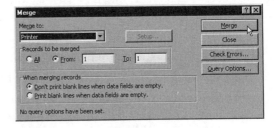

2. Select Printer from the drop-down list under Merge to.

3. Click From and type in 1 in both the From and To boxes to try a test run. You're telling Word which records to print. In this case you want Word to begin and end with record 1 to get a single page.

TIME SAVER

If you don't put anything in the To box, Word assumes you want everything from the first record you specified to the end of all of the records. In this case, if you entered a 1 in the From box and left the To box empty, all of the letters would print.

If your test letter comes out correctly, you can repeat the process and select All under Records to be merged, or you can type 2 in the From box and leave the To box empty since you already printed the first letter as your test case. Leaving the To box empty means that all records from 2 to the end will print.

15

Mailing Labels

You can also use merge for mailing labels. To print mailing labels from the same data source you used for the letters:

1. Select Tools | Mail Merge.
2. Click Create, and select Mailing Labels.
3. Select New Main Document.
4. Click Get Data and select Open Data Source.
5. Find and select the name of the data source file from the Open dialog box that you created for the form letter. Click Open.
6. Click the Set Up Main Document button that appears. The Label Options dialog box, shown in Figure 15.13, comes up. Click on your printer type under Printer information.

Figure 15.13.

Selecting label options.

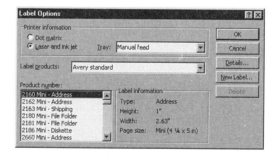

7. Select the type of label you are using from the Product number list.
8. Click OK.

The Create Labels dialog box opens. You can build a picture of the way you want the labels to print by adding fields from the Insert Merge Field list just as you did in the form letter (see Figure 15.14). Add spaces between fields where you need them and press the Enter key at the end of each line. Click OK when you have all the relevant fields added to the labels.

Word builds a page of labels that includes field codes on each label. Again, it's a good idea to go through the checking process as you did with the form letter.

☐ Check for errors (click the Check for Errors button).

☐ View merged data (click the View Merged Data button).

☐ Print a test page.

Figure 15.14.
Adding fields to the label.

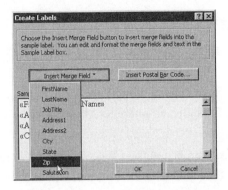

It's especially important to do a trial run for labels. Print a sample on paper before printing on labels. Labels are expensive. Put the sample in front of a label page and hold them up to the light to see if things line up properly. If everything looks good, click the Mail Merge button on the Mail Merge toolbar to set up the print specifications, or you can click the Merge to Print button that prints all of the records.

Envelopes

Creating envelopes is quite similar to creating mailing labels. To create an envelope main document:

1. Select Tools | Mail Merge.
2. Click Create and select Mailing Labels.
3. Select New Main Document.
4. Click Get Data and select Open Data Source.
5. Find and select the name of the data source file from the Open dialog box. Click Open.
6. Click the Set Up Main Document button. The Envelopes Options dialog box, shown in Figure 15.15, will appear.
7. Select an envelope size from the drop-down list. Size 10 is the normal business envelope size, but you can specify other sizes.
8. Change the font types and sizes for the delivery and return addresses if you want to use something other than the default font. Click the Font buttons to change one or both of the fonts.
9. Click OK.

15

Figure 15.15.

Setting envelope options.

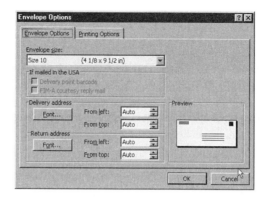

Start building the envelope as you did the mailing labels by inserting fields one at a time. You may want to add a postal barcode above the address lines to speed delivery. To add a barcode:

1. Click the Insert Postal Bar Code button.

2. You must tell Word which field contains the zip code so that it can build the barcode from these numbers. In this data source, the postal code is in the Zip field. Figure 15.16 shows the dialog box that comes up when you insert a postal barcode. Select Zip from the drop-down list at the top. The message above the box says Merge field with Zip code, showing that it builds the postal bar code from the information in the Zip field.

Figure 15.16.

Adding a postal barcode to envelopes.

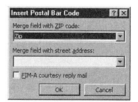

Continue to build the other lines of address as you did when you created labels.

JUST A MINUTE

You can also insert postal barcodes in labels, but they often take up more space than the label allows, and it can be a little trickier. Experiment with different fonts and font sizes to get a label form that works if the barcodes on the labels don't fit quite right.

After you've created the envelope, a sample envelope appears with the field names inserted. You can enter a return address in the upper-left corner if there is nothing there, or if the default return address isn't what you want. Again, run through the checking process before printing.

Using Data from Other Sources

You can attach a different data source file to a main document. If, for example, you want to send the Widgets letter (refer to Figure 15.1) to a group of people listed in an Access file:

1. Open the Widgets letter.
2. Select Tools | Mail Merge.
3. Click Get Data.
4. Select Open Data Source.
5. Select MS Access Databases in the Files of type box.
6. Locate the Access file and open it (see Figure 15.17). Note that there are many different kinds of file types that can be used as data sources for a Word main document.

Figure 15.17.

Selecting an Access file for the data source.

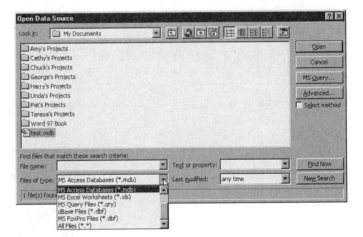

You are returned to the Mail Merge dialog box. Click Close to return to the main document. Make sure that the field names are the same in both the data source and the main document. In this case, the field for the first name in the Access file was called First and the last name was called Last. The fields FirstName and LastName must be deleted from the main document and replaced with First and Last using the fields in the drop-down Insert Merge Field list.

15

Using Query to Print Specific Records

If you have a large data source file, there may be times when you want to print letters for only certain groups of people. For example, say you want to send the Widgets letter to only the people who live in Indiana and Michigan. Query is a powerful tool that lets you select only the records with IN or MI in the State field. To select only these records:

1. From the main document, click the Mail Merge button on the Mail Merge toolbar.
2. Click Query Options.
3. Select State from the first drop-down Field list (see Figure 15.18).
4. Select the Equal to option from the Comparison tab.

Figure 15.18.

Using Query to specify which records to print.

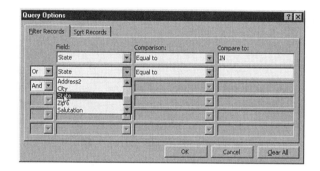

5. Type IN in the Compare to box.
6. Select the Or option from the drop-down list of operators in the box to the left.
7. Select the State option from the second drop-down Field list.
8. Select the Equal to option from the Comparison tab.
9. Type MI in the Compare to box.

Word looks for all the records that contain IN or MI in the State field and prints letters for only those records. These are called conditional statements. The conditional statement, if it were printed, might read something like this:

If the State field contains IN or the State field contains MI, then print the letter. If it doesn't, don't print the letter. If you use the And operator, both conditions must be true. In this case no letters would print because there are no records that have both IN and MI in the State field.

You would use the And operator to narrow the records by two or more fields. For example, you might want all of the records for the people in Lansing, Michigan. Your query would include City, Equal to, Lansing—And—State, Equal to, MI.

You can also specify which Jones you want to send a mailing to by selecting Lastname, Equal to, Jones—And—Firstname, Equal to, Harry. This is helpful if you get a page jammed in the printer and need to print only a specific record. If you know the record number, it's easier to select it in mail merge and specify the record to be merged.

Summary

This hour outlines mail merge, one of the prime functions of a word processor. Merge can be used to create four kinds of documents: form letters, mailing labels, envelopes, and catalogs. Data can come from a variety of sources. You can use a data file you create in Word, one you already have stored, or one from a different source such as Access, Excel, or dBASE.

Q&A

Q I ran a query to select certain records to print, but now I can't print all the records. What should I do?

A Click the Mail Merge icon, then click Query Options. Select Clear All to remove the query.

Q I wanted to use a dBASE file as a data source, but I don't have an option in the list of file types for dBASE, and I can't use All Files to select the file. Word doesn't recognize it.

A You may not have installed the converters for dBASE when you installed Word (or Office). You need to run Setup again to add the converters. Another option is to save your dBASE files as comma- or tab-delimited files. They could then be used as data sources.

Q When I try to print my letters, Word creates another document with all the letters in it, but it doesn't print my letters. What's going wrong?

A Click the Mail Merge icon. In the Merge to box, it may say New Document. Select Printer from the drop-down list. If New Document is selected, Word merges the letter with the data and creates a new document with every letter in it. Some people like to work this way. After the letters are merged to a single document, click the Printer icon, or select File | Print from the menu to print the letters.

15

Hour 16

Automating Tasks

This hour explains how to use AutoText and macros to take care of repetitive tasks. AutoText has taken on new meaning in Word 97. Using AutoText is about as easy as using Copy and Paste to insert frequently used text or graphic elements. If you're thinking about skipping the section on macros because you've always thought of them as something only programmers can figure out, don't! If you can turn on a tape recorder to record music, you can use macros. There's nothing to it.

The highlights of this hour include

☐ What kinds of items you would save as AutoText

☐ How AutoText can save your time

☐ What you would use a macro for

☐ How to assign a macro to a toolbar button or a shortcut key combination

AutoText

AutoText has been around in some form since the very early versions of Word. It used to be called the Glossary. Word 97 has expanded the AutoText feature. You can save frequently used text or graphics to AutoText entries. After they are saved, they can quickly be inserted in a document any time you need them.

You may have noticed AutoText working and didn't even realize it. Start typing today's date. After you type the first three or four characters, a yellow screen tip appears above the text with the complete date. This is AutoComplete working in the background. If you press Enter when you see the screen tip, AutoComplete will finish typing the rest of the date. If your name is entered in the User Information under Tools | Options, start typing your name. Word recognizes you after you've typed a few letters and brings up the screen tip. Press Enter to have Word finish typing your name.

AutoComplete works with AutoText to make AutoText entries even easier to enter than in the past. There are several items that AutoComplete automatically recognizes and offers to finish for you:

☐ Days of the week

☐ Months

☐ Current date

☐ The name listed in User Information

☐ AutoText entries

Because AutoComplete recognizes the shortcut names you've given your AutoText entries, you will also get screen tips for these items.

Adding Entries to AutoText

You may not want the AutoText toolbar open all the time, but the quick access is helpful if you're adding several items to AutoText or using a document where you will be inserting AutoText items frequently. To activate this toolbar, select View | Toolbars and click AutoText. It's a very simple toolbar with three buttons: AutoText, All Entries, and New. Unless something in the document is selected, the New button is grayed out. Think of something you type routinely that could be added to AutoText. The first thing most people think of adding to AutoText is their signature block (the closure lines of a letter that include the sender's name). To add a signature block:

1. Type the signature block as you normally do.

2. Select the signature block.

3. Click the New button on the AutoText toolbar.

16

A dialog box comes up asking you to name the AutoText entry. Word usually suggests the first words in the selected text, but it helps to make the names short. You will see why when you learn how to insert AutoText.

4. Type in a short name for the signature block, such as sig (see Figure 16.1).

Figure 16.1.

The AutoText toolbar.

AutoText options —

Drop-down list of entries —

Add new entry —

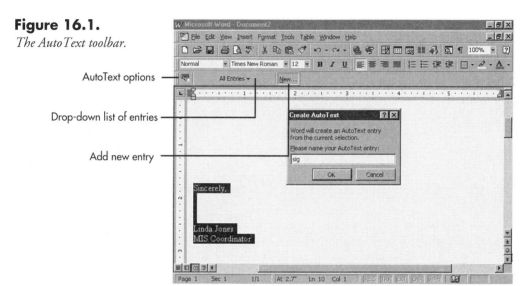

You now have an AutoText entry with the name sig that includes your signature block.

Inserting AutoText Entries in a Document

To insert the newly created sig AutoText entry in a letter:

1. Position the cursor where you want the closure to begin.

2. Type sig, then press the F3 key. Word automatically inserts your signature block.

Typing the shortcut name and pressing F3 is the quickest way to insert an AutoText entry, but you can also insert it from the drop-down list of All Entries from the AutoText toolbar. Word categorizes AutoText entries, and you can see in Figure 16.2 that it places the new sig AutoText entry under the Normal category. Word categorizes AutoText entries by the style that is applied to the first paragraph in an AutoText selection. If a selected paragraph has a Heading 2 style applied and is saved as an AutoText entry, a new Heading 2 category is created and the AutoText entry is saved in that category.

There are several entries that Word designed for you as AutoText. If you look through the other menu options, there are AutoText entries for a lot of common phrases used in correspondence. You may remember the discussion in Hour 8, "Setting Up the Page," about inserting AutoText entries in headers and footers. Header/Footer is one of the categories in the All Entries list. These categories are predefined.

Figure 16.2.

Adding an AutoText entry from the All Entries list.

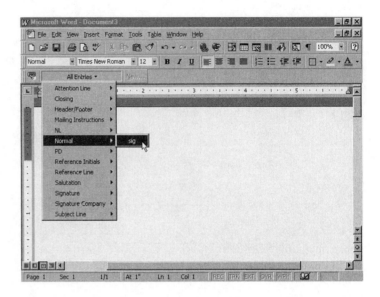

A third way to enter an AutoText entry involves AutoComplete. Rather than saving an AutoText entry with an abbreviated name like sig, accept the longer name that Word suggests or type an abbreviated name that is at least four characters. AutoComplete does not work with AutoText entries that have names shorter than four characters.

You might want to insert your city, state, and zip code in an AutoText entry. Type this information, select it, and click the New button on the AutoText toolbar. When the dialog box opens asking you to name the AutoText entry, give it an abbreviated name of at least four characters or accept the suggested name and click OK. The next time you start typing the city name, Word displays a screen tip with the AutoText entry as shown in Figure 16.3. Press the Enter key, and Word will complete the typing for you. This is a great new feature in Word 97.

If you've been a Glossary/AutoText user through several generations of Word, you may be so accustomed to using the shortcut names and the F3 key that AutoComplete is a nuisance to you. To turn off the AutoComplete tips, click the AutoText button on the AutoText toolbar and uncheck the box for Show AutoComplete tip for AutoText and dates.

Figure 16.3.

AutoComplete will fill in an AutoText entry when you press Enter.

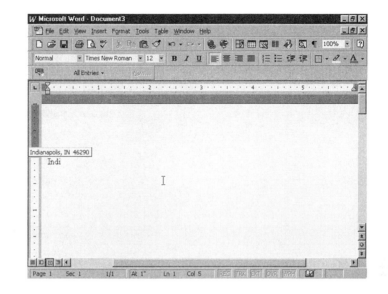

16

Deleting AutoText Entries

If you've set up several AutoText entries for a specific project, you might want to delete them when the project is over. There may be certain terms or elements that you use over and over—like the city and state names as mentioned previously or long technical terms. Anything that requires a lot of repetitive keyboarding could be targeted for an AutoText entry. You can also save graphics, such as an electronic signature or a company logo as AutoText entries. If you want to clean up these AutoText entries and get rid of the ones you're not using

1. Click the AutoText button on the AutoText toolbar (or select Insert | AutoText | AutoText to bring up the same dialog box).

2. Select an AutoText item from the list (see Figure 16.4). The Preview box lets you see what the complete AutoText entry looks like so you know which item you have selected. You may have several entries with similar names. In this case, Telecommunications Project Engineers, which was used for a specific document, is no longer needed.

3. Click the Delete button to remove the selected AutoText entry. You can also remove any of Word's built-in AutoText entries that you never use.

Figure 16.4.

Deleting an AutoText entry.

Modifying an AutoText Entry

Once in a while you may need to change an AutoText entry. Say you get a promotion and want to change your title in your signature block:

1. Type the new signature block as you want it to appear, and select it.

2. Click New on the AutoText toolbar (or use Insert | AutoText | New).

3. Type the same name you used previously for the signature block (sig was used in the previous example).

4. You will get a message asking whether you want to redefine the AutoText entry. Click Yes, and your AutoText entry will be changed to reflect your new job title.

As you use AutoText, you will think of terms and even whole paragraphs that you use over and over. If you type similar letters but include different paragraphs depending on your audience, you could add these paragraphs as AutoText entries. You could even name them as simply as P1, P2, P3, and so on.

To build the letter, type the shortcut name for the paragraph you want first (for example, P2), and then press the F3 key. Add all the paragraphs you need for a particular letter in this way, and then add your AutoText signature block. You can create a letter in a matter of minutes.

16

Macros

One of the greatest ways to build your efficiency quotient is with macros. A macro can record your actions step by step, save the actions, and repeat them back to you on demand. Although macros can be used for the same kinds of things you do with AutoText, AutoText takes care of those functions so efficiently that you probably don't want to use a macro simply to insert a signature block.

Instead, think of the times you access a menu to change certain settings for a particular project. You may actually change options in several different menus. Anything you do repetitively is a candidate for a macro. All you have to do to create a macro is record your keystrokes. When you want to perform these steps again, just play the macro.

Recording a Macro

The Macro Recorder is the tool that is used to memorize the steps you go through to accomplish a task. After the Macro Recorder has memorized the steps and you have given the macro a name, it can repeat back those steps time after time. To turn on the Macro Recorder, select Tools | Macro | Record New Macro or double-click the REC button on the Status bar.

Figure 16.5 shows the dialog box that comes up. You are asked to supply a name for the macro. This macro will be called Letter. Unlike with filenames, you cannot include spaces in a macro name. If you want to be able to use this macro in all documents, leave the setting on All Documents in the Store macro in box. You can add information in the Description box that tells what this macro does. This can be helpful if you set up two similar macros. The Letter macro sets the top margin to 2.5 inches, prints from the Manual Feed tray, and includes a date field, salutation, and signature block.

Figure 16.5.

Naming a macro.

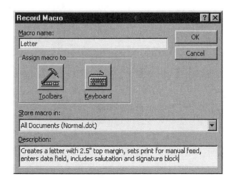

When you click OK in the Record Macro dialog box, the macro recorder starts. The pointer changes to resemble a cassette tape, and a box opens to allow you to stop the recorder when you finish or to pause during parts of the recording as in Figure 16.6. To create the Letter macro now that the recorder is turned on:

1. Select File | Page Setup.
2. Change the top margin to 2.5 inches in the Margins tab.
3. Change the tray setting in the Paper Source tab to Manual Feed.
4. Click OK.
5. Select Insert | Date and Time.
6. Select a date format from the list and check Update Automatically; then click OK.
7. Press Enter twice to enter two blank lines.
8. Type Dear, then press Enter twice.
9. Type the signature block or insert the AutoText entry for the signature block.
10. Click the Stop Recording button.

The Macro Recorder records each of your steps. When you stop the recorder, all of the steps are saved to a Macro called Letter. You never have to repeat those steps again. The macro does them for you.

Figure 16.6.

The Macro Recorder at work.

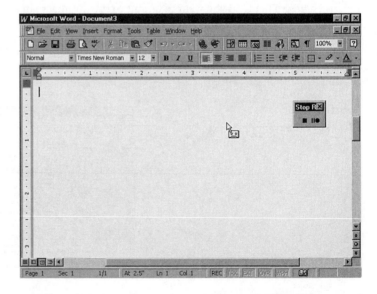

JUST A MINUTE

The Macro Recorder will not allow you to use the mouse to position the cursor or to select text as part of the macro. You can use the keyboard combinations to position and select text.

16

Macros are created with a programming language called Visual Basic. If you want to edit a macro after it has been created, you probably need to know a little about Visual Basic or another similar programming language. Alternatively, you can re-record the macro with the same name as the one you recorded earlier. Word asks whether you want to replace the existing macro. Click Yes and record over the previous version.

Using a Macro

Using a macro is like using the playback feature on your tape recorder. To use the Letter macro:

1. Open a new document.
2. Select Tools | Macros.
3. Select Letter.
4. Click Run.

KEYBOARD
SHORTCUT

Alt+F8 brings up the Macro list without going through the menus.

Running the macro gives you a letter like the one in Figure 16.7. All you need to do is fill in the text of the letter and the inside address.

Figure 16.7.

The document created by the new Letter macro.

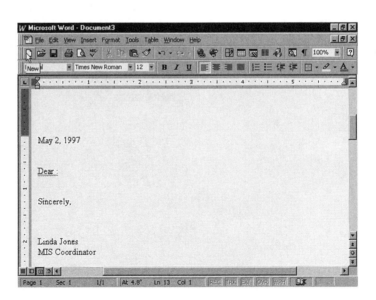

Adding a Macro to a Toolbar

You may develop macros that you use so routinely that you'd like the convenience of assigning them to buttons on a toolbar. You could add them to the new toolbar you created in Hour 11, "Customizing Word to the Way You Work." If you do a lot of work with e-mail files, for example, you might want to create a macro for the process used in Hour 7, "Manipulating Text," to get rid of extra paragraph marks. If this is a daily activity for you, you could add this macro to a toolbar by following these steps:

1. Select View | Toolbars.

2. Select the toolbar to which you want to add the macro.

3. Select View | Toolbars | Customize.

4. In the Commands tab, scroll down in the Categories list to Macros and select it.

5. Locate the macro in the Commands list, click, and drag it to the toolbar as shown in Figure 16.8.

6. Click Modify Selection to change the button. `Normal.NewMacros.FormatEmessage` makes for a very long toolbar button name. Modify the button as prescribed in Hour 11 to use one of the standard button images, or click the Name box near the top of the menu and type the word `Emessage` to replace the long name with a shorter one (see Figure 16.9).

Figure 16.8.

Adding a macro to a toolbar.

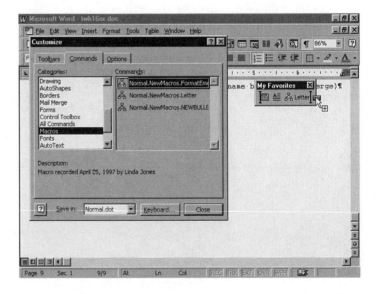

Figure 16.9.

Changing the button text for a macro.

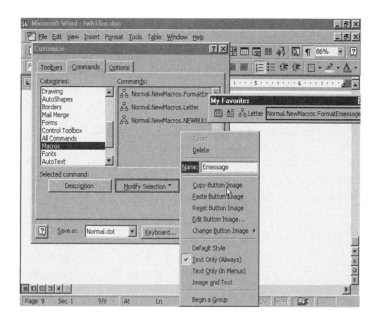

TIME SAVER

If you want to use an image for a toolbar button but none of the pictures seems to fit, Word has a great new feature to let you use any picture as a button image. To use a picture as a button image:

1. Copy the image to the clipboard (insert the picture in a Word document, select it, and click the Copy button).

2. Follow steps 1–6 of the previous instructions to add the macro to the toolbar.

3. Click Paste Button Image from the Modify Selection drop-down menu. The image from the clipboard is pasted as the button image.

4. Click Close.

Assigning a Macro to a Shortcut Key Combination

You can also assign a macro to a shortcut key combination. You use shortcuts like Ctrl+C to copy and Ctrl+V to paste. You can assign functions to any key combinations that are not already programmed. Many of the Ctrl key combinations have functions associated with them, but several of the Ctrl+Alt+letter/number combinations (such Ctrl+Alt+A and Ctrl+Alt+4) are not currently assigned. To assign a macro to keyboard shortcut:

1. Select Tools | Customize.
2. Click the Commands tab.
3. Click the Keyboard button.
4. Scroll down in the Categories list to Macros and select it.
5. Select a macro from the Macros list.
6. Click in the Press new shortcut key box and press the key combination you want to use (see Figure 16.10). The message under the Press new shortcut key box tells you whether this combination is currently unassigned. If the key combination you select is already used by a Word function, the message tells you what the keys are currently assigned to do.

CAUTION

Figure 16.10 shows the Alt+E combination in the Press new shortcut key box. The message under the box does not indicate that this key combination is currently assigned. The Alt+letter combinations are used as shortcuts to the menus (for example Alt+E is the shortcut to the Edit menu), but the Customize Keyboard dialog box does not tell you this. It is a good idea to avoid using these combinations.

7. Click the Assign button.
8. Click Close, then click Close again to exit the Customize dialog box.

Figure 16.10.

Assigning a macro to a shortcut key combination.

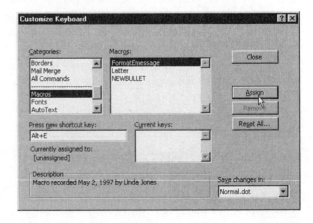

When you assign shortcut keys, look for combinations that are unassigned. For example, if you press Ctrl+E, the description under the Press new shortcut key box shows that this key combination is currently assigned to CenterPara (Center Paragraphs). You probably don't want to change the shortcuts Word already has assigned.

Sample Macros

Here are ideas for other actions you might want to save as macros:

- ☐ Insert a table, resize the columns, insert decimal tabs set for specific columns, and add a border to the table.
- ☐ Open a specific file, print it, and close it.
- ☐ Add bullets of a particular style to selected paragraphs, format the paragraphs with specific indents (for example, both right and left indents), and format the font and font style.
- ☐ Create a header and/or footer you use routinely.
- ☐ Set up a document in two sections with specific page numbering, margins, and headers and footers defined for each section.

The next time you start a task that involves several steps, turn on the Macro Recorder as you work. You'll enjoy the freedom from tedium that macros can give you.

Summary

This hour shows how to save time and effort by turning on the Macro Recorder and recording repetitive tasks so that you never have to do them again. Macros can be added and assigned to shortcut keys or toolbar buttons. AutoText is a big time saver. Save blocks of text or graphics as AutoText entries that can be quickly retrieved by using the AutoText Entries list, the AutoText entry name+F3, or AutoComplete and the Enter key.

Q&A

Q **Sometimes when I click the AutoText Entries drop-down list on the AutoText toolbar or choose AutoText from the Insert menu, I see only one or two of my AutoText entries instead of the whole list. Why?**

A Your cursor is probably in a paragraph that has a specific style applied that has AutoText entries associated with it. In the example earlier in the hour, an AutoText entry was created from text in a Heading 2 style. The entry was placed under a new category called Heading 2. If, for example, your cursor is positioned on a paragraph formatted in Heading 2 style, the drop-down AutoText list button and the Insert | AutoText menu will display the Heading 2 style name, and only the AutoText entries in that category are available. This will happen only if there are AutoText entries that were created in the specified style.

Q **I tried to record a macro and got an Invalid Procedure Name error. What did I do wrong?**

A You probably tried to save a macro with a name that included a space or another invalid character. Try again and give it a name without any spaces or punctuation.

Q **Can I include another macro in the one I'm creating?**

A Definitely. Insert as many as you want. Save yourself as many keystrokes as you can. You can also insert AutoText entries in a macro.

RW **4**

Word in Real Time

Creating a Catalog

Mail merge has a main document type called *Catalog*. Catalog is a useful feature for creating lists. You could always type a list into a Word document, but you may want to keep a database-type listing in a data source that includes lots of information. You can pick and choose which information to use for certain reports using mail merge and the Catalog feature.

This project involves creating an employee listing for Widgets Enterprises. It includes

☐ Creating a mail merge catalog

☐ Creating a data source for the catalog

☐ Using a table in the catalog document

☐ Inserting a header above the table with AutoText

☐ Sorting the list alphabetically

Setting Up the Catalog and Data Source Files

The first step begins like any other mail merge: Select Tools | Mail Merge. For this project, select Catalog from the list of Main document options in the Create drop-down list as in Figure R4.1.

Figure R4.1.

Select Catalog as the Main document type.

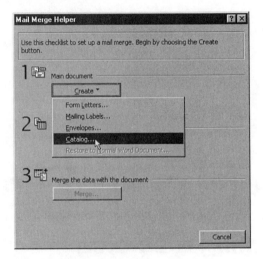

Select Active Window if you just opened Word and have a new document open. If not, select New Main Document to start a new document for the merge file.

The next step is to set up the data source. To do so:

1. Click Get Data and select Create Data Source.

2. Delete unwanted fields (Title, Address1, Address2, City, State, PostalCode, Country). FirstName, LastName, JobTitle, WorkPhone, and HomePhone should be left.

3. Add new fields that pertain to employees, as in Figure R4.2 (Room, Birthday, Spouse, EmergencyContact, HireDate, JobClass, HomeAddress, HomeCSZ). HomeCSZ is a field that combines City, State, and Zip for ease of entry.

JUST A MINUTE

> HomeCSZ is not always useful. Luckily, you can keep the City, State, and Zip fields separate if you need to. But for our purposes, it's okay to combine them.

Figure R4.2.

Changing field names for the employee listing.

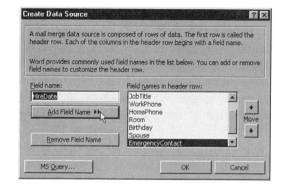

4. Use the Move Up and Move Down functions to place the fields in an order that makes sense when you're doing the data entry. For example, you may want the HomePhone and HomeAddress fields together because they are probably grouped together in the paper copy you are using for this information.

5. Click OK to exit the Create Data Source dialog box.

6. The Save dialog box opens. Name the data file and click Save.

7. Click Edit data source.

Enter the information in the data form for each employee. Use either the Tab or the Enter key at the end of each line to move to the next entry box. Notice the scrollbar to the right of the entry lines, shown in Figure R4.3. This scrollbar indicates that there is more information in each record than you can see in one screen. You can scroll down to see the other fields. At the end of each record, press Enter to start a new record. When you have the records entered, click OK.

Figure R4.3.

Adding records to the data source.

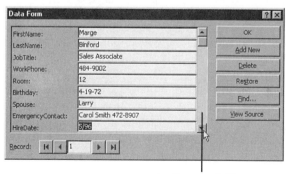

Scroll to other fields

Inserting a Table

Return to the main document after you complete the entries in the data source. The main document will only include one line of field codes even though you want to list all records. Form letters are set up to print one record per page or letter, but the Catalog function creates a list with all records on the same page. If there are more records than will fit on one page, Catalog creates as many pages as necessary to complete the list.

In this sample, you'll put the field names in a table. To build the table and insert the field names:

1. Click the Insert Table button on the Standard toolbar.
2. Insert a table that is four columns wide and has only one row.
3. Position the cursor in the first cell.
4. Click Insert Merge Field and select LastName.
5. Insert a comma and a space after the LastName field, then use Insert Merge Field to insert the FirstName in the same cell.
6. Insert the JobTitle field in cell 2, the Room field in cell 3, and the WorkPhone field in cell 4 (see Figure R4.4).

Figure R4.4.

Inserting merge fields in a table.

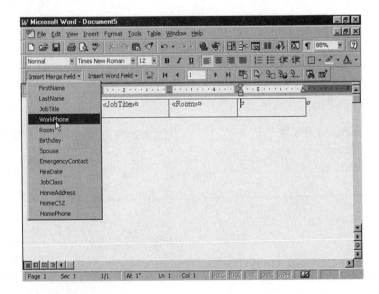

Adjusting the Table

The name and job title columns need to be wider than the room and phone columns. Use the Move Columns buttons on the ruler to adjust the column sizes, as shown in Figure R4.5.

Figure R4.5.

*Adjusting columns
in the table.*

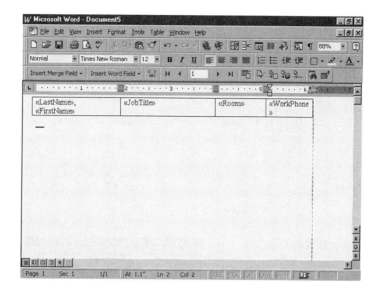

Adding a Heading

If you create a heading in the body of the document, Word inserts a heading before each
record when it merges, as in Figure R4.6. Instead of using one heading to top the entire
column, you have a heading for every record. This is not how you want Catalog to operate.

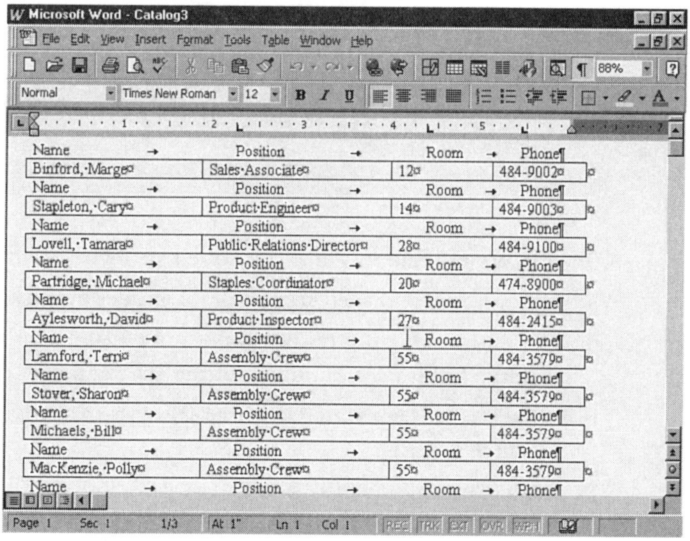

Figure R4.6.

*Adding a title to
a catalog produces
unsatisfactory results.*

One of the best solutions is to use the header area for the title. A header doesn't have to be positioned at the top edge of the page. You can move it down so it appears to be part of the document. Select View | Header and Footer and follow these steps to use the header as the title for the employee listing:

1. Select File | Page Setup.
2. In the Margins tab, change the measurement under Header to 1.2 inches. This will set the header down 1.2 inches from the top of the page rather than the standard .5 inches.

   The Widgets Enterprises employee created an AutoText entry for previous publications that can be inserted from the Insert AutoText list. Figure R4.7 displays the AutoText list and the WEL entry being inserted in the header.

Figure R4.7.

Inserting an AutoText entry in the header.

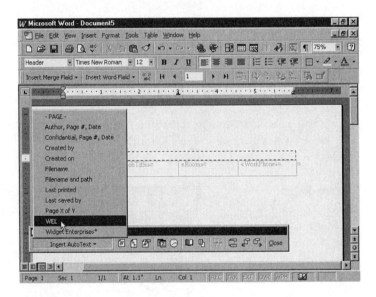

3. The Widget Enterprises title is added to the header from the WEL AutoText entry.
4. Add the date to the left section of the header by clicking the Insert Date button.
5. Tab to the right edge of the header and type the word Page, then a space, and then click the Insert Page Number button (see Figure R4.8).
6. If the fonts do not match the title, select the date and page line and format the font to match the title.
7. Click Close.

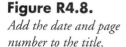

Figure R4.8.

Add the date and page number to the title.

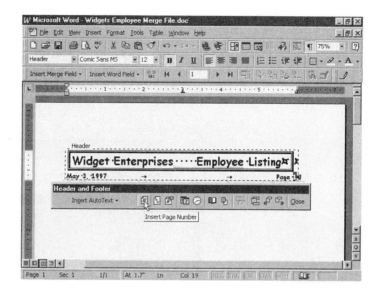

Adding Row Headers

It's helpful to know what each column contains. This information can go into the header. To add column headers, Select View | Header and Footer, and then follow these steps:

1. Position the cursor after the page number field and press Enter to add a new line.

2. Remove any tabs that appear on the ruler by clicking and dragging them from the ruler. Refer to Hour 6, "Formatting Paragraphs," for details on adding and removing tabs.

3. Type the title for the first column (Name) and press Tab.

4. Type the title for the second column (Position) and press Tab.

5. Type the title for the third column (Room) and press Tab.

6. Type the title for the fourth column (Phone).

7. The headings don't line up where you'd want them with the columns, but you can easily drag the tab markers across the ruler so that they do. The vertical line that appears down the page helps identify where the tab (and the heading that follows the tab) will be.

8. Click Close or double-click in the typing area to exit the header.

Figure R4.9 shows what the header will look like after the headings have been inserted and the tabs have been aligned with the columns.

Figure R4.9.

*Adding column titles
to the header.*

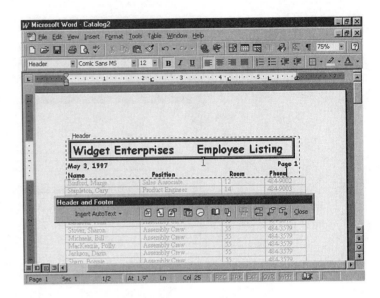

Putting It All Together

You're ready to merge, but this time merge the file to a new document. Click the Merge to New Document button on the Mail Merge toolbar. If the document is merged to a new document, the table can be sorted. In this example, it makes sense to sort the table so that the employees are listed alphabetically. To sort the table:

1. Select the first column (position the mouse above column 1 until you see the dark black arrow pointing down and click the mouse button).

2. Select Table | Sort.

3. Column 1 appears as the Sort by option because it is selected (see Figure R4.10). Click the No header row option at the bottom of the Sort dialog box if it isn't already selected. In this case, there is no header row because you have placed the headings in the header rather than in the table.

4. Click OK to start the sort.

You're ready to print your new employee listing. You could also modify this report by adding different field names and making slight changes to the header. You might, for example, create a list with employee home addresses and phone numbers or a report with the emergency contact names for each employee. One data source—many reports.

Figure R4.10.

*Sorting the list
alphabetically.*

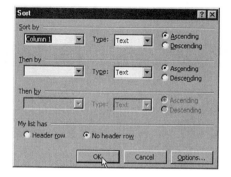

Part

V

Word the Desktop Publisher

Hour

Hour 17

Working with Graphics

This hour explains Word 97 graphics. Two major breakthroughs in Word 97 are the Web tools and the graphics functions. The new graphic capabilities have changed dramatically from previous versions. This chapter explores the new features such as custom word wraps and brightness and contrast controls that make it a whole new product in terms of images.

The highlights of this hour include

- [ ] How to add your own pictures to Clip Gallery
- [ ] How to use the Picture toolbar to enhance graphics
- [ ] What's new and improved in WordArt

Clip Gallery

The former ClipArt Gallery has been renamed Clip Gallery because of the new multimedia add-ins such as sounds and videos. For those who were disappointed with the scant clip art collection in the last version of Word, the new additions of clip art will be a welcome sight. The included photographic art is also a nice touch, though probably more usable in PowerPoint, where the final product is usually displayed onscreen rather than in print.

To open the Clip Gallery, select Insert | Picture | Clip Art. Figure 17.1 shows the Clip Art tab in the Clip Gallery. When you insert clip art, you are automatically switched to Page Layout view.

Figure 17.1.

The Clip Gallery.

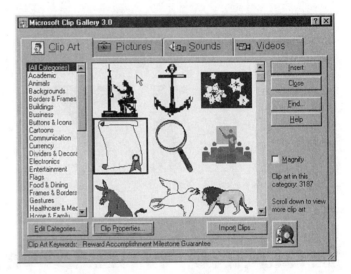

When you view the entire list (All Categories), you look through a very long list of pictures. To narrow your options, click one of the categories in the category list to see only the clips under that heading.

The clip art is indexed on keywords. If you're looking for something in particular, click the Find button and type a word in the Keywords box, as shown in Figure 17.2. Click Find Now, and Word searches through the index and brings up the pictures that are indexed on that term.

Figure 17.2.

Finding clip art on a subject.

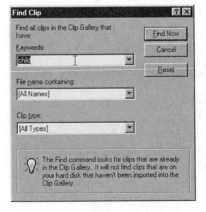

17

A search of clip art using the keyword Child brings up all the matches in all categories that are indexed on this word. Depending on how you install Word, you will get more or fewer clip art selections. If you installed Word from a CD-ROM, and the CD-ROM is currently in the CD-ROM drive, Clip Gallery displays the extra pictures that are included on the CD-ROM. There are more clip art selections on the Office 97 CD-ROM than the Word 97 CD. When you find a picture that fits your project, click the Insert button to bring it into your document.

More Clip Art!

If the clip art that comes with the Gallery doesn't have what you need, you can connect to Microsoft's Clip Gallery Live site on the Web at http://www.microsoft.com/clipgallerylive. You must be connected to the Web in order to grab these extra Clips and add them to your Clip Gallery. Hour 24, "Working with the Web," tells how to get connected. This involves a process of connecting and logging in.

If you are connected, you can jump directly to Clip Gallery Live by clicking the Connect to Web for additional clips button in Clip Gallery. To add a clip to your collection from the Clip Gallery Live selections, do the following:

1. Select Insert | Picture | Clip Art from the menu.
2. Click the Connect to Web for additional clips button.
3. Click the Accept button to accept the terms for using any clip art from this site.
4. Click the arrow beside the Select a category box to choose a broad category from which to search for clips.
5. Click the Go button.
6. When you find something in Clip Gallery Live that you'd like to add to your collection, click the filename beneath the clip (see Figure 17.3). The clip is automatically added to your Clip Gallery.

You can also add clip art or pictures you have gathered from other sources to the Clip Gallery. You need to know that there are two main kinds of computer graphics in order to understand what's happening when you add items to the Clip Gallery.

Vector Graphics

Vector graphics are clip art. This kind of art consists of shapes grouped together to form a larger picture. It does not lose quality when it is resized. Advanced drawing programs like Adobe Illustrator, CorelDraw, and Macromedia Freehand can create vector art. WMF files are Microsoft's clip art graphics that are created with their own program. WordPerfect does the same to create WPG files. All these real clip art formats retain their quality when resized.

Figure 17.3.

*Add to your clip collec-
tion from Microsoft Clip
Gallery Live.*

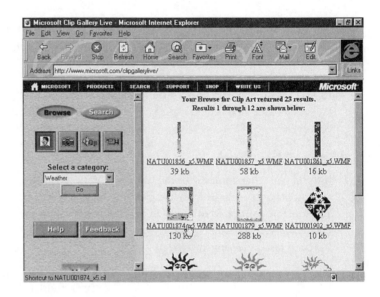

Raster Graphics

When a raster graphic is saved to a file, the program essentially looks at the individual dots (pixels) that make up the picture and saves a picture of the dots. Raster art is subject to distortion when it is resized as in Figure 17.4. Photographs, scanned images, and art created with programs such as Paint and Photoshop are raster graphics. They are not necessarily photo art. Common graphic types such as TIF, BMP, JPG, GIF, and PCX are raster graphics.

One of the reasons this is important is that Clip Gallery saves the two types of images in two different places. If you import a vector graphic, Word places it with the art in the Clip Art tab. If you import a raster graphic, Word puts it in the Pictures tab. Because all the existing art in the Pictures tab is photographic, it may be a bit confusing when your imported art ends up under pictures instead of clip art.

To add a picture to the Clip Gallery:

1. Select Insert | Picture | Clip Art from the menu.
2. Click the Import Clips button in the Clip Gallery dialog box.
3. From the Open File dialog box, locate the file you want to add to the Clip Gallery and select it, then click the Open button.
4. Type keywords to add to the clip index for this file (see Figure 17.5).
5. Click the box beside the category (or categories) that the clip would fit in, or click New Category to create one.
6. Click OK.

17

Figure 17.4.

Raster graphics are distorted when enlarged.

Figure 17.5.

Adding your own pictures to the Clip Gallery.

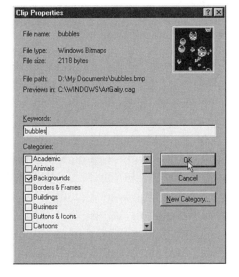

JUST A MINUTE

There are not as many categories in the Pictures tab as in the Clip Art tab, but all the categories appear when you are saving clips to the Gallery. If you import a raster graphic and select a category that doesn't exist in the Pictures tab, Word creates a new category in Pictures and places your clip in it.

Modifying Pictures

Word has a host of new graphic manipulation tools to modify not only clip art, but other graphics as well. When you're working with a picture, the Picture toolbar automatically comes up to give you access to these tools (see Figure 17.6).

Figure 17.6.

Use the Picture toolbar to alter pictures.

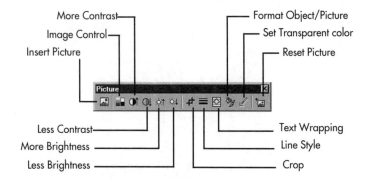

Resizing

The picture you insert in a document is often too small or too large for the space you want to use it in. To resize a picture:

1. Click the image. Sizing handles (small squares) surround the object.

2. Click one of the corner sizing handles; a double-headed arrow appears. Resizing from a corner handle keeps the width-to-height ratio the same as the original.

3. Click and drag the handle away from the object to make it bigger or toward the center of the object to make it smaller.

   A dotted outline displays the position and size that the object will be when it is resized, as shown in Figure 17.7. Release the mouse button when the object reaches the size you want.

To resize a picture to an exact size:

1. Select Format | Picture or click the Format Picture button on the Picture toolbar to display the Format Picture dialog (see Figure 17.8).

2. Click the Size tab.

3. Select Lock aspect ratio to keep the picture proportionally correct. If you need a specific width or height, change that measurement. The other measurement changes automatically when Lock aspect ratio is selected.

17

Figure 17.7.

A dotted outline shows how big the resized object will be.

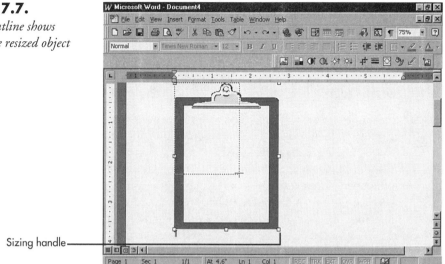

Sizing handle

Figure 17.8.

Setting a picture to an exact size with the Format Picture dialog.

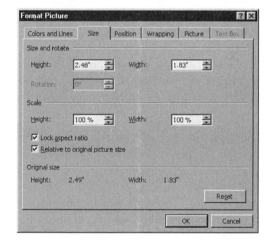

4. Click OK. If you want an exact width and height, do not check Lock aspect ratio. You can specify both the width and height measurements.

   You can also scale the picture to a certain percentage of the original. For example, set Scale to 200% and the picture will be twice as large as the original. Again, if the Lock aspect ratio box is checked, both scales change when you change one of them.

After you've resized the picture, place it anywhere you want by clicking it and dragging it from one location to another. The pointer changes to a four-sided arrow when you select and move pictures or objects.

Step-Up

Previous versions of Word required that you put a frame around a graphic in order to move it. In Word 97, graphics inserted normally "float" over text and do not have to be in a frame to be moved. The Float over text option can be changed so that the graphic is actually on the text layer. It is called an inline graphic when it is positioned with text on the same layer. An inline graphic must be inserted in a text box that must then be converted to a frame in order to be capable of movement. It's much easier to take advantage of the Float over text option for graphics.

One of the reasons you might want to use an inline graphic is to insert it in a table. If you want to insert a graphic in a table, it *must* be an inline graphic rather than one that floats over text. If you've inserted a clip in your document and want to change it to an inline graphic:

1. Select the clip.
2. Click the Format Object button on the Picture toolbar. If a picture is one of the Clip Gallery selections, the button name is Format Object rather than Format Picture (because the clips are not all pictures).
3. Select the Position tab.
4. Uncheck the Float over text checkbox.
5. Click OK.

Crop

Cropping is a way to cut off part of a picture that you don't want (the old "cut the disfavored relative out of the picture" scenario). In earlier versions of Word, cropping was a hit-or-miss affair. You had to specify a certain amount of space to crop from an edge. If you cropped too much or not enough, you had to go back to the menu to increase or decrease the measurement until the picture looked about right. The addition of the cropping tool to the Picture toolbar eliminates the guesswork. To crop a picture:

1. Select the picture.
2. Click the Crop button on the Picture toolbar.
3. Click one of the sizing handles.
4. Drag the handle in a direction that removes the unwanted section of the picture, as shown in Figure 17.9.

17

Figure 17.9.

Use the cropping tool to eliminate part of a picture.

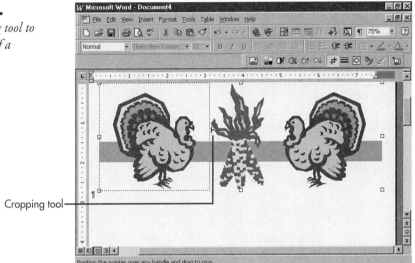

Cropping tool

The dotted outline shows how much of the picture will be left after the picture is cropped. Release the mouse button to complete the cropping. You can crop from any edge or corner. If you crop more than you want:

1. Click the Crop button. Position the cropping tool on the sizing handle you used to crop the picture.

2. Click and drag the sizing handle back in the opposite direction to restore part of the picture. The complete picture is still there; cropping just hides part of it from view. A common misconception is that the file size can be decreased by cropping a picture. This is not the case because the entire image is really there.

Cropping is a good way to eliminate extra whitespace or unwanted portions of the graphic such as borders. For example, you might scan a signature and save it. When you try to insert it in a signature block, you may find you saved the image with too much whitespace on the top and bottom to allow it to fit nicely in the block. Cropping the picture from the top and bottom gets rid of the unwanted space. Sometimes graphics have an existing border (a picture frame effect) that you don't want to include. You can crop from all sides to eliminate the picture frame.

Brightness and Contrast

The new brightness and contrast features offer a lot more control over the image. These are features that you would expect to find in a graphic manipulation package or a desktop publishing program.

If a picture is too dark, select it and click the More Brightness button on the Picture toolbar. Click the button again to increase the brightness one step at a time. Similarly, the Less Brightness button darkens the picture.

Contrast is the ratio of dark to light tones within the picture. Decreasing the contrast eventually fades the picture to gray. Increasing contrast heightens the difference between lights and darks.

CAUTION

Clip art in the Clip Gallery is optimally set for contrast and brightness. What you see onscreen may not be what you get in print. Try a test page before adjusting contrast and brightness settings. If you increase the brightness before printing to a color printer, you may get unsatisfactory results (for example, faded colors and annoying horizontal lines). This is a known problem that seems to affect only color printers. If you make changes to a graphic that cause distortion or unwanted results (color, brightness, cropping, resizing, and so on), select the graphic and click the Reset Picture button on the Picture toolbar to restore the original.

Add a Picture Frame

You can dress up a picture by adding a custom frame or border around the outside edge. To place a box around a picture:

1. Click the picture.
2. Click the Line Styles button on the Picture toolbar.
3. Select one of the predefined line styles, or click More Lines to vary the line width, color, and style. The Format Picture dialog box, shown in Figure 17.10, appears.

Figure 17.10.

Framing a picture with line styles.

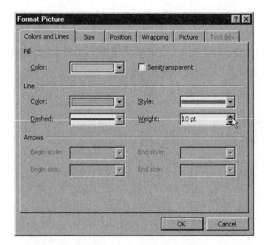

17

4. Select Color and Style from the drop-down lists. Add a dashed line style if you like. Weight determines how thick or heavy the line will be. Use the default or modify the point size in the Weight box.

Add or Change the Background Color

A picture can go from simple clip art to a work of art with some of Word's new custom background options. Photoshop-like background effects can bring a graphic to life. Figure 17.11 shows a piece of clip art that has one of the new gradient fills applied to the background.

Figure 17.11.

Clip art with a gradient-fill background.

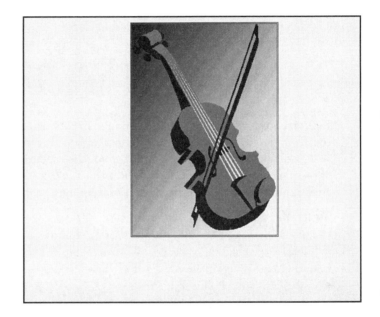

To add a special background fill to a picture:

1. Select the picture.
2. Click the Format Picture icon on the Picture toolbar or select Picture from the Format menu.
3. Click the Colors and Lines tab.
4. Click the Color drop-down list under Fill.
5. Select Fill Effects.
6. Click the Gradient tab to select fills like the one that was used to create the illustration in Figure 17.11. Figure 17.12 shows the Gradient Fill options.

Figure 17.12.

Selecting a gradient fill.

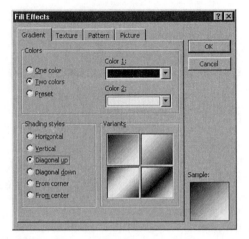

Experimenting with the different fill options is the best way to learn how they work and how they look in print. Textures and patterns also provide interesting background choices. If you'd like to use another picture as a background, select the Picture tab and open the picture. While it may sound strange to use another picture for a background, there is a wealth of clip art that has been designed especially for backgrounds.

Text Wrap

Another of the fun things about Word 97 is its capability to wrap around text in new ways. Word has always had the old standards—text on top and bottom, text to the left, text to the right, and a few other variations. Word 97's new text wrap options are much less constricting with the Edit Wrap Points feature.

Select a picture and click the Text Wrap button on the Picture toolbar to see what wrap options are available. The last item in the list is Edit Wrap Points. When you insert one of the clip art pictures and select Edit Wrap Points, Word outlines the item as shown in Figure 17.13. Text flows up to the edit points.

The wrap points are the darkened squares on the dotted line that surrounds the picture. You can click and drag any of the wrap points in any direction for some unique text-wrap effects.

The Wrapping tab in the Format Picture dialog box gives greater control over text wraps, including adding more whitespace between the graphic and the text (see Figure 17.14). Increase the measurements in the Distance from text section to provide more whitespace. Not all options are available for every wrapping style. The Distance from text and Wrap to options are grayed out and cannot be selected if they do not apply to a specified wrapping style.

17

Figure 17.13.

Edit Wrap Points brings text up to the picture.

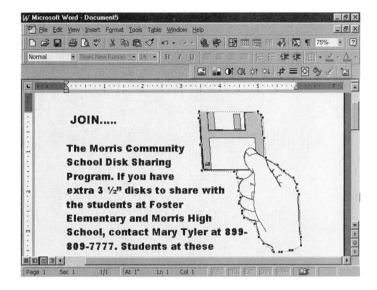

Figure 17.14.

More text wrap options from the Format Picture dialog.

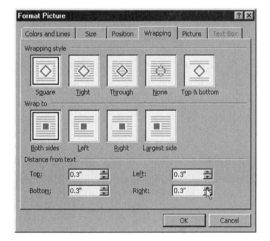

Image Control

The Image Control button on the Picture toolbar lets you change the image type, as shown in Figure 17.15. Automatic is the format the image is already in when it is added to a document. You can convert the image to:

- ☐ Grayscale—changes every color to a shade of gray
- ☐ Black and white—changes every color to either black or white (line art)
- ☐ Watermark—changes the image to a faded image that can be used behind text. The image in Figure 17.15 has been converted to a watermark.

Figure 17.15.
Converting an image to a
watermark.

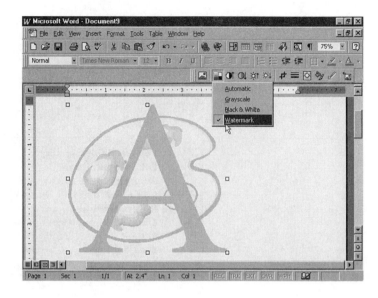

WordArt

Word 97's WordArt is strikingly different from previous versions. It has great-looking 3D effects for headings and titles. They're sharp enough to be standalone graphics anywhere in your document. To add WordArt to your document:

1. Select Insert | Picture | WordArt.
2. Select one of the WordArt designs, as shown in Figure 17.16, and click OK.

Figure 17.16.
WordArt comes with a
whole set of 3D designs.

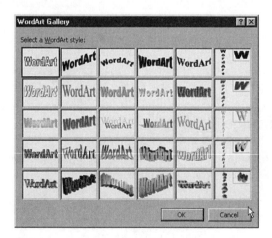

17

3. Type the text you want to use as a WordArt object.

4. Select a font and a font size.

5. Click OK.

Your WordArt title is created, and the WordArt toolbar opens to give you quick access to lots of editing features. Click the WordArt Gallery button if you want to apply a different style. From the toolbar, you have the following options in addition to changing the style:

☐ Format WordArt—gives almost the same options as Format | Picture. You can set colors and lines (and fill effects), text wrapping, position, and size.

☐ WordArt Shape—offers a menu of over 30 different shapes that you can apply to the WordArt (see Figure 17.17).

Figure 17.17.

Change the shape of a WordArt object.

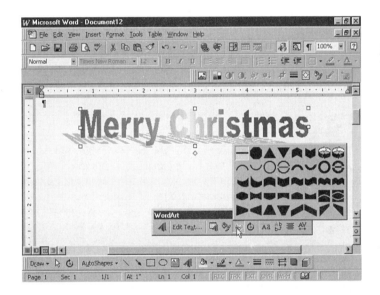

☐ Free Rotate—lets you grab a corner of the WordArt and change its direction on the page. (Hour 18, "The Drawing Tools," explains the Free Rotate tool.)

☐ WordArt Same Letter Heights—makes every letter the same height.

☐ WordArt Vertical Text—lets you flip the WordArt on its side so that it runs vertically rather than horizontally.

☐ WordArt Alignment—aligns WordArt as you would other text with a couple of other special additions (word justify, letter justify, and stretch justify).

☐ WordArt Character Spacing—lets you increase or decrease the amount of space between letters.

Other Pictures

Many other types of graphic files can be used in Word. A huge variety of art is available on disk, CD, or through the Internet in many forms. Most of these file types can be used in Word. To insert a graphic that is not part of Word's Clip Gallery:

1. Select Insert | Picture | From File.
2. Select the source where the graphic is located from the Look in box. It might be on a CD in your CD-ROM drive, on a disk in your floppy drive, or on your hard drive.
3. Select the name of the graphic.
4. Click Insert.

   If the graphics are vector graphics, they work exactly like the pictures you inserted from Clip Gallery. Other graphic files (raster graphics) work in nearly the same way. You can't apply fills to raster graphics, and the text wrap options will be less flexible. Raster art will always be rectangular, so the only edit points will be the four corners.

CAUTION

> Most art on the Internet is copyrighted. Even some of the art you purchase on disk or CD-ROM is copyrighted. A common misconception is that this art is free for the taking. Be sure to check any restrictions that apply before using any art. You will sometimes see the term *royalty free*, which means that you can use the art without charge. It is important to read the documentation to find out how you need to reference the source of the art and any other restrictions the producer has on its usage.

Summary

This hour is devoted to the way Word 97 works with art. The new and improved Clip Gallery has hundreds of pieces of clip art (over 3,000 if you have the Office 97 Professional CD) that can be inserted in your documents. New text wraps and the splashy effects added to WordArt make Word 97 well worth the investment. Hour 18, "The Drawing Tools," contains many functions that expand on what you've learned in this chapter. The drawing tools work in conjunction with clip art and other pictures to round out the Word graphics package.

17

Q&A

Q **Is there any way to change the colors in a clip art graphic?**

A Yes, but it takes patience. Clip art is a series of many objects and shapes that have been grouped together. We'll look at "ungrouping" these elements and recoloring along with another possible solution to recoloring clip art in the next hour.

Q **I tried both the Tight and the Through Text Wrap options. I can't see any difference. Is there anything different about them?**

A Tight goes closely around the edge of the object. Through works exactly like Tight but has an added feature to allow text to move into empty space within a graphic if you manipulate the wrap points correctly. For example, you could run text into the center of a wreath so that you have text both inside and outside of the wreath. It's probably easier to use a text box, however. Text boxes are covered in the next hour.

Q **I can't connect to the extra clip art in the Clip Gallery. When I click the button to get additional clips from the Web, Microsoft Internet Explorer opens but nothings happens.**

A You can't use Internet Explorer unless you have Internet access and go through the process to connect. See Chapter 24 to find out how you can get connected to make this function work.

Q **Should I avoid using raster art because it distorts the images when they're enlarged?**

A There are certain kinds of graphics, such as photographic art and scanned images, that are always raster art; you will probably have many occasions to use them. There may also be raster art available and suitable for your project that may not be available as vector graphics. Anyone can create raster art with inexpensive software, so there's a lot of it.

Q **When I print a WordArt object to my color printer, it works fine. I often have trouble printing to my laser printer, however. Sometimes I get a printer overrun error. I also can't get the color gradations. The text shows up as solid black. Is there some way to make WordArt work better with my laser?**

A WordArt requires a lot of printer memory when using a laser printer. The printer overrun occurs when there is not enough printer memory to complete a print job. Depending on your printer, you may be able to set an option to print graphics as raster rather than vector graphics. Select File | Print. In the Print dialog box, click Properties. If there is a Graphics tab, click it. Under Graphics mode, select the Use raster graphics option. The color gradation for WordArt seems to work in this mode.

17

Hour **18**

The Drawing Tools

This hour is a lesson in lines, shapes, and objects. The drawing tools are not just for drawing simple shapes. They can be used to modify existing graphics. There are powerful 3D imaging tools that give pictures depth. AutoShapes includes many new shapes. Create callouts, flow charts, and stylized arrows from the new collection of AutoShapes. Text boxes create moveable text. Position text on top of graphics or in a box that is independent from other text in a document.

The highlights of this hour include

- ☐ How to use layers to place graphics behind text
- ☐ How to link text boxes
- ☐ What kinds of things you would put in a text box
- ☐ How to turn a flat picture into a 3D object

Shapes

If you've ever used Paint or another simple drawing program, the primary drawing tools in Word 97 for performaing tasks such as drawing a line or rectangle will look very familiar. The main headquarters for working with the drawing tools is the Drawing toolbar. Select View | Toolbars and click Drawing to open the toolbar.

It seems there is a toolbar for every significant function. You don't need the Drawing toolbar up all the time, but when you're working with graphics, it's essential. Figure 18.1 shows the Drawing toolbar positioned at the bottom of the screen. It really helps to have the toolbar available, but out of the way while you're working.

Figure 18.1.

Placing the Drawing toolbar at the bottom of the screen for quick access.

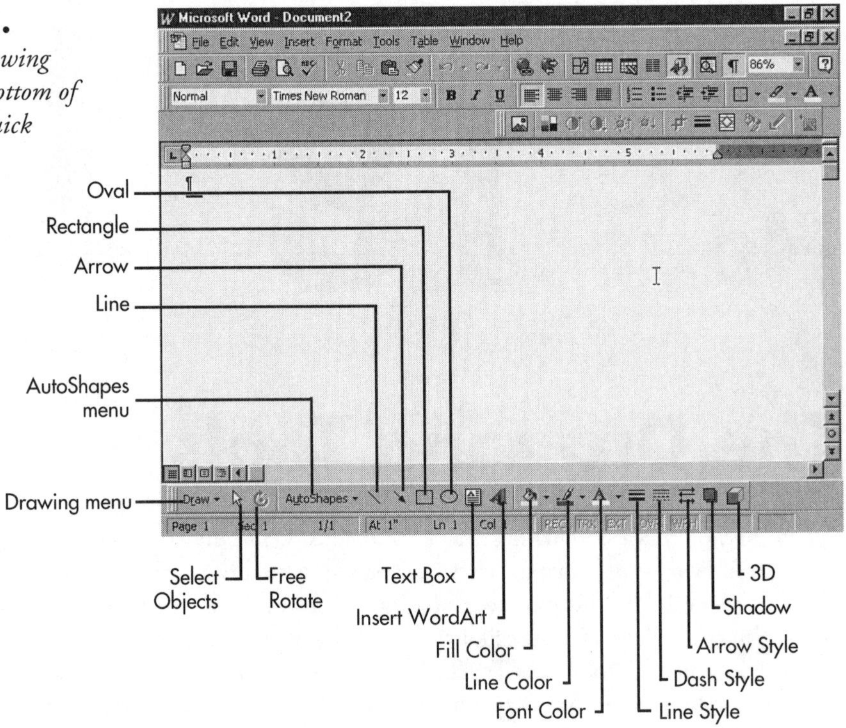

Rectangles, Squares, Ovals, and Circles

Rectangles and squares are created from the Rectangle button on the Drawing toolbar. To add a rectangle or square to a document:

1. Click anywhere in the document.
2. Click the Rectangle button on the Drawing toolbar.
3. Move to the typing screen; the mouse pointer turns to a crosshair. Click and drag the mouse across and down to create a rectangle (see Figure 18.2).

18

Figure 18.2.

Move the crosshair across and down to create a rectangle.

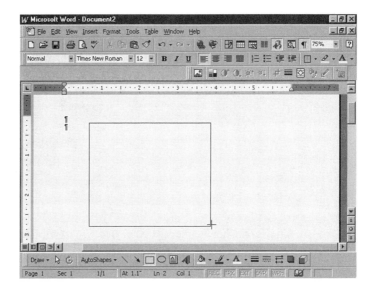

4. If you want a square, you can eyeball your rectangle and try to make it square as you click and drag, but this is not an easy task. If you hold down the Shift key while clicking and dragging the crosshair from the top-left corner to the lower-right corner, the shape will be proportionally the same height and width.

5. The same process is used to insert an oval or a circle. The Shift key in combination with the Oval tool creates a circle. Using the Shift key while clicking and dragging any of the AutoShapes maintains the width-to-height ratio.

Fills and Lines for Shapes

You don't have to settle for a plain rectangle or circle. You can fill it with color, modify the line style of the outer edge, and change the line color. The paint bucket icon on the Drawing toolbar is standard to many graphic programs. This is the Fill button. To fill an object with color:

1. Click the object.

2. Click the drop-down list beside the Fill Color button and select from one of the colors, or click the More Colors button to bring up a color wheel.

3. Click one of the colors shown in Figure 18.3 to select it, or click the Custom tab to do some color mixing to create other colors.

18

Figure 18.3.

Selecting a Fill Color from the color wheel.

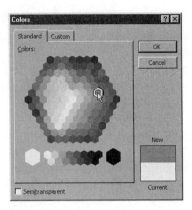

4. Click OK when you have a color that you're satisfied with.

You may have noticed the Fill Effects entry in the drop-down list of fill choices. These are the same options that were discussed in the last hour for adding backgrounds to clip art—Gradient, Texture, Pattern, and Picture Fills. Fill effects can turn a simple box or circle into a custom backdrop for a title or an accent graphic. Figure 18.4 displays three objects with different fills:

☐ 1 has a pattern fill

☐ 2 has a texture fill (woven rug)

☐ 3 has a gradient fill (Colors option = One color, Shading Styles option = From center)

Figure 18.4.

Using different fill effects in drawing objects.

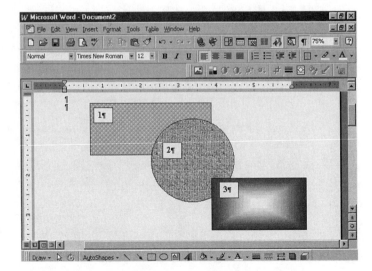

18

Grouping and Ungrouping Objects

If you wanted all of the objects in Figure 18.4 to act as a single object, you could group them together. Grouped objects can be moved around as though they are a single object. To group objects together:

1. Hold down the Shift key and click each object without releasing the Shift key between selections. The positioning handles appear for each selected object. This is called the multiple select method.

2. Click the Draw menu on the Drawing toolbar.

3. Click Group as shown in Figure 18.5.

Figure 18.5.

Group several drawing objects to make them one object.

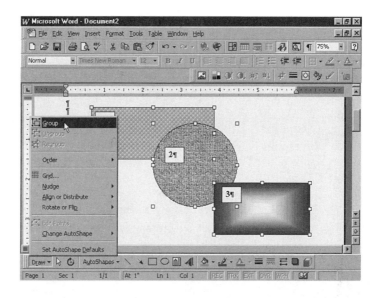

Grouped objects become a single object that can be moved as one (see Figure 18.6). Click anywhere on one of the objects and drag it to another area. The outline in Figure 18.6 shows that all three items are being moved together. You can no longer click the individual items to format or move them. Any new formatting applied, such as a background, applies to all of the objects. If, for example, you applied a gradient fill to the grouped object, the fill in all three objects would be changed.

Figure 18.6.

All of the objects that are grouped can be moved together.

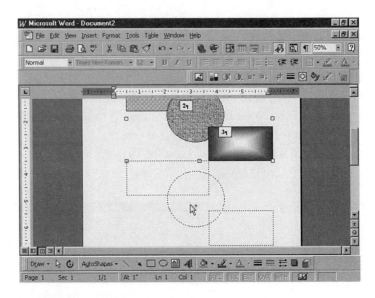

TIME SAVER

It can be difficult to reposition drawing objects, clip art, or text boxes in small increments with drag-and-drop. To inch the object slightly in one direction or another:

1. Select the object.
2. Select Nudge from the Draw menu on the Drawing toolbar.
3. Click the direction you want the object to move (Up, Down, Left, or Right).

Nudge moves a selected object in increments of five pixels. The arrow keys on the keyboard do the same thing. To move items more precisely (one pixel at a time), hold down the Ctrl key while pressing an arrow key on the keyboard.

If you decide you need to make changes to one or more of the objects, click anywhere on the grouped object and select Ungroup from the Draw menu. Each object can again be formatted, resized, or moved individually. Clip art is made up of a series of grouped objects. There may be dozens of small pieces in a single clip art picture. Those objects can be modified if you ungroup them. To change portions of a clip art image:

1. Click the clip art picture.
2. Select Draw | Ungroup from the Drawing toolbar.

18

3. Hold down the Shift key and click each object you want to include in the selection (multiple select).

4. To change the color of the objects, select a fill color from the drop-down list on the Drawing toolbar.

JUST A MINUTE

> Clip art is often made of so many separate objects that it is very difficult to recolor it. PowerPoint includes a feature on its Picture toolbar specifically for recoloring. It would be much easier to insert the clip art in PowerPoint to recolor it, then copy and paste it into your Word document.

5. To move the objects, click and drag them to a new location.

6. To remove the objects entirely, press the Delete key.

Changing the Order of Objects

Word uses a layering system that lets you determine whether an object is in front or in back of another. If you have text that flows through an object, you can specify that the text is on top. Use Order from the Draw menu to change the layer a selected object is placed on. If you select Send to Back, the object is placed on a layer behind the other objects in the document. Select Bring to Front, and the item is placed on a layer above the other objects (and/or text). Use the Behind and In Front of Text options to place an object on a layer above or behind text.

You may have more than two layers. In this case, the Send Backward option sends an object back one layer at a time. If you refer to Figure 18.4, you'll see that there are three objects on the page. The rectangle labeled 3 is on the top layer. The circle is on the second layer, and the rectangle labeled 1 is on a third layer. Click the number 3 rectangle and choose Send Backward to place it behind the circle. Click the circle and choose Send Backward to place it behind the number 1 rectangle. If all three objects were touching, you could select rectangle number 3 and choose Send to Back. This would place it behind both numbers 1 and 2.

AutoShapes

Figure 18.7 displays the kinds of AutoShapes that can be inserted from the AutoShapes drop-down list under the flowchart options. You can essentially build a flowchart using flowchart AutoShapes and a series of connecting lines.

18

Figure 18.7.

Building a flowchart
with AutoShapes.

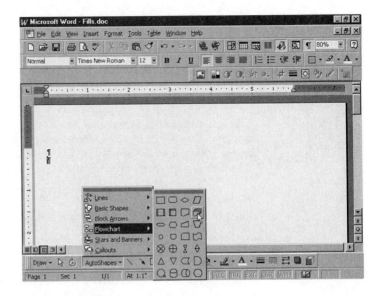

Here are some tricks for building a flowchart with AutoShapes:

☐ You usually want all of the same size boxes for one level of a flowchart. Instead of
    inserting and drawing each box, draw one box. Hold down the Ctrl key and click
    and drag the box to another location to make another copy of it. Continue this
    process until you have as many boxes as you need.

☐ When you draw connecting lines, it is often difficult to get the line to stop right at
    the edge of the flowchart box. Don't worry about making it exact. If the line is a
    little longer than it needs to be and spills into the box, click the line and select
    Order from the Draw menu on the toolbar. Select Send to Back. This places the
    line in back of the box so the spillover isn't visible.

☐ Use the Nudge feature or the Ctrl+arrow key combinations to position the flow-
    chart boxes more precisely. Selecting and nudging an object moves it in very small
    intervals.

☐ You may have three or four boxes that are supposed to be on the same level of the
    flowchart, but it's hard to get them to line up exactly and Nudge can take too long.
    To get them evenly spaced and lined up:

    1. Hold down the Shift key and click each of the boxes (multiple select).

    2. Select Draw | Align or Distribute | Align Top.

    3. Select Draw | Align or Distribute | Relative to Page from the Drawing
       toolbar.

    4. Select Draw | Align or Distribute | Distribute Horizontally.

18

5. Use the multiple select procedure to reposition all of the boxes and keep them aligned (Shift+click the objects to select and move them as in Figure 18.8). Using multiple select is like temporarily grouping objects. When you do something to one, you do it to all of them.

Figure 18.8.

Lining up and moving boxes in a flowchart.

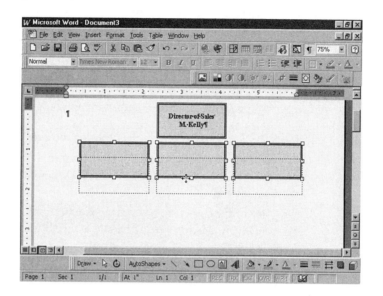

Figure 18.9 displays some of the other types of AutoShapes. When callouts are inserted, they include a text box because they were designed to hold text like the thought bubbles in cartoons. The callout in Figure 18.9 shows the outline of the text box.

Figure 18.9.

More AutoShapes to choose from.

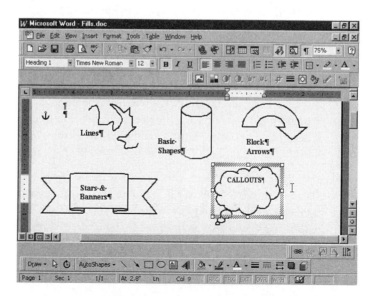

Text Boxes

You have already seen text boxes in the figures used in this hour. All of the text in Figure 18.9 was inserted using text boxes, as was the title in the top box of the flowchart in Figure 18.8. The numbers in Figure 18.4 were also included in text boxes. You can see the outline of the text boxes in Figure 18.4. This is what text boxes look like when they are inserted. The default is a thin line border with a white fill color.

Adding and Resizing Text Boxes

You have an idea what text boxes do from the examples used previously. To add and resize a text box:

1. Click the Text Box button on the Drawing toolbar.

2. Position the mouse pointer on the typing screen; it turns into a crosshair. Click and drag the mouse pointer just as you would if you were drawing a rectangle (to the right and down).

3. Drag one of the corners to resize the box proportionally or resize it vertically or horizontally by clicking a sizing handle on one of the edges and dragging it to make it smaller or larger.

4. Move the text box by clicking the box and positioning the mouse on one of the edges until the four-sided arrow appears. Click and drag the text box where you want it.

Inserting Text in a Text Box

A text box is essentially a container for text. It combines graphic elements with text. You can move both a text box and the text inside it at the same time. If you select a text box and press the Delete key to remove it, the text is gone too. This is a handy way to insert instructions within a document. When the user is finished with the instructions, it only takes a click and Delete to remove the entire text box.

Unlike using Rectangle to insert a box, a text box is created with a paragraph mark inside it so that you can add text to it. If a text box is selected, all the text can be formatted at once using Format | Font or using the Formatting toolbar. Text alignment applies to everything in the box. To apply formatting to only certain sections of the text box, select those portions individually.

If you type more text than will fit in the text box, it will seem to disappear. Click one of the edges or a corner to resize the box and make it big enough to display all the text or resize text to make it small enough to fit in the box. You can rotate the text vertically in a text box like you can with WordArt as outlined in Hour 14, "Working with Tables." To change the orientation of text in a text box:

18

1. Select the text box. The Text Box toolbar, which is available only if a text box is selected, will appear. If you don't see it onscreen, select View | Toolbars and select the Text Box toolbar.

2. Click the Change Text Direction button as in Figure 18.10. Keep clicking until you have the text orientation the way you want it.

3. Click one of the alignment buttons on the Formatting toolbar to align the text.

Figure 18.10.

Change the direction of text in a text box.

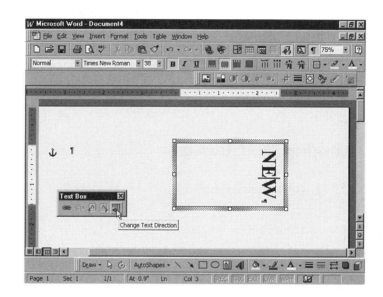

Removing or Changing the Text Box Border and Fill

You will often want to place a text box on top of another object to provide a label for the object as in the numbers that were used in Figure 18.4. You usually want to remove both the line and the fill when you're using the text as a label. To remove the line and then the fill:

1. Click the text box.

2. Select Format | Text Box from the menu.

3. Click the Fill Color drop-down list and select No Fill.

4. Click the Line Color drop-down list and select No Line, as in Figure 18.11.

5. Click OK. Both the line and the fill will be removed.

Figure 18.11.

*Removing the line and
fill from a text box.*

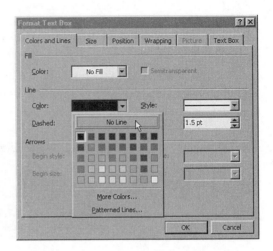

Linking Text Boxes

Linking text boxes is a great way to create newspaper-like reports that flow from one column
to a section on another page. It's also a way to jump from one place to another in a document.
To create a link between two text boxes:

1. Create the first text box.
2. Create a second text box elsewhere in the document.
3. Click the first text box.
4. Click the Create Text Box Link button on the Text Box toolbar. The mouse
   pointer will look like a water pitcher.
5. Move to the second text box and position the mouse pointer over the box. The
   pitcher looks like it is pouring, as in Figure 18.12. Click the text box to complete
   the link.

When you type text in the first text box and space runs out, the text spills over into the second
text box. To jump between text boxes, use the Previous and Next Text Box buttons on the
Text Box toolbar. You can lay out an entire document as you would a newspaper and have
articles flow from one page to another.

CAUTION

> The second text box must be empty in order for you to create the link to it.

18

Figure 18.12.

Linking two text boxes.

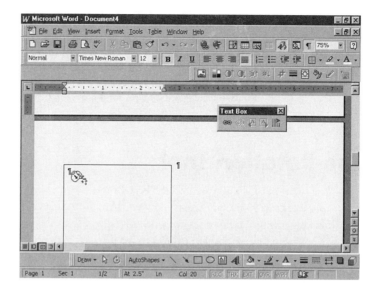

JUST A MINUTE

The Text Box toolbar is only visible when you are in a text box. It hides as soon as you move out of the box.

18

Lines and Arrows

Creating a line or an arrow is as simple as creating a rectangle or circle. To create a line:

1. Click the Line button on the Drawing toolbar.

2. Click in the document.

3. Drag the crosshair in any direction and release the mouse button when the line is as long as you want it.

4. Use the same process to create an arrow with the Arrow button. To modify either a line or an arrow, the object must be selected. The Line Style button brings up a list of line styles, the Dash Style button gives options for dashed lines, and the Arrow Style button contains the arrowhead styles. The line style of the arrow is selected from either the Line Style or Dash Style button.

Hold down the Shift key while dragging to draw a straight line. You can rotate the line in 15 degree increments as you move the mouse pointer, and the line will always be straight. Lines that are rotated without the Shift key may appear jagged, but they will print as straight lines. It is important to have the lines look straight if they will be viewed onscreen.

The Rotation Tool

The rotation tool is accessed via the Free Rotate button on the Drawing toolbar. Free Rotate only works with drawn objects like WordArt, AutoShapes, and other objects created using the Drawing toolbar. It does not work with clip art, text boxes, or pictures inserted from files. That's probably being held in reserve for the next version of Word.

To rotate an object:

1. Click the object.
2. Click the Free Rotate button on the Drawing toolbar or the WordArt toolbar for WordArt rotation. The sizing handles change from squares to small colored circles.
3. Click one of the circles; the pointer turns to four arrows rotating in a circle.
4. Drag the mouse in the direction you want the object to rotate. A dotted line appears as you move the mouse, showing where the object will be repositioned. Release the mouse when the text lays the way you want it (see Figure 18.13).

Figure 18.13.

A dotted line shows where the rotated object will be.

18

TIME SAVER

You can rotate clip art if you ungroup it first. It then becomes a series of drawing objects. Rotate the objects, then immediately regroup them.

Special Effects

The new Shadow and 3D effects add a great touch to simple graphics. They also work with WordArt to create some dramatic effects. It will look like you spent hours on a project when you touch it up with special effects here and there.

Shadows

Add a shadow to a selected drawing object by clicking the Shadow button on the Drawing toolbar. For example, when you're creating flowcharts or titles placed in boxes, you can accent them with shadows. Figure 18.14 shows some of the standard shadow effects you can apply. When you apply a shadow style, it creates the smallest shadow possible. Sometimes it is even hard to tell that there is a shadow at all. Select Shadow Settings to nudge the shadow by small increments up, down, left, or right. The button on the right side of the Shadow Settings toolbar lets you change the shadow color. The button on the left lets you toggle the shadow on or off. You will not see the Shadow samples when you're working with the Shadow Settings toolbar. They are both shown in Figure 18.14.

18

Figure 18.14.

Adding a shadow to an object.

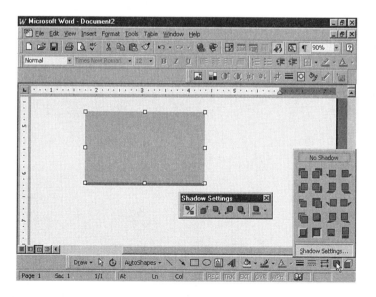

3D Effects

You can have a lot of fun with the 3D options. Figure 18.15 shows a simple rectangle with a gradient fill and a WordArt object that have 3D effects applied. Click the 3D button on the Drawing toolbar to apply a 3D style to a selected object. To further enhance or define the style, use the 3D Settings toolbar, shown in Figure 18.15; the 3D Settings toolbar can be accessed from the 3D button.

Figure 18.16 shows examples of 3D settings that have been modified. The 3D Settings toolbar lets you make these changes:

☐ Tilt—changes the angle from which the object is displayed. Increase the amount of tilt by clicking repeatedly on one of the Tilt buttons.

☐ Depth—increases the perspective or depth of the object. The higher the specified point size, the greater the depth.

☐ Direction—select from nine presets to display the object from different directions.

☐ Lighting—changes the direction the light hits the object. Also choose Bright, Normal, or Dim lighting settings.

☐ Surface—select from Wire Frame, Matte, Plastic, or Metal. (It may be hard to distinguish much difference other than brightness between the last three options in some objects.)

☐ 3D Color—changes the color of the 3D effect. This does not change the color of the original object. It only changes the color of the part of the picture that is added to make it look 3D.

Figure 18.15.
Apply 3D effects to drawing objects and WordArt.

18

Figure 18.16.

3D settings offer many ways to modify 3D effects.

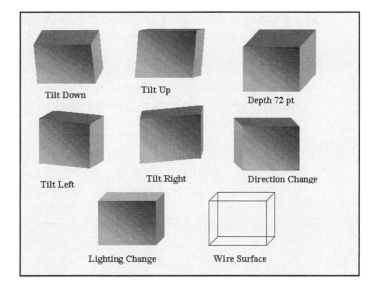

Summary

This hour offers a synopsis of the drawing tools. You can draw shapes or use AutoShapes. Enhance them with colors, shadows, and 3D effects. Label them with text boxes. Group them to move simultaneously or format them as a single object. Link text boxes to create a newspaper-like format that allows text to continue from a box on one page to a box on another page.

Q&A

Q **I used linking text boxes to create a newsletter. I'd like to add a page reference in the text box such as "continued on page 3," but this shoves the text into the other box. How can I do this?**

A You will probably not display the outline border for the text box in the final form. Simply type the *continued to* statement on the line below the first text box and the *continued from* statement on the line above the linked box on the other page.

Q **I want to insert a rectangle and rotate it, then I want to put text in it, but I can't rotate the text in a text box. Is there any way around this?**

A Instead of a text box, use one of the simple WordArt designs and position it in a rectangle. Group the rectangle and the WordArt, then rotate them as a single object.

18

Q **I'm trying to move the WordArt up into the rectangle, but I keep grabbing the rectangle instead. I can't get WordArt into the rectangle. Is there an easier way to do this?**

A If you have one of the drawing objects selected, pressing the Tab key allows you to move from one object to another. If there are four drawing objects on a page, you can easily toggle between them using the Tab key. Once an object is selected, it can be easily moved.

Hour 19

Jazzing Up Your Documents

This hour details some of the ways you can give your documents a cosmetic overhaul. Columns of different sizes can be applied to remodel a document and give it greater readability and eye appeal. Borders and shading can add accentuating lines, colors, and shading. They add the professional decorator's touch to documents.

The highlights of this hour include

- ☐ How to insert columns in only part of a page
- ☐ How to create columns of uneven widths
- ☐ How to apply new whole-page border designs
- ☐ How to use headers and footers for more than page numbers

Columns

Multicolumn documents can't be beat for readability. People are more likely to read the short lines they are used to seeing in newspapers and magazines. Most newsletters use some variation of columns for their basic design. Hour 5, "Working with Words," discusses the message that fonts portray. Serif fonts, for example, depict a more formal, conservative message. Likewise, column styles reflect a certain tone. A page layout consisting of two columns of equal size is seen as a conservative, formal style. A page layout with three columns of equal size, though still conservative, has a less formal, even friendly appearance. Uneven column widths portray a modern, informal tone.

Training documents with one narrow and one wide column allow for explanatory notes or definitions in the narrow column. Although the content may be very technical in nature, the layout makes it less formidable. This is an interesting format for reports of any kind. Use the short column as a sidebar with a sidelight story or explanation. The short column is often referred to as a *scholar's margin*.

You can work with columns in Normal view, but they will appear as one long column. Switch to Page Layout view to see the columns as they are actually laid out.

Placing Existing Text in Columns

The easiest method for inserting columns is to type the text first. As with many of the other Word functions, columns can be applied to text using a menu option or a toolbar button. To place text in columns using the toolbar button, perform the following steps:

1. Select the text to be placed in columns.
2. Click the Columns button on the Standard toolbar.
3. Drag the mouse across the number of columns you want, as in Figure 19.1.

As soon as you release the mouse button, the selected text is placed in columns, as shown in Figure 19.2. Notice that a double-dotted line with the words *Section Break (Continuous)* is placed between the title and the rest of the text. The title was not part of the selection that was placed in columns, so it is not formatted in columns.

Each section can be formatted differently, as outlined in Hour 8 "Setting Up the Page." For example, the title section could have .5-inch left and right margins and the other section could be set up with 1-inch margins.

If you had selected all the text and applied columns, the title would have appeared in the first column. You can correct this by selecting the title, then clicking the Columns button and selecting one column. Word will create the section break that divides the sections. You cannot mix the number of columns within a single section, but you can have different numbers of columns on the same page. When you use this method to place selected text in columns, Word inserts a continuous section break.

19

Figure 19.1.

Select the number of columns from the Columns button.

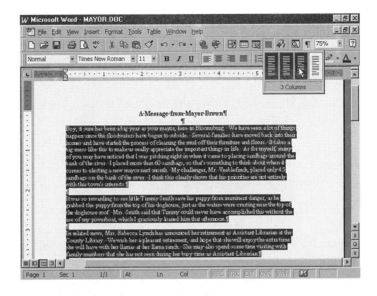

Figure 19.2.

A section break is inserted when selected text is placed in columns.

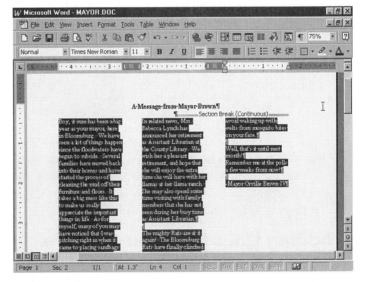

You can also add columns using the Format | Columns menu. If you want something other than the standard columns of equal width, use the menu rather than the toolbar button. There are many options that you can specify through the menu that can't be applied with the toolbar button.

Formatting Column Widths

Sometimes you'll want columns that are not all the same width. Use Format | Columns to vary the column options. Figure 19.3 shows the changes you can make from the Columns dialog box. At the top of dialog box are five presets:

- ☐ One—the standard single column used for most normal documents
- ☐ Two—two columns of equal size
- ☐ Three—three columns of equal size
- ☐ Left—two columns; the one on the left is half the size of the one on the right
- ☐ Right—two columns; the one on the right is half the size of the one on the left

The Left and Right presets use the scholar's margin layout mentioned earlier.

Figure 19.3.

Use the Columns dialog to select column layouts.

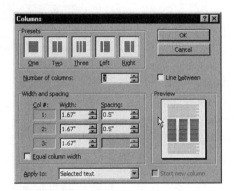

You are not limited to the preset options; you can design your own layout. Type a number or use the arrows in the Number of columns box. Specify the width of each of the columns in the Width and spacing section. Spacing is the amount of space between columns. You cannot specify any of these numbers unless the Equal column width box is unchecked. If it is checked, the columns cannot be different widths.

Adding Lines Between Columns

A nice touch is to add a line between columns. It's also a good separator between two sections of a publication. To insert a line, check the Line between option in the Columns dialog box to create a document such as the one in Figure 19.4. This document uses the Right preset, which lays out the columns with a scholar's margin on the right. Calendar information is added as a sidelight to the mayor's article on the left.

19

Figure 19.4.

Adding a line between columns.

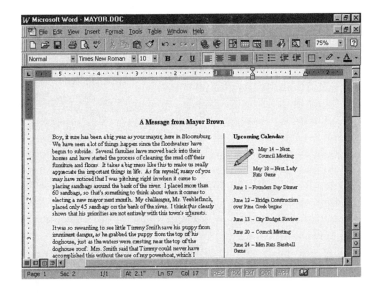

Adding Column Breaks

Sometimes the columns don't break in appropriate locations. To force a break at a certain point, position the cursor in the line ahead of the text you want to move to the next column. Select Insert | Break | Column. This forces the text from that point forward into the next column.

JUST A MINUTE

Although this method is the quick and easy way to create a column break, later adjustments to text may cause some problems. Another way to ensure that text you want to keep together stays in one column is to select the text, then select Format | Paragraph. In the Line and Page Breaks tab, check the Keep lines together box. Keep lines together does not work for text that is in tables, however. You must use the Table | Cell Height and Width option. In the Row tab, uncheck the Allow row to break across pages box.

19

Figure 19.5 shows how the document in Figure 19.4 appeared as it was first typed. The Upcoming Calendar section needed to be placed in the second column. Placing the cursor just ahead of Upcoming Calendar and inserting a column break forced the calendar section into the second column.

Figure 19.5.

Inserting a column break to push text into another column.

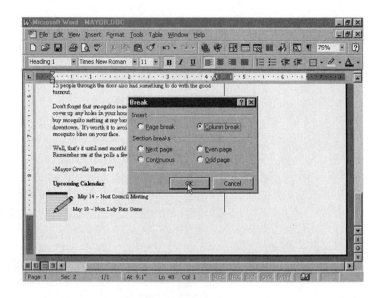

Adjusting Columns from the Ruler

The system for moving columns on a page is similar to the methods used for moving columns in a table. If the ruler is not visible, select Ruler from the View menu. If you position the mouse pointer on the ruler in the gray area between two columns, the pointer changes to a double-headed arrow that says Move Column. Click and drag the Move Column marker either to the right or the left. To see the column measurements as you drag the column marker, hold down the Alt key while you drag the marker (see Figure 19.6).

Figure 19.6.

Resizing columns from the horizontal ruler.

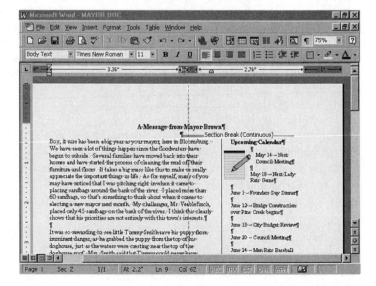

19

Borders and Shading

Borders are frames and lines that set off a title, divide sections, outline parts of a table, or in other ways make use of lines to create visual breaks. Shading can be used with or without borders to create similar effects of division or accent. Borders and shading are also ways to enhance tables.

Adding Emphasis Lines

When working with borders and shading, it's a good idea to bring up the Tables and Borders toolbar for quick access to many of the borders and shading features. To display the Tables and Borders toolbar, click the Tables and Borders button on the Standard toolbar or select View | Toolbars | Tables and Borders from the menu. Some of these toolbar features were covered in Hour 14, "Working with Tables."

To add a line under a heading, use the Tables and Borders toolbar or the Format | Borders and Shading menu. To insert a line using the toolbar, perform the following steps:

1. Select the paragraph that will be underlined.
2. Click the Line Style drop-down list (see Figure 19.7) to choose a line style. The pointer changes to the Draw Table pencil. Don't be confused by this. As soon as the pointer moves back to the Tables and Borders toolbar, the pointer reverts back to the selection arrow.

Figure 19.7.

Selecting a line style.

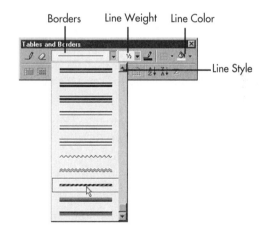

The line selected in Figure 19.7 is one of the new lines added to Word 97's expanded collection of line styles.

3. Click the arrow beside the Borders button for a drop-down list of the border choices (see Figure 19.8). Select the Bottom Border option.

Most of the line styles can be weighted or made thicker by changing the measurement in the Line Weight box. Some of the styles, like the one in Figure 19.8, are preset to a certain size and can't be changed.

Figure 19.8.

Selecting a bottom border.

If you have a color printer and want to add a touch of color, click Border Color to change the color of a line. If you decide you don't like the line and want to change it, do the following:

1. Select the paragraph to which the line style is applied.
2. Select a new style from the Line Style list.
3. Make changes to line weight and border color, if desired.
4. Click the Border icon to activate the new line style (in this example, the Border icon displays the Bottom Border option).

If you want to delete a line, position the cursor in the paragraph to which the line is applied and click the Borders button to remove the line. The Borders button appears lighted when a line or border is applied to a paragraph. Clicking it darkens it and removes the line from the selected paragraph.

Placing Boxes Around Text

To place a box around a paragraph, use the same technique as for creating a line, except select the Outside Border option from the Borders drop-down list. First select the paragraph. Select a line style, line weight, and color as you did for a line, then click the arrow beside the Borders button to display the drop-down list of borders. Select the Outside Border option.

If you want to place a box around the text in a title but not the whole paragraph, select the text in the line without the paragraph mark at the end. After you select a line style, weight, and color, and click the Borders button to select Outside Border, the box encloses only the text. Figure 19.9 shows an example of a border applied to the paragraph in the first line as well as an example of a border applied to the selected text in the second line.

If you don't like the way either of these options looks, you can always set the line style and use the Draw Table feature to draw a table with a single cell and type the text in it, but it would probably be easier to use a text box. Text boxes are more moveable.

19

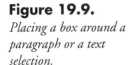

Figure 19.9.

Placing a box around a paragraph or a text selection.

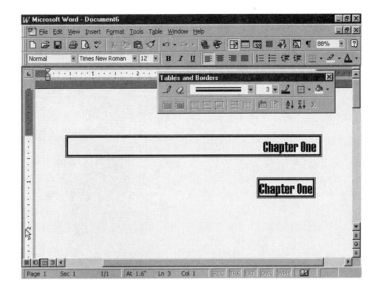

Full Page Borders

If you're responsible for the one-page flyers, announcements, and invitations for your business or organization, you probably keep looking for borders to accent the entire page. You may have even resorted to buying packaged clip art that includes borders. Microsoft must have recognized that this is one of the big things people do with a word processor. Word 97 has added a Page Borders tab to the Format | Borders and Shading options. To add a page border:

1. Select Format | Borders and Shading.
2. Click the Page Borders tab.
3. Select from any of the line styles, or choose one of the art borders (see Figure 19.10).
4. Click OK to apply the border style.

Figure 19.11 shows the art border applied to the one-page message from the mayor. Even though there are lots of border and shading options, it's always better to err on the side of too little than too much ornamentation. A little accent dresses up your document; a lot makes it look like a menagerie. A simpler border style would have been a better choice for this document. This border looks like something more appropriate for a certificate or award. It seems out of place in a newsletter from the mayor.

19

Figure 19.10.

Apply new full-page art borders.

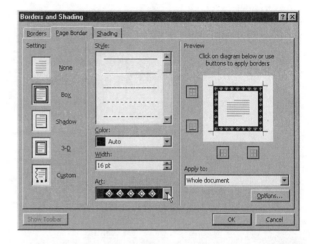

Figure 19.11.

A whole-page border added to a one-page newsletter.

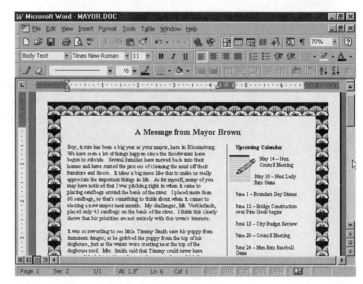

Extra Border Options

The Borders tab in the Format | Borders and Shading dialog box gives you a few extra options that don't appear in the Tables and Borders toolbar. You can apply shadow and 3D effects to borders. Click one of the icons under Setting to choose a border effect or remove an existing border. The dialog box offers options similar to those on the toolbar to apply a line style, color, and weight. Select which lines you want to apply borders to by clicking the Border buttons in the Preview box or clicking the edges of the sample picture where you want to apply lines. If a border is already applied and you want to remove specific border lines, click the Border buttons for the lines you want to delete, or click the lines themselves.

Shading

Shading can be applied with or without a border. As with most other features, you get the fast food from the toolbars, but the menus offer a full-course meal. The most common shades are available from the Shading Color drop-down list on the Tables and Borders toolbar. Select other shading options, including several patterns, from Format | Borders and Shading in the Shading tab (see Figure 19.12).

Figure 19.12.

Select shading colors and patterns from the Borders and Shading dialog.

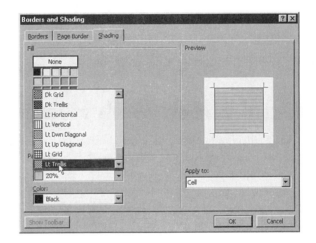

The Shading button on the Table and Borders toolbar looks like the Fill Color bucket on the Drawing toolbar. They work in the same way, but the shading color is applied to the text layer, while the fill color is applied to objects on the graphics layer. You can't use them interchangeably.

Figure 19.13 shows how black shading with white text is used in the Professional Report template to accent the chapter number and a title. These accents draw the reader to the page by creating focal points.

19

Figure 19.13.

White text with black shading creates accents for the page.

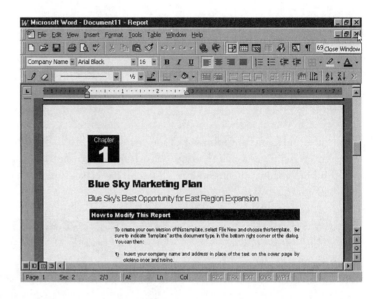

Special Effects with Headers and Footers

Use borders and shading in headers and footers to provide a sense of consistency throughout a document. Figure 19.14 shows a header that was created with borders and shading. It has a pushbutton look that is accentuated by the font that appears to be etched in the button.

Figure 19.14.

Creating a 3D header.

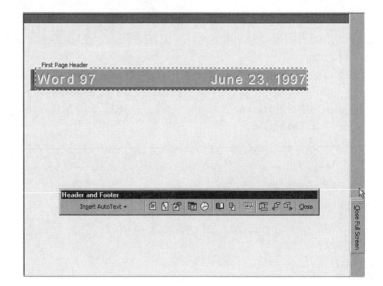

19

To create this special-effect header, do the following:

1. Select View | Header and Footer.

2. In the header pane, use the Tables and Borders toolbar to add medium-gray shading by clicking the Shading Color button and selecting one of the shades of gray.

3. Select one of the new shadowed lines from the drop-down list of line styles and increase the line weight to make it one or two sizes thicker.

4. Click the Borders button and select Bottom Border and Left Border. This gives the 3D appearance.

5. Add text to the header using a sans serif font such as Arial or Helvetica, and increase the font size. Use Format | Font to apply the engrave effect.

6. Select File | Page Setup. In the Margins tab, increase the Header margin to about .8 inch to bring the header down slightly.

Use the same technique to create a footer in a similar style. If you want a scaled down version of the first page header to appear on the rest of the pages of the document, do the following:

1. Select File | Page Setup.

2. In the Page Layout tab, check the Different first page box under Headers and Footers.

   Figure 19.15 shows a sample footer and second page header created to go with the first page header. There is no need to re-create the border and shading each time.

3. Copy and paste the first page header to the second page header, then replace the existing text. Do the same for the footer.

4. Add a page number to page two so that the document will start numbering on this page.

You could also use the drawing tools to dress up the header and footer. Figure 19.16 was created with a rectangle formatted with the 3D effects, a WordArt title, and a text box with no line or fill for the date. The date font was enhanced with an outline effect.

Insert your company logo or other trademarks that uniquely identify you or your organization in the header or footer.

19

Figure 19.15.

Coordinating the footers and second page header.

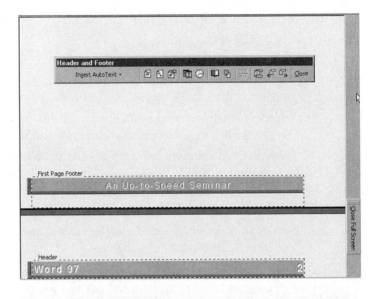

Figure 19.16.

Creating a header with the drawing tools.

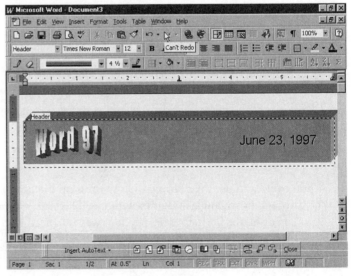

TIME SAVER

Create personalized stationery with monograms to use or give as gifts. Use Word's alphabet clip art or create your own with WordArt. Creating a single letter in WordArt usually renders a distorted image, but using two or three initials or a last name looks pretty impressive. These would not need to be placed in a header if you're printing out the stationery for gifts. It works well, however, if you are going to type the letter and print it out

19

> with the header at the same time. This would be a good candidate for a
> template.

Summary

This hour shows the functionality of columns and how they can change the look and tone
of a document. With a little help from borders and shading, documents can move from plain
to professional with minimal effort. Borders and shading create natural visual breaks and
accents. The new page borders can frame certificates, flyers, and announcements with fun or
fancy designs. Headers and footers can be used for more than inserting page numbers and
dates. Use them to insert titles, borders, and graphics.

Q&A

**Q I tried to change the border around a text box, but it seems to be inside the
text box. When I make the box bigger, the border doesn't move or get bigger.**

A You must have applied the border from the Tables and Borders toolbar. This
formats a border only around selected text. Text box borders are applied through
the Format | Text Box menu. The Format Text Box dialog box includes the
options for lines that can be applied to text boxes.

**Q I like to use borders, but the lines are always too close to the text. Is there any
way to get more space between the lines and the text?**

A Yes. Select the paragraph or section that includes the border. Select Format |
Borders and Shading. In the Borders tab, click Options. You can specify (by point
sizes) how much whitespace is placed between the border and the text. Select space
for top, bottom, left, or right or any combination of the sides (for example, you
may only want more space left and right but not on the top and bottom).

**Q I changed a line style using the Tables and Borders toolbar, but the line didn't
change.**

A You would assume changing the style would change the selected object, but you
need to click the Borders icon to reapply the new line style.

19

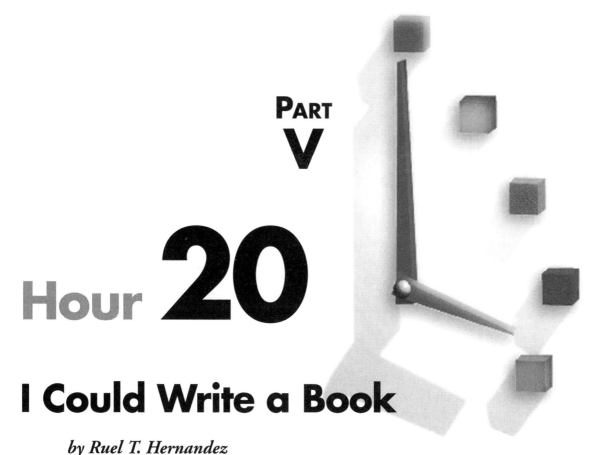

Hour 20

I Could Write a Book

by Ruel T. Hernandez

If you have been itching to write the next best-selling book, you can do so with Word 97. In fact, Word 97 is being used to write this book!

You may already have all the basic text written for the main part of your book or document, but now you want to set up a professional-looking table of contents, index, footnotes, and captions for pictures. Can you do all of that with Word 97? Yes, you can! And that's what I cover in this jam-packed chapter. These are the sorts of things you will need to know how to do if you are writing a book, a school thesis or paper, or some other document requiring a table of contents, index, footnotes, or captions.

So in this hour, you will learn how to do the following:

- ☐ Set up a table of contents
- ☐ Set up an index
- ☐ Set up footnotes and endnotes
- ☐ Set up captions for figures
- ☐ Set up a table of figures

Creating a Table of Contents

A table of contents will help you inform readers about how your book or document is organized. What is really nice about Word 97 is that it can build the table of contents for you.

Check the Headings

To set up the style area width so you can see the style of the headings and text in a column on the left side of your Word 97 screen, do the following:

1. Select Tools | Options.
2. On the View tab, set the Style Area Width option in the Windows section at the bottom of the dialog to .5" or .6" and click OK. (To turn off the style area, reset the style area width to 0.) You should see a column to the left with various styles listed.

Instead of viewing the style area, you can switch to Outline view to check the headings. Nevertheless, you may find viewing the style area while in Normal view to be very convenient.

To ensure that the headings in your document are correct, you should look at the heading levels listed in the style area column. Also look at the style settings for the paragraphs in your document; make sure they are set to normal or body text so they will not show up in the table of contents. You can switch between Normal view and Outline view to demote/promote the headings. If any paragraph in your document is set to a heading level, demote the paragraph to body text so the paragraph will not show up in the table of contents.

Selecting and Inserting the Table of Contents

To begin creating a table of contents, follow these steps:

1. Set up the Styles view area as discussed previously. Alternatively, you can check the headings by switching back and forth between Normal view and Outline view.
2. Move your cursor to wherever you want to place your table of contents and then click Insert | Index and Tables.

   You might want to insert a new page at the beginning of your document by going to the top of your document and pressing Ctrl+Enter to insert a page break. Place your cursor before the place where you want the page to break. You may want to press Enter a few times to put in some blank lines.

   To change the page number format for the table of contents pages, select Insert | Page Numbers and then click the Format button on the Page Numbers dialog. This invokes a Page Number Format dialog; in the Number Format pull-down selection list, you can select different page numbering formats. For instance, you can select the i, ii, iii page number format and then switch to regular numbers for the regular pages of your document after the table of contents.

20

3. Click the Table of Contents tab; you should then see a dialog similar to the one shown in Figure 20.1.

Figure 20.1.

Select a table of contents format for your book or document.

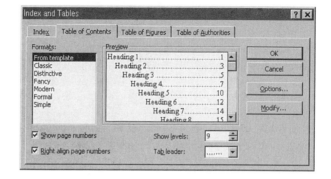

4. From this dialog, select a format, such as From template.

5. You should adjust the number of heading levels by increasing the number of levels in the Show Levels area on the Table of Contents tab. The default is three levels. If you leave the number of levels at three, your table of contents will show only the top three heading levels. Increase the number of levels shown if you want a more thorough table of contents.

6. You can then select the tab leader. A tab leader can be blank space, periods or dots, dashes, or a solid underline between a heading and the page number. A tab leader helps the reader trace the heading to the appropriate page number.

7. Click OK, and a table of contents will be inserted in your document.

There are also Options and Modify buttons on the Table of Contents tab on the Index and Tables dialog. If you click the Options button, you will get the Table of Contents Options dialog. Do so if you want to include paragraphs with styles other than the usual heading styles in the table of contents. You may wish to use the Modify button if you want to modify the table of contents format, but you will only be able to modify the From template format.

If you have the style area column enabled, you will see that elements in the table of contents are designated by the TOC style label with a number indicating the heading level. For instance, TOC 1 would indicate a TOC heading with heading level 1. You can change the fonts or edit the text in the table of contents as you would any other text in your Word 97 document. For instance, you could select some text in the table of contents, select Format | Font, and then change the font.

As you can see, making a table of contents is easy! Figure 20.2 shows you a sample table of contents.

20

Figure 20.2.

A sample table of contents using the From template format.

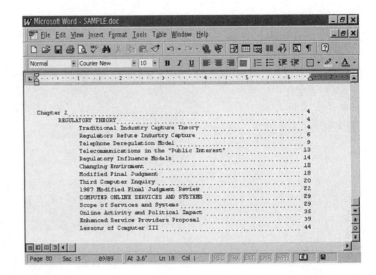

<table>
<tr><td>Chapter 2</td><td>4</td></tr>
<tr><td>REGULATORY THEORY</td><td>4</td></tr>
<tr><td>Traditional Industry Capture Theory</td><td>4</td></tr>
<tr><td>Regulators Refute Industry Capture</td><td>6</td></tr>
<tr><td>Telephone Deregulation Model</td><td>9</td></tr>
<tr><td>Telecommunications in the "Public Interest"</td><td>13</td></tr>
<tr><td>Regulatory Influence Models</td><td>14</td></tr>
<tr><td>Changing Environment</td><td>18</td></tr>
<tr><td>Modified Final Judgment</td><td>18</td></tr>
<tr><td>Third Computer Inquiry</td><td>20</td></tr>
<tr><td>1987 Modified Final Judgment Review</td><td>22</td></tr>
<tr><td>COMPUTER ONLINE SERVICES AND SYSTEMS</td><td>29</td></tr>
<tr><td>Scope of Services and Systems</td><td>29</td></tr>
<tr><td>Online Activity and Political Impact</td><td>35</td></tr>
<tr><td>Enhanced Service Providers Proposal</td><td>39</td></tr>
<tr><td>Lessons of Computer III</td><td>44</td></tr>
</table>

Building an Index

Using Word 97, you can set up an index to help readers find topics in your book or document. An *index* is an alphabetized list of words and phrases that includes the page numbers where each word or phrase can be found. Like a table of contents, an index can help readers find certain topics right away, but an index gives a reader more specific direction on where to find certain items.

Main Entries for the Index (and Generating a Quick Index)

To build an index for your book or document, do the following:

1. You'll probably want to begin your index on a separate page at the end of your document. Place your cursor where you want the index to appear, then press Ctrl+Enter to place a page break to start a new page. You might want to center the word *Index* at the top of the new page and press the Enter key a few times to insert some blank lines.

2. Click Insert | Index and Tables, and click the Index tab. You should see a dialog similar to the one shown in Figure 20.3.

3. Click Mark Entry to invoke the Mark Index Entry dialog (see Figure 20.4).

20

Figure 20.3.

Select an index format for your book or document.

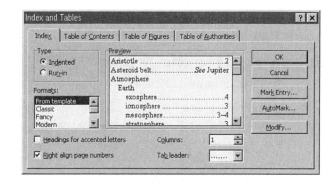

Figure 20.4.

Enter the index entries you want listed in your index.

4. In the Mark Index Entry dialog, in the Main entry blank, type or simply select the words from your document that you want indexed. (The Mark Index Entry dialog will stay open so you can also type other words or select words or phrases in your document to be inserted in the Main entry blank.)

5. Click the Mark button on the Mark Index Entry dialog. You may find that blocking words or phrases and then clicking the Mark button is an easy way to build your index. For each index entry you make, you will see an entry like the following inserted in your text after the word or phrase being indexed:

{XE "word or phrase"}

The words or phrase within the quotation marks is what is indexed. Onscreen, the index entry would have a dotted underline to indicate that it is a hidden font code.

TIME SAVER

To hide this code (and other formatting codes), click the Paragraph icon on the Standard toolbar under the menu bar. (Or you can hide the formatting codes by clicking Tools I Options and, on the View tab, unclicking Hidden Text or All in the Nonprinting Characters section of the View tab.)

6. After you have marked all the words or phrases that you want to index, close the Mark Index Entry dialog.

Subentries for the Index

You can also enter a subentry of a main entry. To do this, perform the following steps:

1. Position your cursor after the words or phrase in the text that you want to be a subentry. Do not block the words or phrase.

2. On the Mark Index Entry dialog, enter the words or phrase in the Subentry field, and enter the words or phrase for the main entry in the Main entry field. For instance, if you have a main entry for dogs and you want a subentry for show dogs, place your cursor after the words *show dogs* in your document. On the Mark Index Entry dialog, enter the word dogs in the Main entry field, then enter the words show dogs in the Subentry field.

3. Click the Mark button. Repeat these steps for other subentries you might want to make.

Cross-References

You can enter cross-references in the Mark Index Entry dialog. A *cross-reference* is used to alert the reader to similar items that are related to an indexed item. To make a cross-reference, perform the following steps:

1. Place your cursor by the words or phrase you want cross-referenced (you can block this text if you want this to be a main entry). Make sure the words or phrase show up in the Main entry or Subentry field (with the appropriate main entry typed in for a subentry).

2. After the word *See* in the Cross-reference field, type the cross-reference. Be sure the Cross-reference option is enabled.

Current Page, Page Range, and Bookmarks

The Current page option (the default) indicates that the index entry is to be on the page your cursor is currently on. The Page range option lets you specify a range of pages, such as pages 32 to 39, where a particular topic is discussed. The Page range option requires that you insert bookmarks prior to marking text for the index. A *bookmark* is a selection of text that you mark for the page range. This is how you would insert a bookmark and set up a page range:

1. Click Insert | Bookmark (you might have to click the down arrow at the bottom of the Insert menu to find Bookmark).

2. On the Bookmark dialog, type a bookmark name, and then click the Add button.

3. Place your cursor by the text you want to index (or select the text) and choose Insert | Index and Tables.

20

4. Enter the main entry (and subentry, if applicable), then click the Page range option

5. Select the bookmark.

6. Click the Mark button to insert the index code.

The Mark All Button

Think of the Mark All button as a shotgun approach to marking all the occurrences of a word or phrase in a document. If you want every occurrence of a word or phrase in a document to be listed in the index, you would use the Mark All button to insert an index entry code next to each and every instance of the word or phrase in the document. For instance, if you are writing a document about dogs and you have repeated the words *dog house* many times in the document, you can use the Mark All button to mark all of the instances of that phrase without having to search for each instance. This is probably one of the easier ways to build an index; you may find yourself using the Mark All button quite a bit. To use the Mark All button, do the following:

1. Select or place your cursor on the text you want to index.

2. In the Mark Index Entry dialog, ensure that the text is in the appropriate Main entry and Subentry fields

3. Click the Mark All button.

Page Number Format

You can set the index page number format to bold, italic, or both. To do so, simply click the Bold and/or Italic options on the Mark Index Entry dialog.

Creating the Index

To create the Index, do the following:

1. Mark all the index entries.

2. Place your cursor wherever you wish to place the index (usually at the end of your book or document).

3. Click Insert | Index and Tables.

4. On the Index tab, select the index format you want to use, such as the From template format.

5. Select how many columns you want for your index. Word 97 selects two columns as the default. You may instead want to set up the index for one column.

6. Click OK.

The index will be couched between a couple of hidden section break lines that will not print. You can change the fonts and manipulate the index as you would the rest of your Word 97 document. Figure 20.5 shows a sample index.

20

Figure 20.5.

A sample index created using the From template format.

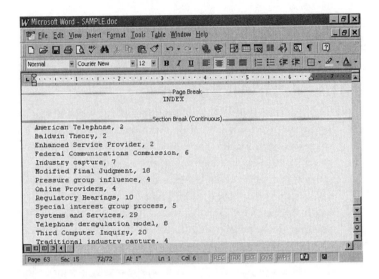

To change the formatting of the index, you must adjust the index's style. You must select the From template format to be able to make any formatting changes. This is what you do:

1. From the Index tab on the Index and Tables dialog, select the From template format and click the Modify button.

2. In the Style dialog, select the style you want to change and then click the Modify button.

3. In the Modify Style dialog, make whatever changes you desire and then click OK.

4. Repeat this for any other formatting changes you would want to make. When you are finished, click the Apply button.

5. Click the OK button to insert your index.

Creating a Concordance File

An easy way to build an index is to create a concordance file. To do so, you must create a new document and make a two-column table:

1. Start with a new blank document.

2. Select Table | Insert Table. The default is two columns by two rows, which is acceptable for our purposes. Click OK.

20

3. In the first box in the first column, type the words or phrase for which you want Word to search and mark index entries in your document. Press Tab to move to the next column.

4. Type the index entry to correspond with the text in the first column. This is what you want to appear in the index. Press Tab. If there is no second row of boxes, pressing the Tab key will create a new row for you.

5. Repeat the previous two steps for each index reference and entry.

6. Save your concordance file.

7. Open the document you want to index.

8. Click Insert | Index and Tables.

9. Activate the Index tab.

10. Click the AutoMark button.

11. Type the name of your concordance file (or search for and select your concordance file).

12. Click the Open button. Word will input an index entry code on each occurrence of the words or phrases you want indexed.

13. Select the place where your index is to appear, such as at the end of your document. You may want to press Ctrl+Enter to start a new page.

14. Click Insert | Index and Tables.

15. Activate the Index tab.

16. Select your index format, number of columns, and so on (as described previously), then click OK to insert your index.

Many users feel that creating a concordance file is the easiest way to build an index in Word 97. This is particularly true if you are working on a large document with numerous words and phrases you want to index. But you may want to use the other index-building techniques when you work on smaller documents.

Footnotes and Endnotes

Footnotes and endnotes are for documenting your sources for facts or quotations you have in your book or other document. *Footnotes* can be of the usual type that you find at the bottom of pages, or they can be set up as *endnotes*, which are placed at the end of your document.

Inserting a Footnote/Endnote

To insert a footnote/endnote, perform the following steps:

20

1. Place your cursor at the place where you want to indicate the presence of a footnote (usually after a quotation or a fact whose source you want to note).

2. Click Insert | Footnote and, from the Footnote and Endnote panel, click either Footnote or Endnote; your screen should then be divided into two sections (as shown in Figure 20.6). In the main text (upper) area, type your main text. In the footnote/endnote (lower) area, type your footnote/endnote text.

Figure 20.6.

Word will divide the screen so that you type your main text in the upper area and your footnotes/endnotes in the lower area.

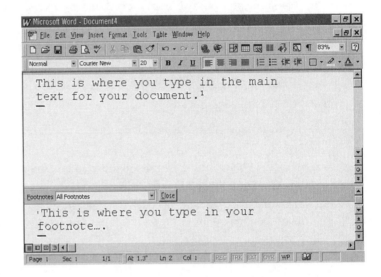

3. In the footnote/endnote entry pane area, type your footnote or endnote.

4. Click the Close button when you finish typing your footnote or endnote. A superscript footnote/endnote reference number should show up in the main body of your text.

If you are in Page Layout view, you may notice that the mouse pointer turns into a flag when passed over a footnote/endnote number. You may also see a screen tip with text of your footnote/endnote. This can be helpful if you need a quick reference to the text you have entered.

Editing and Deleting a Footnote/Endnote

To edit a footnote/endnote, double-click the reference number. The editing pane will show up at the bottom of the screen, and you can edit the footnote/endnote. Alternatively, you can click View | Footnote or View | Endnote to open up the footnote/endnote pane and then search for the footnote/endnote you want to edit.

If you have a lot of footnotes/endnotes, you can use the Go To command:

1. Click Edit | Go To (or use the Ctrl+G shortcut command).

20

2. Select Footnote or Endnote.

3. Type the footnote/endnote number you want to edit.

Delete a footnote/endnote by deleting the footnote/endnote reference number in the main text of your document.

Numbers or Symbols

Word 97 will automatically number your footnotes/endnotes. You can select different numbering or lettering options in this way:

1. Click the Options button on the Footnote and Endnote dialog. A Note Options dialog will pop up. The two tabs, one for All Footnotes and the other All Endnotes, are identical.

2. Select where you want to place the footnotes/endnotes by clicking the Place At pull-down selection list.

3. Select the numbering format.

4. Select whether to start your footnotes/endnotes at number 1 or at a different number.

5. Select whether to have the numbering be continuous, restart with each section of your document, or restart with each new page of your document.

6. After you finish, click OK two times.

7. Type your footnote/endnote text in the footnote/endnote entry pane area at the bottom of the screen. You may want to be in Normal view to see the footnote/endnote entry pane area. If you switch to Normal view and don't see the footnote/endnote entry pane area, select View | Footnotes to see the area where you can type your footnote/endnote.

8. Click Close after you finish typing your footnote/endnote.

You'll usually want to use numbers when creating footnotes/endnotes, but there may be times when you want to use symbols instead. You can use symbols instead of numbers, but you must change the symbols manually. That is, if you use numbers, the numbers increment automatically from footnote to footnote (or endnote to endnote). If you use a symbol such as an asterisk (*) to designate one footnote/endnote and then another symbol to designate the next footnote/endnote, you must manually select which symbol you want to use for each footnote/endnote like so:

1. Click Symbol.

2. Select the symbol you want to use.

3. Click OK.

20

If you have many footnotes or endnotes, consider using automatic numbering. If you use a random combination of symbols, you may confuse yourself or your reader.

Moving and Copying a Footnote/Endnote

Whenever you move text in Word 97, footnotes/endnotes associated with the text you are moving should move with it. If the footnotes/endnotes do not move with their associated text, locate the footnote/endnote reference number you want to move. Select that reference number and move it to the location where you want to place it. It's just as easy as moving regular text.

Similarly, you can copy an existing footnote/endnote to another location in your book or document. Again, find the reference number for the footnote/endnote, select that reference number, copy it, go to the new location in your document, and then paste it in. Word 97 will automatically give the copied footnote/endnote a new number. If you want to edit the copied footnote/endnote, do so as you would any other footnote/endnote.

Footnote/Endnote Separators and the Continuation Notice

The footnote/endnote editing pane has a pull-down menu that lets you switch between editing footnotes/endnotes, changing the footnote/endnote separator or continuation separator, and editing the footnote/endnote continuation notice. Think of these as different views. You can change the separators, but you might want to stick with the defaults. That way, you'll probably only have to edit the footnotes/endnotes and set up the footnote/endnote continuation notice. For the continuation notice, where the footnote or endnote continues on the next page, enter something like (Continued next page) in the footnote/endnote continuation notice field of the editing pane.

Captions for Pictures, Graphs, and Diagrams

Captions are for figures (such as pictures, graphs, and diagrams) in your book or document. A *caption* is like a text description of a figure to help the reader understand what the picture or diagram is and why it appears in your book or document. For instance, say you're writing a document about dogs, and you insert a picture of an award-winning show dog. You may want to use a caption to state the breed (and maybe the name) of the dog. To insert a caption, select Insert | Caption. This invokes a dialog similar to the one shown in Figure 20.7.

20

Figure 20.7.

Captions help you describe a picture or diagram for your book or document.

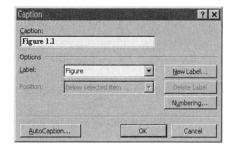

Captions and Tables of Figures

After you set the captions in your document, you can set up a table of figures, which is similar to a table of contents except that it lists only figures. You must first decide where you want to place the table of figures. You might place it after the table of contents or the index. To set up a table of figures, do the following:

1. If you want to place the table of figures after the table of contents, press Ctrl+Enter to start a new page, press Enter once or a few times, and then press Ctrl+Enter again to separate the table of figures from the subsequent text in your document.

2. Click Insert | Index and Tables from the menu bar.

3. On the Table of Figures tab, select a table style, such as From template.

4. Click OK.

Summary

In this hour, you have learned how to set up a table of contents and an index, to create footnotes and endnotes, and to assign captions for figures to illustrate your best-selling book, award-winning report, or grade A+ paper.

Q&A

Q Why can't I see all of the levels of my table of contents?

A Increase the number of levels to show in your table of contents by clicking Insert | Index and Tables and, in the Show Levels area, increasing the number of levels.

Q Can I convert footnotes to endnotes and vice versa?

A Yes. To convert only one footnote/endnote, display it in the footnote/endnote editing pane, right-click it, and then click the Convert to footnote/endnote selection. To convert all your footnotes to endnotes, select Insert | Footnote, click

20

Options, and then click Convert. Select the conversion you want (Convert all footnotes to endnotes or Convert all endnotes to footnotes) and then click the OK button. When finished, click Cancel until you get back to your document.

Q Can I set up a subentry of a subentry in an index?

A Yes. The trick is to use semicolons when you type the subentries. For instance, if you want a main entry of pets, then a subentry of dogs, and then a further subentry of show dogs, type `pets` as the main entry in the Mark Index Entry dialog, and then type `dogs; show dogs` as the subentry.

RW 5

Word in Real Time

Design a Newsletter

This project will pull together several graphic and page layout options to build a newsletter. You can always use Word's Newsletter template, but it's more fun to design your own and use it for future editions. This project will involve these features:

- ☐ Columns
- ☐ Clip art
- ☐ WordArt
- ☐ Borders

It's a good idea to lay out your ideas before you sit down at the computer to generate a publication. Create a mock-up drawing of how you want the publication to be laid out. Figure out who your audience is. Are you trying to appeal to a conservative or a liberal audience? You don't have to get political, but you need to be aware of what will be effective with the majority of your readers.

Think about readability and the visual contact points on the page. Will columns make it easier to read? Will specific fonts make the text more legible? Do text and graphics flow together in a way that draws the reader from one place to another, or does it look like little chunks pasted together?

JUST A MINUTE

A good rule of thumb is to use no more than two fonts in one publication. Newsletters usually work well with sans serif fonts for headings and serif fonts for the body of the newsletter. The best advice is to keep it simple.

Create a Heading

A good header is essential to draw the reader in. It may make the difference between whether the newsletter gets read or tossed. Figure R5.1 shows the first stages of the header. The chalkboard and apple are two separate clips from the clip art collection. The title was created in WordArt, and all three items were grouped. To group objects, do the following:

1. Hold down the Shift key and click each of the objects.
2. From the Drawing toolbar, select Group from the Draw menu.

Figure R5.1.

Using clip art and WordArt for the title.

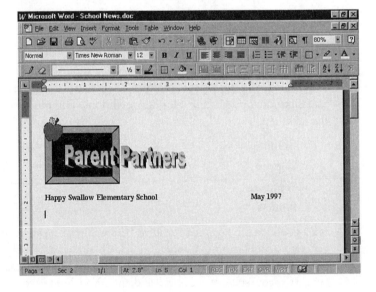

In addition to allowing you to move the objects as one unit, grouping your graphics makes it easier for you to add a text wrap. This example uses a top and bottom style text wrap so that text does not flow around or next to the graphic. To add a top and bottom text wrap:

1. Click the drawing object.
2. Select Format | Object from the menu.
3. In the Wrapping tab, select the Top & bottom option.
4. Click OK.

A line of text was added below the title and formatted with a font similar to the one used in the WordArt object.

This letter will be sent to parents of elementary school children. Give it a festive look with a decorative line beneath the last line of the heading. Figure R5.2 displays the line style that will be added. The key to remember is that the line is not applied until you make a selection from the Borders drop-down list. This tells Word where you want the line (top, bottom, and so on).

Figure R5.2.

Adding a decorative line.

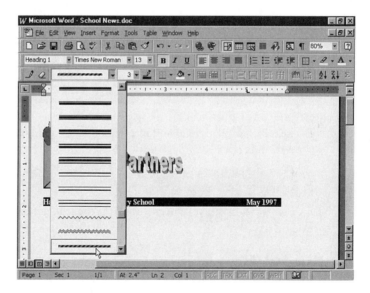

In the paragraph after the header, insert a break by selecting Insert | Break. Select a Continuous Section break. Section 1 is the heading, and section 2 is the text for page 1.

Adding Columns

A change of pace for newsletters is to use something like a scholar's margin. This example is set up with a scholar's margin on the left for page one and a mirrored image on page 2 with the scholar's margin on the right. That means you'll need a section break at the end of page 1 so that the columns can be different for page 2. To add columns to section 2 of page 1 (the section after the heading):

1. Place the cursor in section 2.

2. Select Format | Columns and choose the Left option in the Presets section (see Figure R5.3).

Figure R5.3.

Setting a scholar's margin for page 1.

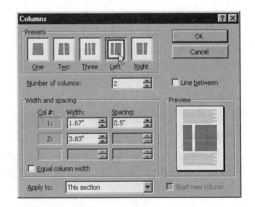

3. Leave a few blank lines and insert another section break (for page 2). Make this section break a Next page section break.

4. Place the cursor in section 3 (page 2) and use Format | Columns to set a Right option in the Presets section.

Type the articles in the larger column and use the scholar's margin (the short column) for the article titles.

Final Touch

A nice touch is to use symbols between articles to mark the end of one section and the start of another. The symbols used between the articles in this newsletter were pictures of an open book found in the Wingdings symbol set. Select Insert | Symbol from the menu and choose from the interesting symbols for fonts like Monotype Sorts or Wingdings. Increase the symbol's size by selecting it and increasing the font size from the Formatting toolbar. The newsletter is complete (see Figure R5.4).

Figure R5.4.

The finished newsletter.

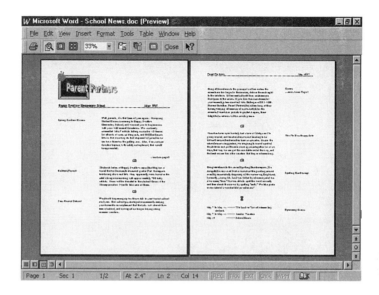

PART
VI

Word Has Connections

Hour

Hour 21

Bookshelf and Word's Editing Tools

by Ruel T. Hernandez

Word 97 has several easy-to-use editing tools that you can use to hone your documents. This hour covers the Undo/Redo command, the spelling and grammar checker, the AutoCorrect capability, and Bookshelf. The Undo/Redo command can be found under the Edit menu on the menu bar, and the other functions can be found under the Tools menu on the menu bar.

The highlights of this chapter include

- ☐ The Undo/Redo command
- ☐ The spelling and grammar checker
- ☐ The AutoCorrect function
- ☐ Bookshelf

JUST A MINUTE

Bookshelf Basics is included with the professional edition of Office 97, but not with the standard or small business editions. Bookshelf is also not included in the standalone version of Word 97. If you wish to use Bookshelf, you will have to get the professional edition of Office 97 or get the standalone Bookshelf program.

Undo/Redo

Think of the Undo command as your "oops" function. Say you accidentally delete a word or a paragraph. You can undelete what you have deleted using the Undo command. Try it! Type something in Word, and then delete it. Then select Edit | Undo Typing or press Ctrl+Z to undelete the words you have deleted. When you select Edit | Undo, Undo may show up as Undo Clear, Undo Typing, or something similar, with the word after Undo describing the action last completed.

Undo is very useful for undoing almost anything, including typing or deletions. Word keeps track of all your actions as you type your document. For instance, if you type a whole paragraph and then decide against using it, you can press Ctrl+Z to undo what you have typed instead of deleting the paragraph. Essentially, you are going back a step, or going in reverse, to the point where you were before you typed the paragraph (you may have to press Ctrl+Z or click Edit | Undo several times to get there). Use the Redo command to redo what you have undone using the Undo command. To use the Redo command, select Edit | Redo or press Ctrl+Y.

JUST A MINUTE

You cannot use Undo/Redo to perform multiple undelete commands. Some people cheat by using the undelete command in other word processing programs to perform a copy/move/paste maneuver. In Word 97, you must use the regular Copy/Paste commands to copy and move sections of your document.

You can also undo and redo by clicking the Undo and Redo buttons on the Standard toolbar. The Undo button is designated by an arrow going counter-clockwise, and the Redo button is designated an arrow going clockwise. To the right of each button is a pull-down list of the actions you have taken in the writing of your document that you can undo or redo. These actions generally include almost all the word-processing actions you have taken since you opened your document.

21

JUST A MINUTE You usually lose the record of your undo/redo actions when you close your document. To save those actions for the next time you open and work on your document, select File I Versions to invoke the Versions dialog box, then click the Automatically save a version on close option. This is useful if you want to see the progression of how a document was constructed. To see the undo/redo actions of a previous version of a document, select File I Versions to open the previous version of the document, and then trace the undo/redo activity that occurred in the drafting of the document.

Spelling and Grammar Checking

Word 97 has a wonderful spelling and grammar checker that can help you draft your documents. The spelling and grammar checker can be found under the Tools menu on the menu bar (listed as Spelling and Grammar); you can also activate this function by pressing the F7 key on your keyboard. When a spelling or grammatical error is found, a Spelling and Grammar dialog box similar to the one shown in Figure 21.1 pops up on your screen.

Figure 21.1.

Word 97 has a spelling and grammar checker that will help you proof your document.

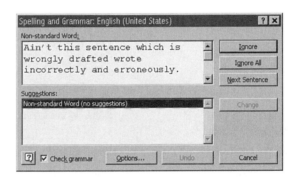

The text containing the spelling or grammatical error appears in the top part of the dialog box. The bottom part of the dialog shows suggested changes to correct the error. You can ignore the error, ignore all of the same errors, go on to the next sentence, or accept the suggested change. This floating dialog remains on the screen until the spell check is complete, at which time a Readability Statistics dialog box will appear on the screen (more on the Readability Statistics dialog later). Until you finish the spell check, the dialog remains on the screen unless you click on the Cancel button; you can continue to type your document while the dialog remains on the screen (the dialog's Ignore button will change to a Resume button that you can click to continue the spelling and grammar check). The spelling and grammar checker is very straightforward and easy to use.

21

Spelling and Grammar Options

You can set several spelling and grammar options. Enable the Check grammar with spelling checkbox in the Spelling & Grammar dialog box if you want the spelling and grammar checker to check spelling and grammar; leave this option unchecked if you want the spelling and grammar checker to check for spelling only. Access more spelling and grammar options by clicking the Options button at the bottom of the Spelling & Grammar dialog box or by selecting Tools | Options from the menu bar. This invokes a dialog box with a series of spelling and grammar options (see Figure 21.2).

Figure 21.2.

*In the Spelling &
Grammar dialog box,
you can set Word 97 to
automatically check your
spelling and grammar.*

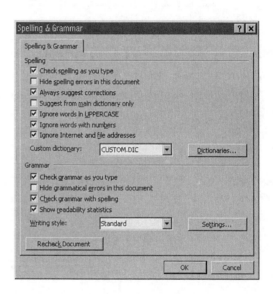

In the spelling section of the options dialog, you can set the following options:

- ☐ Check spelling as you type (Word automatically checks your spelling as you write your document)
- ☐ Hide spelling errors in document (this is so you don't see the red squiggly underline on misspelled words; you must run the spelling and grammar checker to find out about any errors)
- ☐ Always suggest corrections (Word finds correct spellings for you)
- ☐ Suggest from main dictionary only (this is useful if you want Word to point out every error without the help of a supplemental custom dictionary)
- ☐ Ignore words in UPPER CASE (this is useful in the case of proper names that you may want to type in uppercase; otherwise, Word will point them out as errors)

21

- ☐ Ignore words with numbers (such as ignoring F114 and similar words with numbers)

- ☐ Ignore Internet and file addresses (this is to ignore Internet addresses such as `http://www.address.com` and filenames such as `C:\MY DOCUMENT\FILENAME.EXT`)

I suggest you select the Check spelling as you type and the Always suggest corrections options, as well as the three ignore options. You can also specify the name of a custom dictionary that will be used in addition to the main dictionary included with Word 97. The default is `CUSTOM.DIC`, to which you can add your own words.

In the grammar section of the options dialog, you can set the following options:

- ☐ Check grammar as you type (Word automatically checks your grammar as you type)

- ☐ Hide grammatical errors in this document (this hides all grammatical errors; you must run the spelling and grammar checker to find the errors)

- ☐ Check grammar with spelling (if you do not check this, only spelling errors will be looked for)

- ☐ Show readability statistics (this shows you how readable your document is after you have completed a spell and grammar check)

I suggest you select the Check grammar as you type and the Check grammar with spelling options. If you are writing for a particular audience or readership, consider selecting the Show readability statistics option. This prompts a Readability Statistics dialog box to pop up on the screen after the spelling and grammar check is complete. The readability statistics include

- ☐ The number of words, sentences, and paragraphs in your document

- ☐ The average number of sentences per paragraph and words per sentence

- ☐ Readability statistics, including the percentage of passive sentences, to help you determine how readable your document is

- ☐ What percentage of your document contains passive sentences

You can set the grammar checker to one of several different writing styles:

- ☐ Casual
- ☐ Standard
- ☐ Formal
- ☐ Technical
- ☐ Custom

You can switch between these styles to tell Word how critical the grammar check will be. For instance, if you select the Formal writing style, Word will point out more grammatical errors.

21

If you select the Casual option, Word will let certain errors slide. You can edit the a writing style by clicking the Settings button, but I suggest that you edit only the Custom writing style.

Automatically Check Your Spelling and Grammar as You Write

You may want to configure Word 97 so that it checks your spelling and grammar as you type. This way, Word 97 immediately tells you when you misspell a word or write a grammatically incorrect sentence. If the misspelled word or grammatically incorrect sentence is not changed by AutoCorrect, the word or sentence will be underlined by a wavy line. A red wavy line indicates a spelling error and a green wavy line indicates a grammatical error. Right-click the misspelled word or grammatically incorrect sentence to invoke the shortcut menu. For spelling errors, that shortcut menu shows suggested changes in bold text and offers several options:

- ☐ Ignore all similar errors in the document
- ☐ Add the word to the dictionary
- ☐ AutoCorrect to automatically correct the word with a suggested word
- ☐ Spelling to run Word's spell checker on the word

For grammatical errors, the shortcut menu shows suggested changes in bold text and offers the following options:

- ☐ Ignore the error
- ☐ Run the grammar checker

For spelling errors, you may prefer to right-click misspelled words and then click one of the suggested changes as you write instead of waiting to run the spelling checker later. Likewise, for grammatical errors, you may prefer to right-click the incorrect sentence and simply rewrite it until the wavy line vanishes rather than runn the grammar checker after you finish writing. Or you can ignore the errors and wait until you finish writing, at which time you can run the spelling and grammar checker. If you prefer to make corrections later, you don't have to right-click each error that pops up. (If you like, you can even hide the spelling and grammar errors, as discussed in the "Spelling and Grammar Options" section.)

AutoCorrect

AutoCorrect automatically corrects as you type. The difference between AutoCorrect and automatic spell checking is that AutoCorrect automatically searches for and corrects predefined errors as you type. For instance, commonly misspelled words, such as *the* where the *t* and *h* are transposed, are automatically corrected as you type. You can add misspelled words or grammatically incorrect phrases to the AutoCorrect function of Word 97 by clicking Tools | AutoCorrect. You should get a dialog similar to the one shown in Figure 21.3.

21

Figure 21.3.

You can set Word to automatically correct commonly misspelled words or grammatically incorrect phrases.

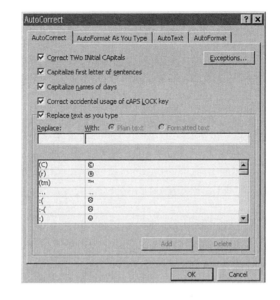

Word has about 500 preset automatic corrections built into its AutoCorrect function. If you often misspell a certain word or use a certain phrase that you know is grammatically incorrect (or that Word tells you is grammatically incorrect), add it to AutoCorrect like so:

1. Click Tools | AutoCorrect. You will get the AutoCorrect dialog box.
2. Click the AutoCorrect dialog tab if it is not the first tab showing on the dialog box.
3. Type the incorrect word or phrase in the Replace field.
4. Type the correct word or phrase in the With field.
5. Click the Add button at the bottom of the AutoCorrect dialog (if the incorrect word or phrase is already in the AutoCorrect list of automatic corrections, the Add button will become a Replace button).
6. Click OK to return to your document.

You can change or delete automatic corrections that are already in AutoCorrect. If there is an automatic correction you want to change or remove, find it in the AutoCorrect dialog and delete it by clicking the delete button on the dialog or change it to suit your needs. One automatic correction you may want to remove or edit is the one for the copyright symbol. If you type (c), Word automatically changes it to a copyright symbol (©). This is a default automatic correction in Word 97. You can avoid the automatic correction by typing an uppercase C, or by inserting the lowercase c between the parentheses (type (), then insert the lowercase c). You can edit this automatic correction by doing the following:

21

1. Click Tools | AutoCorrect.

2. Click the AutoCorrect tab if it is not activated.

3. Scroll through the list of automatically corrected words or phrases. Select the correction you want to edit (in this case, (c)); it should appear in the Replace and With fields.

4. In the Replace field, change the lowercase c to an uppercase C, and then click the Replace button.

5. You will get a dialog box telling you that the AutoCorrect entry already exists and asking whether you want to redefine it. Click the Yes button.

6. Click the OK button to return to your document.

You can also make AutoCorrect ignore errors by specifying AutoCorrect exceptions:

1. Select Tools | AutoCorrect. If necessary, click the AutoCorrect tab to activate it.

2. Click the Exceptions button.

3. In the AutoCorrect Exceptions dialog that appears, you will see two tabs: First Letter and Initial Caps.

   Normally, Word capitalizes the first word that is typed after a period, but what if you want to type an abbreviation in the middle of a sentence? The First Letter tab contains a list of abbreviations for which Word is told not to capitalize the first word after the abbreviation. For instance, say you want to type John Doe lives at 123 Main St. in Springfield. If the abbreviation St. is not in the exception list on the First Letter tab, the first letter of the word after St. in the sample sentence will be capitalized (John Doe lives at 123 Main St. In Springfield).

   The Initial Caps tab contains a list of words wherein the first two letters of each word are capitalized. Although there may be few words whose first two letters are capitalized, this list is useful in other instances. For example, some businesses use a naming convention in correspondence and other types of documents that turns a first name and a last name into a single word (for instance, John Doe becomes JDoe). If your office uses this naming convention, you would enter those words/names as exceptions on the Initial Caps tab. (There is also a three-initial–caps naming convention that will not cause errors in Word.)

4. Click the First Letter tab.

5. In the Don't capitalize after field, type def. (an abbreviation for the word *defendant*).

6. Click the Add button.

7. Click the Initial Caps tab.

21

8. In the Don't correct field, type the first letter of your first name followed immediately by your last name (do not separate them with a space). Be sure that the first two letters of the resulting word are uppercase.

9. Click the Add button.

10. Click OK to return to the AutoCorrect dialog box.

11. Click OK to return to your document.

Type def. in a sentence. The first letter of the word that you type after def. will remain lowercase (if you typed it in lowercase). Then type your name using the two-initial–caps naming convention (as in JDoe). Word will not change the second letter to lowercase.

Using the Word 97 Thesaurus

Think of how many times you've written a word that's close, but isn't quite right for the sentence. (The night was *hot*. No, wait: *humid. Muggy? Sultry.* The night was *sultry.*) You can save yourself a lot of trouble by using the thesaurus that is built into Word 97. To use the thesaurus, do the following:

1. Place your cursor on the word you want to change.

2. Select Tools | Language | Thesaurus or press Shift+F7 (be sure to press the Shift key or you will run the spelling and grammar checker). A Thesaurus dialog box similar to the one shown in Figure 21.4 will pop up; this dialog provides synonyms and related words that you can use to replace the unsatisfactory word in your document.

Figure 21.4.

Word's thesaurus will let you choose synonyms and related words to use in your document.

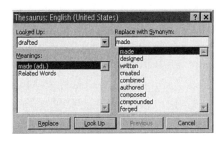

21

Consulting Microsoft Bookshelf

The professional version of Office 97 is packaged with Bookshelf Basics, which is a subset of the full version of Bookshelf. Bookshelf Basics consists of the American Heritage Dictionary, the Original Roget's Thesaurus, and the Columbia Dictionary of Quotations. The full version of Bookshelf offers these reference books as well as the Concise Columbia Encyclopedia, the Concise Encarta World Atlas, the People's Chronology, the World Almanac and Book of Facts, the Bookshelf Internet Directory, and the National Five-Digit Zip Code and Post Office Directory. The Bookshelf Basics version has preview versions of the additional references that come with the full version of Bookshelf. This book limits its discussion to the American Heritage Dictionary, the Original Roget's Thesaurus, and the Columbia Dictionary of Quotations.

If you have the professional edition of Office 97, you must install Office 97 as either a typical or custom installation. If you run Office 97 from the CD-ROM drive, you will not be able to run Bookshelf from the Word menu bar. You can run Bookshelf separately from the Windows Start button by selecting Start | Programs | Microsoft Reference | Microsoft Bookshelf Basics. If you are using the full version of Bookshelf and it does not integrate itself into Word 97 (for example, if you are running Office 97 from one CD-ROM drive and Bookshelf from another CD-ROM drive), you can launch Bookshelf separately from the Windows Start button by clicking the Windows Start button and then selecting Programs | Microsoft Reference | Microsoft Bookshelf 1996–1997.

Using Bookshelf with Word

After Bookshelf is installed, and assuming it is integrated into your Word Tools menu, start Bookshelf (while inside Word) by performing the following steps:

1. Be sure your Office 97 professional edition or Bookshelf CD-ROM is inserted into your CD-ROM drive.

2. Select Tools | Look Up Reference. This invokes the Lookup Reference dialog box.

3. Click Microsoft Bookshelf 1996–97 Edition or Microsoft Bookshelf Basics.

4. Type a word you want to search for in the Search Text field on the Lookup Reference dialog.

5. Click OK.

21

You may find yourself using Bookshelf to look up definitions of words. To do so, right-click a word in Word 97, click Define on the shortcut menu, and Bookshelf will provide the definition of the word according to the American Heritage Dictionary.

You will have to go separately into the Original Roget's Thesaurus and the Columbia Dictionary of Quotations, as well as the other references in the full version of Bookshelf, and use the Copy and Paste functions to use the information from those references in your Word documents. This is discussed in the next section, "Copying/Pasting from Bookshelf to Word."

JUST A MINUTE

All the references in Bookshelf use the same interface. For instance, the Contents tab lets you see what is in the reference by alphabetical order; the Find tab lets you quickly see whether your word or topic is covered in the reference (Figure 21.5 shows the Find tab in the thesaurus); the Gallery tab helps you search for articles that contain audio, animation, video, and images.

Figure 21.5.

By using the Find tab on the Bookshelf's thesaurus, you can find words similar to the word you want to use in your Word document.

Copying/Pasting from Bookshelf to Word

You already know how to copy and paste between documents in Word or from one section of a document to another; copying and pasting between Bookshelf and Word is no different.

21

Say you're in the Columbia Dictionary of Quotations and you find a good one that you want to put in a Word document. If Bookshelf is integrated into your Word menu, do the following:

1. Be sure your Office 97 professional edition or Bookshelf CD-ROM is inserted into your CD-ROM drive.
2. Select Tools | Look Up Reference. This invokes the Lookup Reference dialog box.
3. Select the text in Bookshelf that you want to copy.
4. Right-click the selected text.
5. Click the Copy to option.
6. Select Word.
7. You will automatically be switched over to Word, where you will see a Copy to Word dialog box. Select New Document, Current Document, or End (of an open document that may be listed).
8. Click OK.

The text you selected and copied from Bookshelf will be pasted into your Word document. You may want to change the font of the pasted text to match the rest of your document by selecting that text in the Word document and selecting a new font from the Formatting toolbar. Notice the superscript number at the end of the text that you pasted into your document. This is a footnote. If you move your cursor above the footnote number, a flag and then a screen tip will pop up to tell you where the text came from. You can edit the footnote by selecting View | Footnotes. This invokes a footnote editing pane area at the bottom of the screen, where you can edit the footnote. Click the Close button on the footnotes divider bar when you finish editing the footnote. See Chapter 20, "I Could Write a Book," for more information about footnotes and endnotes.

If Bookshelf is not integrated into Word, do the following to copy and paste text from Bookshelf:

1. Make sure your Office 97 professional version or Bookshelf CD-ROM is in your CD-ROM drive.
2. Go to the Columbia Dictionary of Quotations by selecting Books | Quotations from the Bookshelf menu bar.
3. Find an article from which you want to copy. Copy whole articles by selecting Edit | Copy from within Bookshelf, or copy only the text you want by selecting it and then choosing Edit | Copy.
4. In Word, place your cursor in the spot in your document where you want the copied text to be placed.
5. Paste the text into your document by selecting Edit | Paste from the menu bar, or by right-clicking and then choosing Paste from the shortcut menu.

21

This method of copying and pasting from Bookshelf to Word is just like what you would do between other Windows programs. Unlike the first method, this method does not automatically create a footnote.

Summary

This chapter instructed you about how to use Word 97's editing tools. These tools include the Undo/Redo functions, the spelling and grammar checker, the AutoCorrect function, the thesaurus, and the Bookshelf references. The Undo/Redo functions are for undoing what you've written and redoing what you've undone. You can use the Undo function as a simple undelete function, but you can use the full power of the Undo/Redo functions to retrace the history of your document. The spelling and grammar checker, the AutoCorrect function, and the thesaurus are very easy to use. If you set the spelling and grammar checker to automatically check your spelling and your grammar, you will find yourself correcting your writing as you work on your document. And if you want more capabilities than are provided in Word's built-in editing, spelling, and grammar functions, you can go into Bookshelf to look at more references. It's all at your fingertips.

Q&A

Q The Undo and Redo commands in the Edit menu sometimes say Undo Clear or Redo Clear, sometimes Undo Typing and Redo Typing, and sometimes other things. Why?

A It depends on what activity you undid. For instance, if you were typing, the Edit menu will say Undo Typing and Redo Typing. If you were pasting, it will say Undo Paste and Redo Paste.

Q When I type a sentence that I know is grammatically correct, Word 97 says it's grammatically incorrect. What can I do to fix it?

A You can try changing the writing style or set up a Custom writing style to reflect your writing style. Or you can simply turn off the grammar checker by unclicking all the boxes for it in the Spelling & Grammar dialog box.

21

Hour **22**

The Insert Menu— Adding Elements to Documents

by Ruel T. Hernandez

This chapter will show you how to add or insert several different things into your documents, including the date and time, symbols, fields, files, objects, reviewer's comments, and bookmarks. You learned about inserting graphics (clip art, WordArt, charts and graphs, and other pictures) in Hour 17, "Working with Graphics," and covered inserting tables of contents, indexes, footnotes, and captions in Hour 20, "I Could Write a Book." So you already have some experience in inserting various things into Word documents. In this hour, you will start by examining the simplest items you can insert into a Word document and progress to the more complex items (not necessarily meaning they will be more difficult). You will learn how to insert the following into your documents:

- ☐ Date and time
- ☐ Symbols
- ☐ Fields
- ☐ Files
- ☐ Objects
- ☐ Reviewer's comments

Date and Time

Inserting the date and time into your document is easy. To do so, follow these simple steps:

1. Place your cursor where you want to insert the date or time.
2. Click Insert|Date and Time. You will see a Date and Time dialog similar to the one shown in Figure 22.1.

Figure 22.1.

You can select different formats to use to insert the date and time into your document.

3. From the Date and Time dialog box, click one of the available formats for date and/or time.
4. Click the Update automatically checkbox at the bottom of the Date and Time dialog box.
5. Click OK.

Some of the different date formats include

- ☐ 12/31/97
- ☐ Wednesday, December 31, 1997
- ☐ December 31, 1997
- ☐ 12/31/1997
- ☐ 1997-12-31

22

22

Some of the different date and time formats include

- ☐ 12/31/97 12:12 PM
- ☐ 12/31/97 12:12:12 PM
- ☐ 12:12 PM
- ☐ 12:12:12 PM
- ☐ 20:20
- ☐ 20:20:20

If you click the Automatically update box on the Date and Time dialog, the date and/or time format that you select will be automatically printed with the current date and/or time. This is useful if you are printing form letters or similar documents and you do not want to change the date each time you print the letter or document. Some examples of documents in which you may want to insert the date and the time are memos and fax cover sheets. An example of a document in which you would only insert the date might be a letter.

JUST A MINUTE

Make sure that the internal clock on your computer is set correctly. Otherwise, the wrong date and time will be inserted into your document. In Windows 95 or Windows NT 4.0, right-click the time display on your Windows taskbar and click Adjust Date/Time. This invokes the Date/Time Properties dialog panel, where you can adjust the date and the time. Click OK when you are finished.

Symbols

You can insert a whole slew of typographical symbols into your document. These include mathematical, Greek, Hebrew, Japanese, and Wingdings symbols. The number of symbols available to you depends on what fonts are installed on your computer. If you have many fonts installed on your computer, you will have many symbols from which to choose. It is quite easy to insert a symbol. For example, to insert a paragraph symbol, perform the following steps:

1. Select Insert | Symbols. You should see a dialog similar to the one shown in Figure 22.2 (you may have to click the Symbols tab).
2. Click the Font drop-down list and select the normal text option.
3. Click the Subset drop-down list and pick Latin-1.
4. Find and click the paragraph symbol (¶). If you are having trouble seeing the symbols, click the symbol you want to use to view a magnified version of the symbol contained in that cell.

Figure 22.2.

You can insert different typographical symbols into your Word 97 document.

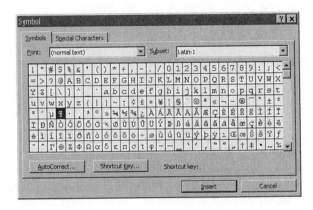

5. Click the Insert button.

6. Click Close to return to your document.

Fields

Fields are like placeholders indicating where data is to be placed in a document. This is useful if you are making form letters or address labels, as well as when you mail merge documents (mail merging is covered in Hour 15, "Mail Merge"). Some examples of fields that you might use include author name and filename. If you want your document's filename to be printed on the document, insert a filename field.

Inserting Fields

To insert a field, do the following:

1. Select Insert | Field.

2. Click a category and then a field name.

For instance, if you want use fields to insert the current date and time, do the following:

1. Click Insert | Field.

2. Select Date and Time from the Categories list.

3. Select a category, such as PrintDate, from the Field names list. Many of the categories are self-explanatory. In this case, the PrintDate field inserts a field for the date when the file was last printed.

4. Click OK.

The field will show up as text within a gray block. You may have to click the field to see the gray shading.

If you want to insert the filename of the document as mentioned previously, this is what you do:

1. Select Insert | Field.
2. Select Document Information from the Categories list.
3. Select FileName from the Field names list.
4. Click OK.

Updating Fields

If you insert a field where the information may change, as would be the case for a field for the time or file size, you can update that information by clicking the field and then pressing the F9 key. Automatically update all fields at once when you are going to print by doing the following:

1. Select Tools | Options from the menu bar.
2. Click the Print tab.
3. Click the Update fields checkbox.
4. Click OK.

Files

Inserting a file into your document is useful if you want to insert the whole file and not just a portion. This is useful if you are working with a report containing multiple documents written by different people (you may be a manager of an office or a unit and need to gather monthly reports into one single document). You would use Insert Files to insert the separate documents (the monthly reports) into one single document.

But if you only want to insert a portion of the file, this is what you do:

1. Open the file from which you want to get text as a separate document.
2. Select the portion of text from the document you wish to insert.
3. Select Edit | Copy.
4. Return to your original document.
5. Select Edit | Copy to paste the copied portion into your original document.

If you know you want to insert an entire separate file into your document, this is what you do:

1. Place your cursor at the point where you want to insert the separate file (this is the insertion point).
2. Select Insert | File.

3. Click the file you want to insert.

4. Click OK.

Objects

An *object* can be just about anything other than a Word document. An object is information created in another software program that you might want to insert into your Word document. For instance, you can insert, or *embed*, an Excel worksheet or chart as an object into your Word document (more on inserting and embedding in Hour 23, "Teaming Up Word with Other Office Applications").

You've already dealt with objects in the form of graphics and pictures that are inserted into documents. Think of inserting objects as similar, except you perform the insertion through the Object dialog box (shown in Figure 22.3) instead of through the Clip Gallery. (You can insert clip art using both the Clip Gallery and the Object dialog box.)

Why insert an object at all? Well, you can add clip art or pictures to help illustrate the point being made in your document. You can add an Excel worksheet or chart to provide numerical information to supplement the information in the text of your document.

Figure 22.3.

You can insert objects into your document using the Object dialog box.

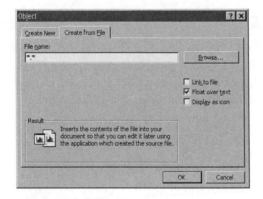

Inserting an Existing Object File

To insert an object, follow these steps:

1. Select Insert | Objects.

2. Click the Create from File tab.

3. Click the Browse button, find and click the file you want to use, and then click OK. If you know the name of the file and the directory the file is in, type it in the File name input field (you'll have to delete or overwrite the *.* wildcard). You might type something like C:\MY DOCUMENTS\FILENAME.OBJ.

22

When you find it, click the file and then click OK. The name of the file with the directory will appear in the File name input field in the Object dialog.

4. Click OK, and the object will appear in your document.

CAUTION

When you insert an object, you insert into your document the entire file in which that object resides. So if you are inserting an Excel worksheet, you may wish to insert only a portion of that worksheet instead of the whole file. In this case, perform a copy-and-paste operation from the Excel worksheet to your Word document.

When you insert an object, you have three options that you can use individually or in combination with each other:

☐ Link to a file—Choose this, and you create a link to the existing object file. If you make any changes to the original object file, the changes will be reflected in your Word document. However, you will not able to make any changes to the linked object while you are in Word. You are only linked to that object; you must go to the software program in which that object was created to make any changes in the object.

☐ Float over text—Choose this, and the object will actually be in your document.

☐ Display as an icon—If you choose this, the object will only appear in Word as an icon. Displaying an object as an icon can save time in loading a text object or a graphic/picture object. Instead of text objects or graphic/picture objects, icons show up on your computer screen.

Creating a New Object

To create a new object, click the Create New tab (see Figure 22.4) on the Object dialog. You must be familiar with the software program that you want to use to create the object. For example, if you wish to create a new Photoshop object, you should have Photoshop installed on your computer and you should know how to use it.

Say you want to create a bitmap image (a BMP file). To do so, follow these steps:

1. Select Insert | Object from the menu.
2. Click the Create New tab.
3. Select Bitmap Image.
4. Pick Float over text or Display as an icon.
5. Click OK.

6. Word will display a Windows Paint program interface from which you can construct a bitmap image to be inserted into your document.

7. To get back to your document and return to the regular Word interface screen, click outside of the object's boxed area. To get back into the object, just double-click it and you'll return to the Windows Paint program.

Figure 22.4.

You can create a new object to insert in a Word document.

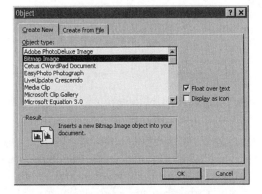

Figure 22.5 shows what the Word interface looks like when you create a bitmap image object.

Figure 22.5.

Word changes its interface to allow you to create objects.

Word's interface changes according to what type of object you wish to create. Unless you know what you're doing, you may want to insert existing objects instead of creating new ones.

22

Reviewer's Comments

Many people insert reviewer's comments into a document to provide suggestions and criticisms they may have regarding the document. For instance, say you're required to review someone else's document before it is sent out. Word 97 allows you to insert your comments into the document; those comments are read onscreen.

Insert comments into a document that you are reviewing by doing the following:

1. Select Insert | Comments.
2. Type your comments in the Comments pane that appears at the bottom of the screen (see Figure 22.6).
3. Click the Close button on the Comments pane divider bar.

If you receive a document that contains comments, you can read them by selecting View | Comments. The Comments pane will appear at the bottom of the screen for you to read. You can see the reviewer's initials, as shown in Figure 22.6, to determine who wrote the comments.

Figure 22.6.

Type your comments in the Comments pane.

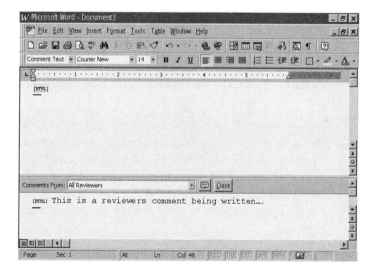

Voice Comments

It's possible to insert voice comments, but doing so requires the use of a microphone and sound card. If you have such equipment and wish to insert voice comments, and if the person who wants to listen to the comments also has the right equipment, follow these steps:

1. Select Insert | Comments.
2. Click the Insert Sound Object button (the one that looks like a cassette tape).

3. The Windows Sound Recorder pops up on the screen. Click the Record button (the one with the red dot), and then speak into the microphone.

4. When you finish speaking, click the Stop button (the button to the right of the Record button).

   You can play what you recorded by clicking the Play button (the middle button with the triangle pointing to the right).

5. When you finish recording, exit the Sound Recorder. You should see a Speaker icon in the Comments pane in Word.

6. To listen to the comments, double-click the speaker icon.

Viewing Comments

To view comments, select View | Comments. The Comments pane will appear at the bottom of the screen; here, you can read the comments. You should also see the insertion codes for the comments in the main text of your document.

If there is more than one reviewer, and if you want to see only one reviewer's comments, click the pull-down menu on the Comments pane divider with the names of all the reviewers, and then click the name of the reviewer whose comments you want to read.

You may be able to see text that is highlighted or blocked in yellow or another color. Move your mouse cursor above the text in that area. If the Comments pane is at the bottom of the screen, a little flag will pop up, and when the mouse is moved over the highlighted text, you should see a screen tip with the reviewer's name along with his or her comments.

You can also right-click the highlighted area to get a menu that will let you edit the comment. If you do not have the Comments pane at the bottom of the screen, you may have to right-click several times to get the correct menu. To make it easier for you to find and read the comments, you should have the Comments pane turned on.

Protecting Comments

Protect your comments to make sure no one deletes or edits them. To do so, follow these steps:

1. Select Tools | Protect Document.

2. Select Comments.

3. To make sure the protection is not turned off, type a password (you'll have to type it again to confirm it).

   When you select a password, pick one that only you will know. Also, you should pick a password that you will remember.

4. Click OK.

22

Printing Comments

Normally, you see the comments onscreen, not on the printed page. But if you want to print the document with comments, this is what you do:

1. Select Tools | Options.
2. Click the Print tab.
3. In the Include with document section, click disable the Comments checkbox.
4. Click OK.

The comments will automatically be printed with your document. If you decide later that you no longer want the comments to be printed, simply enable the Comments checkbox.

To print only the comments (not the document with the comments), do the following:

1. Select File | Print.
2. Toward the bottom of the Print dialog, click the Print What pull-down menu and select Comments.
3. Click OK to begin printing.

Bookmarks

Bookmarks let you quickly jump from place to place in the document. Instead of paging up or down through your document, you can simply jump to a bookmark. Think of bookmarks as reference points in your document. For a bound book, you would place a bookmark, such as a piece of paper, in the book to mark where you read an important or significant passage. You can do the same in Word by leaving an electronic bookmark in your document to mark an important or significant place in the document.

Adding a Bookmark

Inserting a bookmark is simple. This is what you do:

1. Click the point in your document at which you want to place the bookmark, or select a portion of text that you want to bookmark.
2. Select Insert | Bookmark. You may have to scroll down the Insert menu to get to Bookmark. You will then get the Bookmark dialog box.
3. Type a name in the Bookmark name area of the dialog box.
4. Click the Add button.

Repeat this for all bookmarks you want to place in your document.

Changing a Bookmark's Location

You can change the location of a bookmark that has already been inserted in your document. You might want to do this if you think a bookmark name is more appropriate for a different part of the document than where it was originally inserted. To change a bookmark's location, do the following:

1. Click the point or select a portion of text in your document where you want to place the bookmark.
2. Select Insert | Bookmark.
3. In the middle section of the Bookmark dialog, select the name of the bookmark whose location you want to change.
4. Click the Add button.

Deleting a Bookmark

If you have no use for a bookmark that you have inserted, you can delete it like so:

1. Select Insert | Bookmark.
2. Select the bookmark you want to delete.
3. Click the Delete button.

Finding a Bookmark

You can find a bookmark that has already been inserted in one of two ways: by using the Bookmark or the Find dialog box. To use the Bookmark dialog box to find a bookmark, do the following:

1. Select Insert | Bookmark.
2. Click Sort by Name to see an alphabetical listing of your bookmarks or click Sort by Location to see the bookmarks in the order they appear in your document.
3. Select the bookmark you want to go to in the bookmark list in the middle of the Bookmark dialog box.
4. Click the Go To button.

To use the Find dialog box to go to a bookmark in your document, do the following:

1. Select Edit | Find, click the Find button on the Standard toolbar, or press Ctrl+F. This invokes the Find dialog box.
2. Click the Go To tab on the Find dialog box.
3. Click Bookmark on the Go to what list.
4. Pull down the Enter bookmark name list or type the name of the bookmark to which you want to jump.
5. Click the Go To button.

22

Summary

In this chapter, you learned about inserting dates, symbols, fields, objects, and comments into your Word documents. These are really easy to insert; the only tricky aspect is inserting objects. I recommend that you insert existing objects instead of creating new ones unless you know what you are doing. If you only want to insert clip art and pictures, you'll most likely find the Clip Gallery easier to use.

Q&A

Q Sometimes when I'm typing a word that happens to be the name of a month, such as *May*, a little box pops up with today's date. Why?

A That is an automatic date insertion function of Word 97. Whenever you see that, just press Enter to insert today's date. That way, you don't have to type it all yourself. If you do not wish for the date to appear in your document, simply continue typing. For more information about AutoText, see Hour 16, "Automating Tasks."

Q I tried to insert a voice comment in a document that I was reviewing, but it wouldn't work. I can play sound files on my computer, so why can't I record a voice comment?

A Speak into your microphone. Be sure that the microphone is turned on and is plugged into your computer. If these suggestions yield no results, you may have a hardware problem. Consult the manual for your computer or for your sound card.

Q When I insert an object such as a picture into my document, it takes very long for the picture to show up on my computer. How can I avoid waiting so long?

A You may want to insert pictures or other objects as icons in your document to avoid waiting so long.

Q I tried to create an object in my Word document, but my computer crashed on me. Why?

A Word accepts OLE, a program integration technology standard. If the object you are trying to create is not OLE, you may not be able to create that type of object (hence, the crash). You may want to insert an existing object file instead, or create the object outside of Word 97 using whatever programs you may have.

Hour 23

Teaming Up Word with Other Office Applications

By Ruel T. Hernandez

This hour shows you how to do some of the typical things you might do in an office setting. These include binding several documents together, placing spreadsheets and graphical charts in documents, setting up mailing lists of people to whom you want to send documents, and setting up office forms for people in the office to use. Luckily, Word 97 is offered as part of the Microsoft 97 package of programs that includes Word, Excel, Access, Binder, and others. In this hour, you will be introduced to some of these programs. The highlights of this hour include

- ☐ Using Word with Binder to bind documents together
- ☐ Using Word with Excel worksheets and charts
- ☐ Using Word with an Access mailing list database
- ☐ Using Word to create office forms

Using Binder to Organize Projects

Binder lets you set up an electronic computer "binder" to organize related files as separate sections of the binder. For instance, if you have several Word documents on a related topic or for a single report, you can assemble those files as separate sections into a binder using the Microsoft Office Binder program.

As with a regular binder, you can assemble an electronic binder into separate sections. You can start with a blank binder and add files, or you can use the templates that are available with Microsoft Office Binder. In this hour, you are going to place Word documents into a binder. This is what you have to do:

1. Run the Binder program by clicking the Windows Start button, selecting Programs, and then selecting Microsoft Binder.

2. From Binder's menu bar, select Section | Add from File. Binder opens the Add from File dialog (see Figure 23.1), from which you can select files to put in your binder. The dialog opens up to the C:\MY DOCUMENTS directory, which is the default documents directory for all Microsoft Office programs. If you changed your default directory, or if your files are not located in the C:\MY DOCUMENTS directory, you will have to go to the directory where your files are located.

Figure 23.1.

You can add your Word document files to an electronic binder.

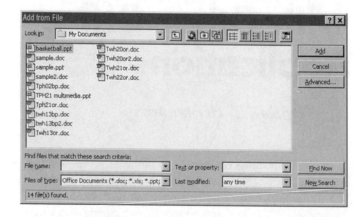

3. Click the Word document files you want to add to your binder, and then click the Add button. You can simultaneously add several files to your binder. Do so by holding down the Ctrl key and clicking each file you want to add as sections to your binder. After you have clicked the Add button, you should see the Microsoft Office Binder program load up the files as shown in Figure 23.2.

23

Figure 23.2.

Binder can load your Word document files as separate sections for a binder.

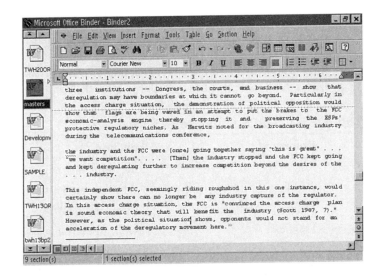

As you can see, the Binder program changes its screen to resemble the Word program's, but subtle differences between the two indicate that you are still in the Binder program. For example, the column to the left shows the separate sections of the binder. You can scroll through that column to see the binder sections. On that column, you will also see arrow buttons at the top and the bottom that you can click. If you click the arrow buttons with the lines, you will either go to the very first or the very last sections of the binder (depending on which button you click). You should also notice a few other differences. For example, the menu bar contains two pull-down menus: Go and Section (I'll discuss these in a moment). You will also notice that if you click File, the File commands refer to binders and not documents.

You can work on a binder section as you would a Word document. The difference is that you are working on a binder section that is a part of a binder. When you save any work you do on a binder section, the whole binder will be saved as an OBD binder file, which will include all of the sections of the binder.

When you save and then close your binder, the Binder program keeps your place. When you open the binder later, the Binder program returns you to the place you were in the binder when it was last saved. This is handy because a binder can become large and may have numerous sections (if you were working on separate Word documents that were not placed in a binder, you would have to wade through each document to find out where you left off).

If you click Go on the menu bar, you will see various commands for opening files or for accessing documents on the World Wide Web. By using a command under the Go selection, you can load the actual program that would normally be associated with the file you are loading. So if you load a Word document, you will actually go to the Word program to edit a document instead of integrating the document as a section into a binder. The Section pull-down menu contains several commands that are useful for working with the different sections of a binder. The commands that appear under the Section selection are listed in Table 23.1.

Table 23.1. The Section selection.

Command	Function
Add	Add a binder (using predefined binder templates)
Add from File	Add to the binder from existing file(s)
Delete	Delete section(s)
Duplicate	Duplicate section(s)
Rename	Rename a section
Rearrange	Rearrange a section (move section to another place in a binder)
Next Section	Go to the next section
Previous Section	Go to the previous section
Hide	Hide a section
Unhide Section	Unhide a section
Page Setup	Set up page formatting
Print Preview	Preview what a print job will look like
Print	Print your binder
Save as File	Save a section to a file
View Outside	View a section using outside program
Section Properties	Provide a summary of the binder
Select/Unselect All	Select or unselect all sections (for duplicating, deleting, and so on)

Binder offers predefined templates with predefined sections that you can use. You might want to explore the different binder templates by selecting Section | Add. If you choose to use the existing templates, you will see a dialog similar to the one shown in Figure 23.3. From this dialog, you can select the template you wish to use.

23

Figure 23.3.

Binder has a multitude of predefined templates that you can use if you do not want to construct a binder from scratch.

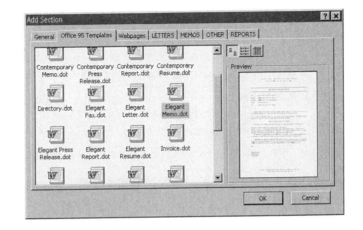

The Duplicate and Rearrange commands will help you copy or move sections around in your binder. Selecting Duplicate or Rearrange invokes the Duplicate Section or Rearrange Sections dialog box, respectively. Figure 23.4 shows these dialog boxes.

Figure 23.4.

You can duplicate and rearrange sections in your binder.

Especially with the predefined templates, you will find that binders are easy to make using your pre-existing Word documents (which you would add to a binder using the Add from File command).

Adding Excel Worksheets and Charts to Word Documents

You can embed (*insert*) a new worksheet, or you can link (*import*) an existing Excel worksheet (also known as a *spreadsheet*) into your Word document. When you embed a new worksheet, you can work with it as you would any Excel worksheet. However, if you link the worksheet, you cannot change the formulas or otherwise manipulate the worksheet.

Embedding a New Excel Worksheet

You can embed a worksheet by using the Insert Object command (this process is similar to what was discussed in Hour 22, "The Insert Menu—Adding Elements to Documents"). To embed a worksheet using the Insert Object command, do the following:

1. Click your cursor in your document where you want to embed the Excel worksheet. You might want to press the Enter key a few times to provide some blank lines between your text and the worksheet.

2. Select Insert | Object to invoke the Object dialog (shown in Figure 23.5).

Figure 23.5.

You can embed an Excel worksheet as an object into your Word document.

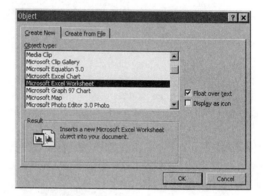

3. In the Create New tab on the Object dialog, click Microsoft Excel Worksheet.

4. Check the Float over text checkbox and click OK.

You can also click the Insert Excel Worksheet button on the Standard toolbar to embed a worksheet:

1. Click the Insert Excel Worksheet button on the Standard toolbar. You will see a 5×4 grid checkerboard.

2. Move your cursor diagonally along the checkerboard, then click when you have selected the number of rows and columns you want for the worksheet.

An Excel worksheet similar to the one shown in Figure 23.6 will be embedded into your Word document.

Double-click inside the worksheet; you will be able use it as you would any Excel worksheet. Click outside the worksheet to work on the surrounding Word document. If you click one time inside the worksheet, you can move the worksheet around your document as you would a picture or graphic object. Manipulate the size of the worksheet by moving the sides as you would with a picture or graphic object.

23

Figure 23.6.

The Excel worksheet will appear inside your Word document.

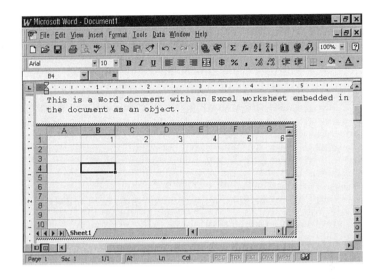

If you check the Display as icon checkbox in the Create New tab of the Object dialog when you embed a worksheet (refer to Figure 23.5), you will embed an Excel worksheet as an icon in your Word document. Double-click that icon to activate Excel so you can work with the worksheet, as shown in Figure 23.7.

Figure 23.7.

You can embed an Excel worksheet as an icon. Double-click the icon work with the worksheet.

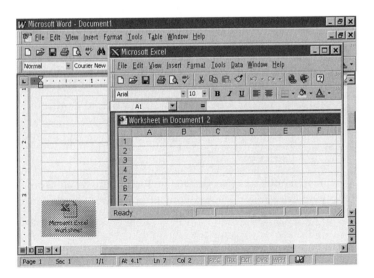

23

Linking an Existing Excel Worksheet

If you have Excel, you can simply copy and paste from Excel to your Word document:

1. Open the worksheet in Excel from which you want to copy.

2. Select the area in your worksheet that you want to copy. To do this, hold your mouse cursor down on the first cell that you want to start copying from and move your cursor to the end of the area. Release your mouse cursor after you have selected the area.

3. Select Edit | Copy.

4. Go to your Word document.

5. Click the point in your document where you want to place the worksheet.

6. Click Edit | Paste.

If you don't have Excel on your machine but want to import an existing Excel worksheet (perhaps one that is on your company's intranet):

1. Click the Open File button on the Standard toolbar or select File | Open.

2. Click the pull-down Files of type menu at the bottom left of the Open dialog and select Microsoft Excel Worksheet.

3. Click the Excel worksheet (XLS or XLW) file that you want to import into your Word document. Then click OK.

4. This invokes the Convert File dialog, shown in Figure 23.8. Make sure Microsoft Excel Worksheet is selected, and then click OK.

5. You should then see the Open Worksheet dialog (see Figure 23.8). Select Entire Workbook from the Open document in Workbook pull-down menu.

6. If you select anything other than Entire Workbook, you can choose a name or cell range if names or cell ranges are available. If available from the Name or Cell Range pull-down menu, specify the number or name of the range you wish to import.

7. Click OK.

You should see a worksheet imported into your Word document. You can move the worksheet around your document as you would any object, but you cannot double-click it to manipulate it as a worksheet.

23

Figure 23.8.

To link a worksheet, you must convert the worksheet, then select either the entire worksheet or a part of the worksheet to be linked.

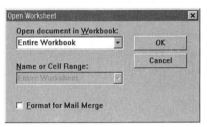

Embedding an Excel Chart

Embedding an Excel chart is very similar to embedding a worksheet. Follow the procedures for inserting an Excel worksheet, but click Microsoft Excel Chart on the Create New tab in the Object dialog (refer to Figure 23.5). You will see a sample chart (similar to the one shown in Figure 23.9) that you can change and manipulate. As you can see, there are Chart and Sheet tabs at the bottom of the worksheet that you can click to switch between the graphical chart and the regular worksheet to change how the chart looks.

Figure 23.9.

When you insert an Excel chart into a Word document, you can manipulate it as you can any Excel worksheet by clicking between the Chart and Sheet tabs at the bottom of the chart.

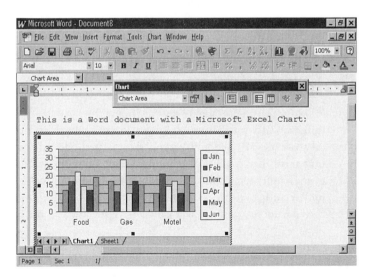

Click between the Chart and Sheet tabs to change the numbers and formulas. Double-click inside the chart to work with the chart, and click outside the chart to work with the surrounding Word document. As with any other object, you can single-click inside the chart to move the chart and change its size.

If you do not have Excel, you can insert a Microsoft Graph 97 chart (see Figure 23.10) by selecting Microsoft Graph 97 Chart from the Object dialog. As with the Excel chart, you get a sample chart with a datasheet that you can manipulate to change the chart (the chart and the datasheet would correspond with the Chart and Sheet tabs for the Excel worksheet).

Figure 23.10.

If you do not have Excel, you can insert a Micro-soft Graph 97 chart.

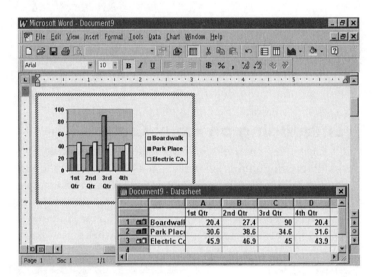

Merging Letters Using an Access Database

Word-processing programs are known for their capability to *mail merge*. In mail merging, information is drawn from a database (in this case, a database made with the Microsoft Access database program) and incorporated into a form document to create multiple copies of the document. Each copy includes information from one record from the database. To perform a mail merge, you would create a database containing records of mailing address information; each record is a collection of fields of specific address data. For instance, a database of all of the addresses of your friends would have specific records for each of your friends. In each

23

record, there would be even more specific fields of data for such items as first name, last name, street address, city, state, zip code, and so on.

Creating a Mailing List Database with Access

If you have Microsoft Access 97 (it is included with the Professional Edition of Microsoft Office 97 or can be purchased separately), you can build a mailing list database with Access. To do so, follow these steps:

1. Run Access 97.

2. Click the New button (or select File | New Database).

3. Select Blank Database and click OK.

4. In the File New Database dialog, give the new database a name with the .mdb extension. Access will provide a default name, such as db1.mdb. After you choose a filename, click the Create button.

5. This brings you to a database dialog that has several tabs (Tables, Queries, Forms, Reports, Macros, and Modules). Click the Tables tab, and then click the New button.

6. In the New Table dialog, you'll see several options (Datasheet View, Design View, Table Wizard, Import Table, and Link Table). Click Table Wizard, and then click OK.

7. In the Table Wizard dialog, select Mailing List from the Sample Tables list.

8. In the Sample Fields list, pick LastName, FirstName, Address, City, State, and PostalCode. Click the > button to select each field. Each field you select appears in the Fields in my new table list.

9. Click the Next button.

10. You will be asked whether Access should automatically pick a primary key for each database record (a record consists of fields). Choose Yes, and then click the Next button.

11. You will be asked how you want to enter your data. Unless you are comfortable with database programs, click the Enter data into the table using a form the wizard creates for me option. You can also click the New Object button (next to the Office Assistant button on the Database toolbar) to get a wizard-created AutoForm, where you can easily input address information.

    Click the Finish button, and you should see a Mailing List dialog similar to the one shown in Figure 23.11.

23

Figure 23.11.

*With Microsoft Access
97, you can easily create
and enter records into a
mailing list database.*

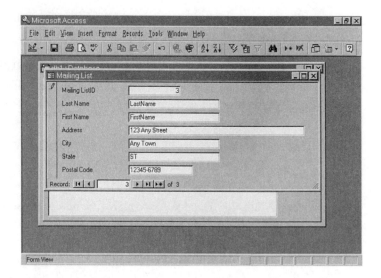

12. Enter address information into the Mailing List dialog. After you finish entering a record, click the button with the right arrow and the asterisk to advance to a blank record so you can enter a new record.

13. Click the exit button on the dialog (the *X* button in the upper-right corner). You will be asked whether you want to save your changes; if you do, click Yes. You will then be asked to provide a name under which the form will be saved. Type a name or use the default name, and then click OK.

Creating Your Mail Merge Document

To create a mail merge document, do the following:

1. Start a new document in Word.

2. Select Tools | Mail Merge.

3. In the Main document section of the Mail Merge Helper dialog (shown in Figure 23.12), click the Create button and select Form Letters.

4. Click Active Window. (If you did not start a new document in Word, click New Main Document.) Click the Edit button that appears next to the Create button, and then click Form Letter.

5. This opens a new document; a Mail Merge toolbar will appear on the screen under the other toolbars.

6. Type the text that you want to merge with your database information. Be sure to leave empty spaces and blank lines between paragraphs where you want the database information to be inserted.

23

Figure 23.12.

Word provides a useful Mail Merge Helper dialog that you can use to merge documents.

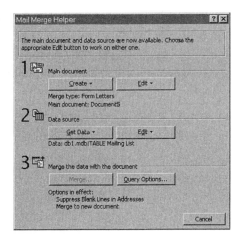

7. Again, select Tools | Mail Merge.

8. In the Data source section of the Mail Merge Helper dialog, click the Get Data button and select Open Data Source (refer to Figure 23.12). This invokes an Open Data Source dialog, which looks very similar to the Open File dialog box.

9. Click the Files of type pull-down menu and select the MS Access Databases option.

10. Go to the directory where you saved your Access mailing list database file. Click that file, and then click the Merge button.

11. You will get a Microsoft Access dialog with two tabs for Tables and Queries. The Tables tab should be active, and should show your mailing list database. If the mailing list is not highlighted, click that and then click the OK button.

12. Because there are no merge fields in your document yet, you will get a dialog box asking you to edit your main document so you can insert merge fields where the database information is to be merged. Click the Edit Main Document button to return to your document. Note that the Insert Merge Field button appears on the Mail Merge toolbar in your document.

13. Click the Insert Merge Field button to pull down the selections for all the fields you can insert into your document. Click the appropriate field to insert them into the appropriate place in your document. For instance, insert the FirstName field after the word *Dear* and before the comma (or before the colon if you use that punctuation in your salutations). Each field will look something like <<Field>>.

14. After you insert all the fields in your document, select Tools | Mail Merge. On the Mail Merger Helper dialog, click the Merge button.

15. This invokes a Merge dialog like the one shown in Figure 23.13. In the Merge to drop-down list, select New document. If you want specific records to be merged, specify the range. If there are blank fields in any of the records in your database, you can specify whether blanks will be printed.

16. Click the Merge button.

Figure 23.13.

You can specify the range of records to be merged into your mail merge document.

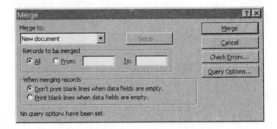

The records in the mailing list database will be merged into the document. For more information about mail merging, review Hour 15, "Mail Merge."

Word's Built-In Data Creator

If you do not have Access, you can still create a mailing list database. From the Mail Merge Helper dialog, click the Get Data button, and then select Create Data. This invokes the Create Data Source dialog, as shown in Figure 23.14.

Figure 23.14.

You can create a data source file with fields for a mailing list in Word 97.

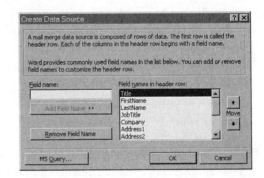

This dialog box contains the basic mailing list fields, some of which you can delete by clicking the Remove Field Name button. Click OK when you are finished; you will then be asked whether you want to edit your data document. Click the Edit Data Source button. In the Data Form dialog, enter the address information (see Figure 23.15).

23

Figure 23.15.

Enter the mailing list address information using the Data Form dialog.

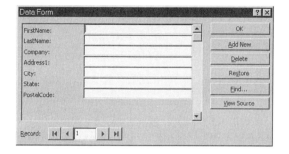

Click the Add New button if you want to add a new record. Click OK when you are finished; you will be asked to make up a name under which to save your mailing list. This mailing list will be saved as a DOC file. Insert the fields into your document and then merge the mailing list data into the document as discussed previously.

Designing Forms

You can design forms for use in your office. There are three types of form fields that you can use:

☐ A *text form field* allows you to insert an input area in your document where you can type text. For instance, you might use a text form field so a user can type name and address information.

☐ A *checkbox form field* allows a user to check a selection. Examples of checkbox form fields are Yes/No boxes that users can check to provide an answer to a question.

☐ A *drop-down* (or *pull-down*) *form field* gives a user a list of selections from which to choose. Drop-down form fields are good for situations where users must answer a multiple-choice question.

Text Form Fields

To insert a text form field into a document, perform the following steps:

1. Create a new document or open an existing one.

2. Click your cursor on the spot in your document where you want to insert a text form.

3. Activate the Forms toolbar (shown in Figure 23.16) by selecting View | Toolbars | Forms.

Figure 23.16.

Use the Forms toolbar to insert text, checkbox, and drop-down form fields into your document.

4. Click the Text Form Field button (the one on the far left). Double-click the gray or black field that appears on your document; this invokes the Text Form Field Options dialog (see Figure 23.17).

Figure 23.17.

You need to set these options when setting up text forms.

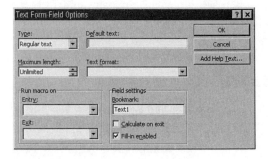

5. The Text Form Field Options dialog contains several options:

☐ Type

    ☐ Regular text

    ☐ Number

    ☐ Date

    ☐ Current date

    ☐ Current time

    ☐ Calculation (for calculating a number from a formula that you would insert)

☐ Maximum length (any number of characters up to unlimited)

☐ Default text (type something or leave this blank)

☐ Text format (uppercase, lowercase, first capital, and title case)

☐ Fill-in enabled (check this box so the user can type something into the text form field, or "fill in the blank")

23

You might want to accept the default options, but you might want to type in some default text. For instance, in a text form field where you expect a first name to be entered, you might simply want to use the words first name as default text. You should also make sure the box for Fill-in enabled is checked. If you do not check this box, the user will not be able to type anything into the text form field (until you protect the form as described in the section titled "Protect Your Forms").

6. Click OK and repeat as necessary.

Checkbox Form Fields

You can use checkbox form fields for simple questions in your documents. This is what you do:

1. Create a new document or open an existing one.
2. Click your cursor on the spot where you want to place the checkbox form field.
3. If the Forms toolbar is not active, select View | Toolbars | Forms.
4. Click the Check Box Form Field button (the box with the check inside it). A gray box should appear in your document.
5. Double click the gray box; this opens the Check Box Form Field Options dialog (see Figure 23.18).

Figure 23.18.

When using checkbox forms, you may only need to select either the Not checked or the Checked radio button.

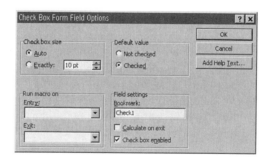

6. Click OK and repeat as necessary.

In a typical Yes/No form, you might type Yes and then No, then insert a checkbox form field after each one. You might want the Yes or No option to be checked automatically as the default answer. Configure this by selecting the Checked on radio button in the Default value section of the Check Box Form Field Options dialog.

Drop-Down Forms

Insert drop-down (or pull-down) form fields into your forms document by following these steps:

1. Create a new document or open an existing one.
2. Click your cursor on the spot in your document where you want to place the drop-down form.
3. Activate the Forms toolbar (if it's not already active).
4. Click the Drop-Down Form Field button (third from the left). A gray field should appear on your document.
5. Double-click the gray field to open the Drop-Down Form Field Options dialog (see Figure 23.19).

Figure 23.19.

From the Drop-Down Form Field Options dialog, you can add items to appear on a drop-down form.

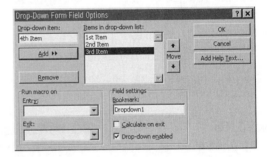

6. In the Drop-down item section, type an item (up to 50 characters) that is to appear in the drop-down form when it is pulled down. Click the Add button. Repeat to add more items.
7. Use the Move arrow keys to move items around. Use the Remove button to remove items.
8. Click OK after you finish adding items. Repeat by adding drop-down forms elsewhere in your document.

Protect Your Forms

When you finish inserting your forms, click the Protect Form button on the Forms toolbar. This will protect your forms from inadvertent changes. If you want more secure protection, add password protection; simply select Tools | Protect Document to invoke the Password dialog box. Type a password that you will remember and click OK; your password will show up as asterisks (*). You will be asked to type in the password again. Do so to confirm the password, and then click OK. To remove the password protection, select Tools | Unprotect Document. Type your password and then click OK.

23

Summary

This hour demonstrates how to use Word with other Microsoft Office programs such as Binder, Excel, and Access. You learned how to make a binder. You learned how to insert Excel worksheets and charts. You also learned how to make a mailing list using Access and Word's built-in data creator, as well as how to merge that mailing list into a document for mass distribution. You learned how to make office forms using text form fields, checkbox form fields, and drop-down form fields. Now you can move on to Hour 24, "Working with the Web," where you will move out of the office and onto the Web.

23

Q&A

Q You didn't go into a lot of specifics of how to use the Excel and Access functions in this hour. Where can I get more information about the specifics of using Excel, Access, and other Office 97 programs?

A You can go to the Help function in Excel and Access for more instruction. You can also use the wizards in those programs for some direction. You can also get copies of *Teach Yourself Microsoft Excel 97 in 24 Hours, Teach Yourself Microsoft Access 97 in 24 Hours,* and *Teach Yourself Microsoft Office 97 in 24 Hours* to learn more about how to use the other Office 97 programs.

Hour 24

Working with the Web

This hour explains how to create Web pages and how to use Word's Web tools. Word 97 includes features that simplify the way that Web pages are created, making it possible for anyone to develop a great-looking Web page.

The hyperlinks tool is not only valuable for creating Web pages, but can also be great for organizing groups of Word documents. Microsoft has given top priority to integrating its products with the Web, and it certainly has come a long way with Word 97's Web capabilities.

The highlights of this hour include

☐ How to use the Web toolbar

☐ How to create hyperlinks and use them effectively

☐ How to turn existing Word documents into Web pages

Connecting to the World

The Internet is a collection of interconnected computer networks that span the globe, allowing a tremendous amount of information to be shared. The World Wide Web (WWW or Web) is a user-friendly system that allows users with Web browser software to find their way through the Internet. Word 97 can open a Web browser program to give you access to information on the Web.

NEW TERM A *Web browser* is a software program that allows you to access the Web. Netscape Navigator and Microsoft Internet Explorer are two popular Web browsers.

You need to have Internet Explorer or another Web browser installed before you can connect to the Web. Word 97 needs to run a Web browser program to open Web pages or to preview your Web page designs.

JUST A MINUTE If you do not have Web access, you can use some of the Web features of Word 97, such as *hyperlinks* in Word documents, but you will not be able to view anything on the Web. If you want to get connected to the Web from home, you will need a modem and an *Internet service provider (ISP)*. Here are a few of the popular ISPs:

☐ AT&T Worldnet (800)967-5363

☐ Microsoft Network (800)386-5550

☐ CompuServe (800)848-8199

☐ America Online (800)827-6364

Most ISPs charge a monthly rate of about $20 for unlimited access, and most have an hourly rate program. You may wish to find a local ISP by looking in your Yellow Pages under Computer Online Services or Internet Service Providers. If you work for an organization that has a computer network, your computer may have Web access through that network.

NEW TERM A *hyperlink* is text or a picture that causes you to jump to another document or Web page when it is clicked. Text that is a hyperlink is underlined and often has a different font color. Pictures that are hyperlinks often have a colored border.

An *Internet service provider (ISP)* is a company that maintains a large computer system to which you can connect. The company has the telephone and computer resources to link to the Web. When you dial in using your modem through your phone line, you can connect to the ISP's computer systems that link to the Web. Most ISPs also have interesting resources that you can use directly from their computers (called *servers*).

Many long distance telephone companies such as AT&T and MCI are starting to offer combinations of telephone and computer services that include access to the Internet. The new trend is moving toward a combination of cable television, telephone service, and Internet access from a single provider over the same lines.

When you subscribe with an ISP, it will supply you with software that needs to be installed on your computer to link to its computers. It will provide the instructions for using the software to connect. Once you have the software installed, you go through a process called *logging in*, where you supply your computer name (or your real name) and a password (of your choosing) each time you connect. This protects you and your ISP from unauthorized use of your account.

Using the Web Toolbar

Clicking the Web toolbar button on the Standard toolbar makes the Web toolbar visible. Many of the capabilities of Microsoft Internet Explorer are included in Word 97 and are represented on the Web toolbar.

The Web toolbar interfaces with the Web browser you have on your computer. For the sake of this discussion, we will assume you are using Internet Explorer. There are similar buttons and functions in other Web browsers, and most are designed in such a way that they are easy to figure out. Figure 24.1 shows Word's Web toolbar.

Figure 24.1.

The Web toolbar.

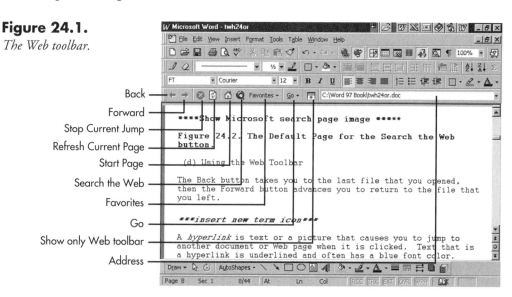

Back
Forward
Stop Current Jump
Refresh Current Page
Start Page
Search the Web
Favorites
Go
Show only Web toolbar
Address

Check Your Connection

Click the Search the Web button on the Web toolbar. Internet Explorer opens with the Microsoft search page as in Figure 24.2 (unless you have changed the default search page). If the search page appeared, you are connected. If you didn't connect and you get an error message, there are a few things you can check:

☐ Are you still connected to your ISP through your phone line? Close Word to see whether you have a Windows message saying you are disconnected. If so, you'll need to log in again to reconnect.

Figure 24.2.

The default page for the Search the Web button.

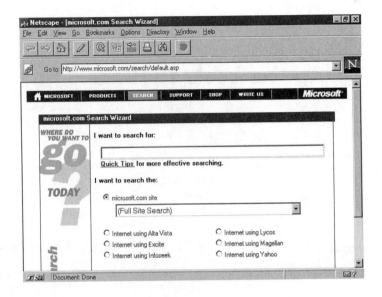

☐ If you don't see a disconnect message, you may need to install a browser. Internet Explorer is included with Word, but if you didn't select the Web options when you installed Word, you'll need to run Setup again to add the Web options.

☐ If neither of these solutions gives you access to the Web, contact your ISP and explain your situation. Your ISP should be able to help with problems specific to connecting to the Web through its service.

TIME SAVER

> If you use the same telephone line for your phone and your modem, you can only use one at a time. If you are online, a disconnection may occur when someone picks up one of the phones on this line. If you lose your connection and aren't sure why, this is probably the first thing to check. Don't be too hard on the culprit. Get in the habit of putting a sticky note on the phones to warn others when you're using the line.

The Web Toolbar Buttons

Microsoft went to a lot of trouble to design the Office 97 toolbars with consistency in mind. Word's Web toolbar mirrors closely what Internet Explorer displays. If you click the Search the Web button on Word's Web toolbar, you actually open Internet Explorer (or your browser). You will see buttons similar to those on Word's Web toolbar, like Back, Forward, and Start Page.

24

Back and Forward

Because of the amount of jumping from document to document that you do, the Back and Forward buttons on Word's Web toolbar are useful with documents that use hyperlinks. These buttons will only take you to files opened from:

☐ The Start button

☐ The Search the Web button

☐ Favorites

☐ A Web address you type in the Address bar

The files become part of the history list, which includes as many as ten of the last documents you opened using one of these techniques. Using File | Open opens a file, but this file is not included in the Web history list.

Stop Current Jump

The Stop Current Jump button is the button that lets you stop a jump when you are opening a Web page. Click this when the Web page is taking too long to open. This button does not work for hyperlinks to documents on your hard drive.

 A *Web page* is a document stored somewhere on a computer that others can link to through the Internet. An organization's or individual's introductory document (the Web site's first page) is called a *home page*.

Refresh Current Page

When you open a file on the Web, your Web browser makes a copy of the file for you to read. If you visited this site previously, what you see may not actually be the newest version of the file. Some sites update constantly, such as the ones that relay sports scores or stock quotes. Clicking the Refresh Current Page button gives you the most recent information.

Start Page

The Start Page button opens the default beginning Web page or document.

To change your Start page:

1. Open the file or Web page that you want to use as your Start page. This should be a document or Web page that you use frequently or one that you don't mind seeing each and every time you search the Web.

2. Select Set Start Page from the Go menu on the Web toolbar.

3. Click Yes to make the current Web page or document your new default Start page. This will now be the page that first opens in your browser if you are using Internet Explorer.

Search the Web

The Search the Web button can be changed in the same way as the Start page. Most people prefer to have a Start page that includes the major search engines. Internet Explorer has an excellent reference to these search engines on the default Start page, so consider carefully before changing the default to another page or document—you'll want to find your way around when you're out on the Web.

NEW TERM   *Search engines* are tools Web developers have created specifically to find information on the Web. Search engines include a box where you can type what you're looking for. By clicking a Search button of some variety, you direct the search engine to look through huge databases to compile a list of places that might have the information you want.

Favorites

Use the Add to Favorites option shown in Figure 24.3 to save the location of the current document to your list of Favorites. Using Favorites from the Web toolbar is much like using Favorites in the Open or Save dialog boxes, but it also includes references to places you link to through the Web.

Figure 24.3.

The Favorites menu.

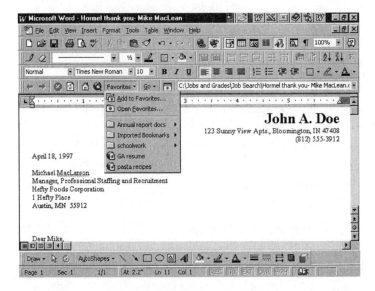

The Favorites folder is also used in Internet Explorer to save the location of favorite Web pages. It is a handy way to quickly open files and Web pages that you use often, but your favorites list can become a crowded mess if you regularly use the Favorites folder. If you put a lot of files in the Favorites menu, you may want to delete some files or create folders to organize the files.

24

To organize the Favorites folder:

1. Select Open Favorites from the Favorites menu.

2. Click the Configure button. This opens the Favorites folder in Windows Explorer (see Figure 24.4).

Figure 24.4.

Organizing the Favorites menu.

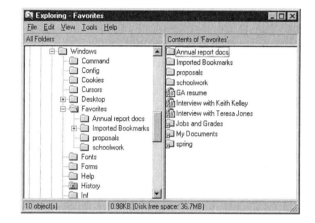

3. Delete any unwanted files by selecting the files and pressing the Delete key.

4. Click Yes if you get a message asking whether you want to send the files to the recycle bin. (You may or may not get this message depending on the way your recycle bin options have been set.)

5. Organize files into folders by selecting New | Folder from the File menu.

6. Type in a name for the folder.

7. Drag the documents that you would like to keep together into that folder.

Go

The Go drop-down menu has an option called Open, which allows you to type a Uniform Resource Locator (URL) or the location of a file on your drive. Be sure to click the Open in new window box if you are opening a file from your hard drive and don't want to close the file that is currently open.

NEW TERM   A *Uniform Resource Locator* is like a mailing address. It tells the Web browser exactly where to go. For example, URLs that begin with HTTP:// go to a site like www.microsoft.com, which is Microsoft's home page, and may go to a specific page or document at the Microsoft site. You can often tell what kind of site you're linking to by the three-character extension at the end of the site address. For example, .com denotes commercial sites, .edu denotes educational institutions, .gov denotes government sites, .org denotes organizations, and so forth.

If you are connected to the Web, here are some examples of URLs (Web addresses) that you can use to visit some good Web pages:

http://www.discovery.com—for inquisitive minds

http://www.disney.com—for the kids

http://www.businessweek.com—business news

http://www.allapartments.com—find an apartment

http://www.amazon.com—buy a book

http://www.switchboard.com—find the phone number, address, or e-mail address of a lost friend or relative

Address Box

The Address box shows the path and name of the document that is currently in use. Clicking the drop-down arrow to the right of the Address box gives you a list of previously used files. Files listed are limited to the ones mentioned earlier in the section on the Back and Forward buttons. Web pages that you have visited in Internet Explorer also appear in the list. You can select a file or Web page from the list, and it opens.

TIME SAVER

Quickly open a Web page or document by selecting whatever filename or URL appears in the Address box and replacing it by typing a different filename or URL and pressing Enter. You may find this quicker than using the Open function from the Go drop-down menu. Also, you don't need to type the http://, and you can often leave off the www that starts many Web addresses. For example, you can type microsoft.com in the Address box instead of http://www.microsoft.com. Notice that the browser adds the http:// for you.

Hyperlinks

Web pages are written in Hypertext Markup Language (HTML), which uses hyperlinks extensively. Word also uses hyperlinks. Hyperlink text in a Word document is blue and underlined, as it is on most Web pages. When you move your pointer over a hyperlink, the pointer turns into a hand. When you click the hyperlink, you jump to the file or Web page to which the hyperlink is linked.

Inserting a Hyperlink

You might have a document that includes information that can be found in another document or from a Web site. Inserting a hyperlink lets you connect to a file or Web page. This is quickly becoming a standard method of conveying information. Rather than

24

including myriads of text in a single document, hyperlinks provide a way to specify other locations from which to gather the information.

To insert a hyperlink:

1. Select some text or a picture. This becomes your hyperlink.

2. Click the Insert Hyperlink button on the Standard toolbar. The Insert Hyperlink dialog box appears (see Figure 24.5).

Figure 24.5.

Inserting a hyperlink in a Word document.

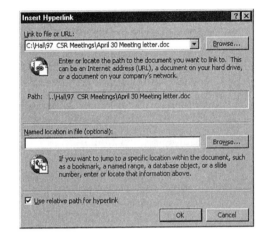

3. Type the name of a file or the address of a Web page in the Link to file or URL text box. If you want to link to a file but aren't sure of its location, click the Browse button to locate the file.

4. Click OK.

KEYBOARD SHORTCUT

Ctrl+K inserts a hyperlink for selected text or pictures.

Clicking the hyperlink automatically goes to the file or Web page that you set as the file path or URL. You do not need any kind of permission to create a hyperlink to a Web page. You only need to know the URL. If you do not have access to the Web, you can use the Insert Hyperlink function to create hyperlinks to other documents on your computer.

TIME SAVER

A quick and easy way to avoid errors in typing long URLs when making a hyperlink follows:

1. Go to the Web page to which you intend to link.
2. Select the entire URL from the Address box of your Web browser.
3. Press Ctrl+C to copy the URL to the clipboard.
4. Click the Insert Hyperlink button on the Standard toolbar.
5. Press Ctrl+V to paste the URL in the Link to file or URL box.

Another easy way to create a hyperlink is to simply type a URL. Try typing any URL in a document; Word recognizes it and turns it into a hyperlink. This is great if you want the URL you type to be a hyperlink. Of course, this feature can be maddening if you are typing URLs that you don't want to turn into hyperlinks. To change a URL to regular text, press the backspace key after you have typed the URL and it has become a hyperlink.

To disable the automatic hyperlink function:

1. Select AutoCorrect on the Tools menu.
2. Select the AutoFormat As You Type tab.
3. Uncheck the Internet and network paths with hyperlinks option, as shown in Figure 24.6.

Figure 24.6.

Removing the automatic hyperlink function.

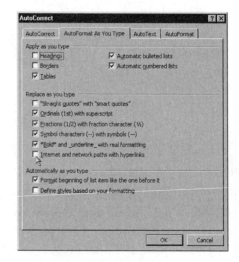

24

4. Select the AutoFormat tab and uncheck the Internet and network paths with hyperlink box if you plan to use AutoFormatting in the document.

You will sometimes want to make a hyperlink jump to another location within the same document. You might also want to jump to a specific place in another document. The easiest way to create these kinds of hyperlinks is by using the drag-and-drop technique.

To create a hyperlink between two documents by using drag-and-drop:

1. Open both documents and select Arrange All from the Window menu. This allows you to see both documents at the same time.

2. Find the start of the text in the document to which you want to link. Select a few words at the beginning of the segment.

3. Click the selected text and hold down the right mouse button while dragging it to the location where you want to place the hyperlink.

4. Click Create Hyperlink Here.

The hyperlink will appear with the name of the selected text. If you want to change the name of the hyperlink, simply select and type over the existing name. Changing the hyperlink name has no effect on the original text. When you click a hyperlink, the referenced document opens and you are placed at the location where you created the hyperlink. You can still access any part of the document, but this is your starting point.

TIME SAVER

When you select a hyperlink to change its name, be certain that the pointer is far enough from the hyperlink to display the I-bar rather than the hand. Otherwise you will activate the hyperlink rather than select the hyperlink text.

Getting Rid of a Hyperlink

If you want to remove the hyperlink attribute that has been assigned to text or a picture, follow these steps:

1. Select the entire hyperlink text or picture.

2. Click the Insert Hyperlink button. The Edit Dialog box opens.

3. Press the Remove Link button. If the hyperlink was text, the text will now be bold.

4. Select the text that was the hyperlink and click the Bold button on the formatting toolbar to remove the bold style from the text.

To get rid of a hyperlink and the representative text or graphic, simply select the hyperlink and press the Delete key.

When to Use a Hyperlink

Hyperlinks are useful in a variety of situations. For example, say you are creating a to-do list for someone who is substituting for you in your job. Using hyperlinks to files in this kind of document makes it easier for someone who is unfamiliar with your computer filing methods to locate the necessary files (see Figure 24.7).

Figure 24.7.

A document with hyperlinks.

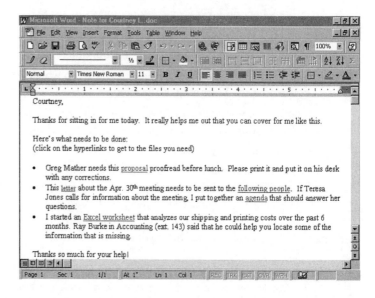

The underlined words appear in blue to signify the hyperlinks. All the substitute has to do is click the hyperlinks to get to the pertinent files.

You could use hyperlinks to interconnect sets of related documents to take the hassle out of opening each document when you work. Hyperlinks could also be used at the beginning of a large document to quickly jump to specific sections of the document. This is part of the principle behind the Master Document format.

CAUTION

> Don't use hyperlinks if you are going to move any of the files and you don't want to redo the hyperlinks. When you move a linked document, the linking document can no longer find it.

Saving Documents in HTML

If you have never created a Web page, now is your chance.

24

1. Open any Word document.

2. Select Save as HTML from the File menu.

3. Click the Save button. You are now a Web page creator.

If you put this new file on a computer that is a Web server, it is said to be "on the Web." Your network administrator or your ISP can help you with the details on how to place your files on the server. Anyone who has Web access can read the file if he knows the address of the file (the URL). It could also be used on a company's intranet system in the same way.

 An *intranet* is like an internal Internet. People within a company or an organization have an interconnected computer system and can share information and resources through a centralized system (a server or servers).

JUST A MINUTE

> When you select Save as HTML, some parts of your Word document will not convert to HTML. Specifically, margins, tabs, columns, and page numbers do not translate. Font sizes and line spacing are also different. The differences come because HTML is incompatible with some of Word's features. For example, Word saves text in the nearest available font size that works in HTML. You will see some differences because there are fewer HTML font sizes than Word font sizes.

24

When you are working with an HTML document, three new buttons appear on the Standard toolbar: the Web Page Preview, Form Design Mode, and Insert Picture buttons, as shown in Figure 24.8.

Figure 24.8.
The Standard toolbar for
HTML documents.

Web Page Preview | Insert Picture
Form Design Mode

Web Page Preview

Click the Web Page Preview button to see what your HTML file looks like in your Web browser. Your page might look very different when you preview it in your Web browser. It is a good idea to click the Web Page Preview button periodically while authoring Web pages with Word to see how they will actually look on the Web. You can edit your HTML file with most of the same tools that you would use to edit a Word document to clean up any conversion problems or to add to the document.

Form Design Mode

Clicking the Form Design Mode button brings up the Control toolbox, which boasts several different icons. If you have ever used Microsoft Access, the Office database tool, you'll notice a striking resemblance. You can create sophisticated HTML documents that include elements such as buttons, drop-down lists, and password requirements (see Figure 24.9).

Figure 24.9.

Use the Control toolbox to add buttons and lists.

The Control toolbar is also available in a regular Word document. Some of the options are different from the ones that are available when working in an HTML document.

You can make your Web pages accept information with the use of form controls. You will be able to add these controls, but you will need to consult with your ISP or Web administrator to make them functional.

To add form elements:

1. Select Forms from the Insert menu (be sure you have an HTML document open) or click the Form Design Mode button.

2. Choose the type of form element you would like to add. The Control toolbox opens, and you can click the properties button to change the attributes of your form element.

Insert Pictures

Pictures on the Web are of two types: JPG and GIF. Word conveniently converts many types of pictures to GIF format when you select Save as HTML. This is a terrific feature for Web page authors, who generally have had to use separate software to convert files to these Web-compatible types.

If you insert a JPG in the Word document, it will not be changed to a GIF in the conversion to HTML. The two drawbacks are that there is no feature that allows you to convert to JPG format, and all converted pictures are renamed to a number, such as `image1.gif`, so you may want to rename the picture to something more descriptive. GIFs look best for drawings and icons, while JPGs look best for photos.

24

TIME SAVER

Graphical images add a lot to Web pages and can make them more appealing. Keep in mind that the quantity and size of graphics affect the time it takes to load your Web page. If your primary aim is to communicate information rather than to look impressive, it may be a good idea to keep graphics to a minimum. People with slower modems are likely to give up before the page loads if there is too much graphical content.

Web Page Wizard

The Save as HTML function is great if you already have a Word document that needs to be put on the Web. If you are starting a page from scratch, it is best to use the Web Page wizard or use a blank Web page. Starting a page this way avoids the conversion problems.

To create a Web page with Web Page wizard:

1. Choose New from the File menu.
2. Select the Web Pages tab.
3. Select Web Page Wizard (see Figure 24.10). If the Web Pages tab does not appear, you need to install Word's Web authoring tools.

Figure 24.10.

Creating a Web page with Web Page wizard.

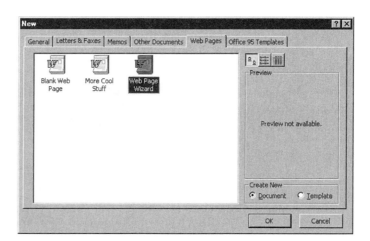

The Web Page wizard will prompt you to select a Web page type, then a visual style as in Figure 24.11. When you have completed the steps in the Web Page wizard, you type over the top of the text on the page with your own information as with other templates to create your Web page.

Figure 24.11.

Choosing a style from the Web Page wizard.

To give your Web page the look you want, there are many ways to customize your page with Word's features. To change the font color of the document text:

1. Choose Select All from the Edit menu or press Ctrl+A to select the whole document.

2. Select Format | Font.

3. Choose a color from the Color drop-down list.

To change the background color or image:

1. Select Background from the Format menu.

2. Choose a color for your background, or if you want a textured background, choose Fill Effects and select one of the Texture designs (see Figure 24.12).

Figure 24.12.

Choosing a textured background style.

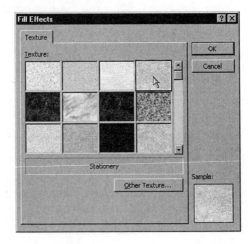

24

To insert pictures:

1. Select Picture from the Insert menu.

2. Select Clip Art or From File.

3. If you're inserting a picture from a file, locate the file and click Insert. If you're inserting from the Clip Gallery, select an image and click Insert.

4. Click the Web Page Preview button on the Standard HTML toolbar to see the image on your Web page. When using images on a page, be sure to keep track of where they are. If you put an HTML file on a Web server, you will also need to place all of the image files that go with it on the server.

To add a horizontal line:

1. Position the cursor where you want to insert a line.

2. Select Horizontal Line from the Insert menu (see Figure 24.13).

3. Click one of the line styles, or click the More button for additional styles.

4. Select a style and click OK.

5. Click the Web Page Preview button on the Standard toolbar to see what the line looks like on your page.

Figure 24.13.

Adding a horizontal line.

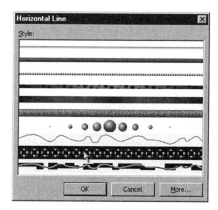

Using Tables in Web Pages

Tables are widely used in Web pages, and can be a useful way to format information on your pages. To create a table:

1. Select Insert Table from the Table menu, as shown in Figure 24.14, or click the Insert Table button on the Standard toolbar. A grid will appear that allows you to specify the size of the table you want.

2. Hold down the mouse button and move across and down to define the number of columns and rows in the table. You can readjust later if you need to add or remove cells.

3. Make any adjustments to the table by selecting the table and using the tools in the Table menu.

Figure 24.14.

Adding a table to the Web page.

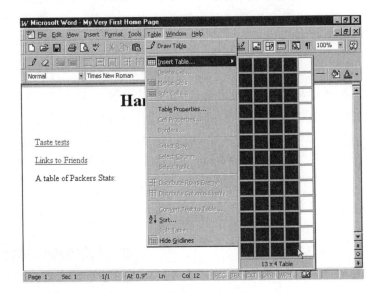

Summary

This hour discusses Word 97's Web features. Many of these features can be useful for simple document sharing without Internet access. The Web toolbar has tools that allow you to search the Web with your browser. Hyperlinks can be used in both Word documents and Web pages to allow the reader to jump to other documents or locations.

The Save as HTML option allows you to convert existing Word documents to Web pages. You can create a new Web page by using the Web Page wizard or a blank Web page.

Q&A

Q How can I work with the actual HTML programming language when making a Web page?

A Choose HTML Source from the View menu to see the source code. This is useful if you know how to program in HTML and would like more precision, or if you are curious to know what HTML is and how it works.

24

Q How can I make a counter on my Web page so that I know how many people have visited my site?

A This requires you to insert a code into your HTML source code. It also requires the help of a site that supplies Web counter services, such as `http://www.digits.com` or `http://www.nosc.mil/planet_earth/info.html`, to update your counter. This is often free unless a large number of people visit your site. The place that supplies the counter will tell you exactly what to put in your HTML source code.

Q How do I put video clips or sound into my Web page?

A Both of these options are under the Insert menu. Select Video or Background Sound to add these types of files to your Web page. Be aware that video and sound files load very slowly from the Web. This discourages many people from visiting a site. Until speedier video comes along, most designers avoid using it on a regular basis. Sound does not slow the process as dramatically, but may be enough to cause you to ask whether it is worth the price of deterring part of your audience.

Q How can I make text that scrolls across the screen?

A Select Scrolling Text from the Insert menu, then type in the text that you want to have scroll. This feature works when viewed in Internet Explorer, but not in Netscape Navigator. The text appears stationary in Navigator.

24

RW 6

Word in Real Time

Building a Web Page

This example uses some of the techniques discussed in Hour 24, "Working with the Web," to develop a simple corporate Web page.

The first step in developing a good Web site is to consider the structure of the site. Think about what information you wish to convey, and how this information could be broken down into a series of interrelated Web pages. This company wants the user to be able to see four things:

- ☐ A price list for the product
- ☐ The number to call to order the product
- ☐ The company's mission statement
- ☐ A link to the Web page of an industry association

All these items will be linked to the first page of the Web site, called the *home page*. The pages developed for each of these can be accessed from the home page.

Step 1—Create a Home Page

A company's home page is its face to the world. When users connect to the company's Web site, this is the first page they will see. A home page usually includes information about the organization and acts as a home base that leads to information on linking pages. The greatest amount of development time is usually spent creating the home page because it is the first thing that visitors to the company's site see. To create a home page for Widgets Enterprises, do the following:

1. Start a new blank Web page from the Web Pages tab in the File | New dialog box.

   You might see a message that asks whether you want to learn about new Web page authoring tools. Unless you are logged on and connected to an Internet server, click No. If you are connected, you can click Yes if you want to look for the tools; click No to move on.

2. Type, in regular text, what you want the page to look like. Use short topic descriptions such as "Order a Widget" for text that you want to use as hyperlinks (see Figure R6.1). Text can be formatted using Word's heading styles. Main headings, for example, should be formatted with the Heading 1 style.

3. Save the file as index.html. Most Web servers automatically look for a file called index.html to call up a home page. Network administrators can point to a file with any name for a home page, but using index.html is a standard practice. It is much easier for people to access your page when you follow this convention.

4. Click the Web Page Preview button to view the page from Internet Explorer or your browser.

Figure R6.1.

The Widget Enterprises home page.

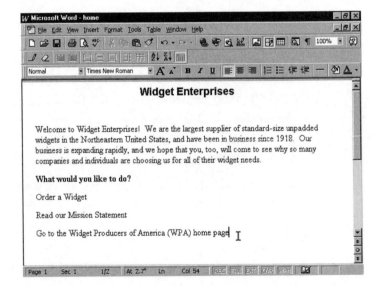

Step 2—Create a Page for Orders

It was previously determined that there would be access to the information for ordering products. To create the document that will be used for ordering purposes:

1. Create another new blank Web page, and give it the filename order.html. It's always a good idea to save all your linking Web pages in the same folder as your home page file.

2. Add a title to the top of the page. Again, format text using Word's heading styles.

3. Add a table to the page to use for a price list using the Insert Table button on the Standard toolbar, or by using Table | Insert Table.

4. Add the information and the toll-free number to the table.

5. Adjust the rows and columns of the table to achieve the look that you want. To add borders to tables in a Web page, you must use the Table | Borders menu. You have only two presets to choose from (with or without a grid). You can also set the line width.

6. Save the file again, and click the Web Page Preview button to see what the table looks like in your browser (see Figure R6.2).

Figure R6.2.

Preview the order.html *page in your default browser.*

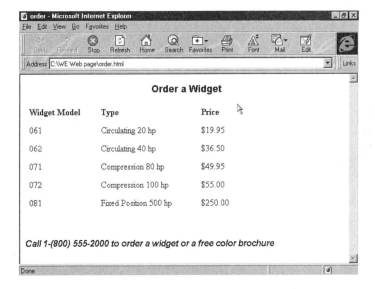

Step 3—Create a Hyperlink from the Home Page to the Order Page

A hyperlink is needed between index.html and order.html so that people can jump from the home page to the order page. To create the link:

1. Select Window | index.html to create a hyperlink from the home page to the order page.
2. Select the text "Order a Widget" and choose Hyperlink from the Insert menu or click the Insert Hyperlink button on the Standard toolbar.
3. Type order.html in the Link to file or URL text box (see Figure R6.3).
4. Click OK.

Figure R6.3.

Make a hyperlink to
order.html.

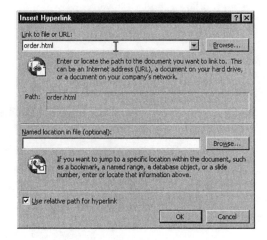

Step 4—Create a Hyperlink to the Company's Mission Statement

The company's mission statement was already created as a Word document. To use it as a hyperlink to the home page:

1. Open the document.
2. Select File | Save As HTML (see Figure R6.4).
3. Name the file (for example, mission_statement). Web page names should not include spaces. In this case, an underscore is used between the words. This is another common Web page naming convention.

Figure R6.4.

Turn this document into a Web page with Save as HTML.

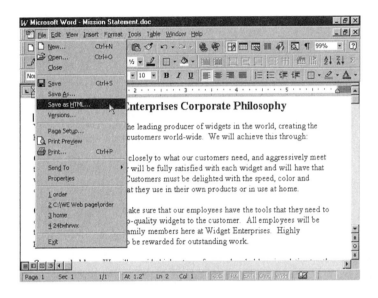

The hyperlink to `mission_statement.html` is created the same way as `order.html` was: by inserting a hyperlink where the text is that you would like to use as the jumping point to the mission statement from `index.html`. On the home page, select the words Mission Statement and create the hyperlink to `mission_statement.html`. Remember that all the files should be saved in the same folder or the path names are needed.

Step 5—Linking to the Widget Industry Association's Home Page

The final hyperlink is to the home page of the Widget Producers of America. Having been to this Web site previously, you know that the URL is `http://www.widgets.org`. To create a hyperlink from Widgets Enterprises to Widget Producers of America:

1. Select the text Widget Producers of America (WPA) on the Widgets Enterprises home page that you want to link to Widget Producers of America.
2. Click the Insert Hyperlink button (or select Insert | Hyperlink).
3. Enter the URL in the Link to file or URL text box as in Figure R6.5.

A URL must be typed exactly, including upper- and lowercase letters.

JUST A MINUTE

Figure R6.5.

*Creating a hyperlink to
another Web page.*

You have now created Web pages that could be put on the Web to use as a company's Web
site. To add some color, you might consider adding an appropriate picture, a horizontal line,
or a background to the Web pages. You get a picture placeholder when adding an image, but
you can see what the page will look like by viewing it with your browser (see Figure R6.6).
When all the changes have been made, be sure to save index.html with all the new additions.

Figure R6.6.

*The finished home page
with a horizontal bar
added.*

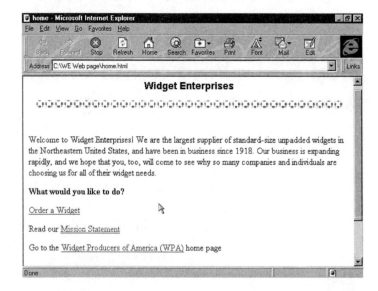

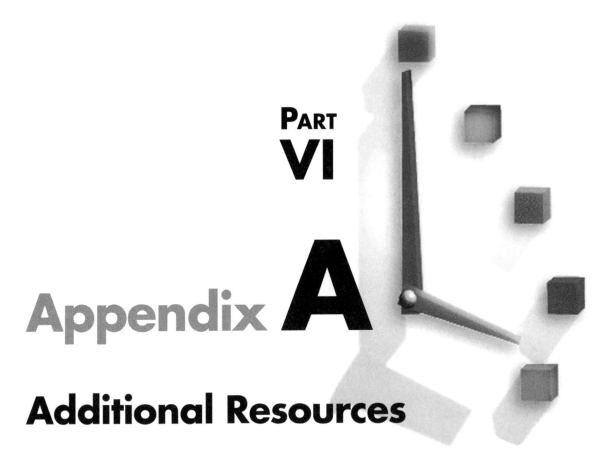

PART
VI

Appendix **A**

Additional Resources

Call for Help

There are many resources available when the help information provided in Word does not provide the answers you need.

Support Engineers

Microsoft offers a wide range of telephone support. A call to a Microsoft support engineer may be worth the long distance charges. These people walk you through a problem step by step in minimal time. It will probably take you more time to get hooked up to the support person than it takes him or her to solve the problem. To reach a support engineer, phone:

- ■ (206) 462-9673 6 a.m.–6 p.m. Pacific time (M–F)

Have Word up and running (unless you're having an installation problem—they can help there, too). Be prepared to give the support engineer your product ID number (this can be found in Word on the Help menu under About Microsoft Word, on the back of the installation CD-ROM, or in the printed materials that came with the floppy disks).

After the first phone call, things will go even more quickly. Microsoft puts you in its system, and you don't have to verify your license.

FastTips

Call first, and Microsoft will send you a map and/or catalog of the technical reports and help files available. It's hard to navigate through the system without the map or catalog, so make the call for these items first. Otherwise, you may go through a maze of phone menus to access the tip you need. Some items can be accessed by phone, others can be faxed or mailed to you. You can listen to recorded messages that answer many commonly asked questions or order technical reports from the FastTips line.

This is a computerized system, and you'll have to be alert to keep up with telephone instructions. To call for the FastTips map and catalog or to use the FastTips system, call:

☐ (800) 936-4100 (24-hour toll-free service)

Visit Microsoft's Web Site

If you have a way to connect to the Internet, there is a wealth of information on the Microsoft Web site. You can easily find your way around Microsoft's site. To save time, go straight to the Word support site at http://www.microsoft.com/mswordsupport/ (see Figure A.1).

Figure A.1.

Word's Web site support.

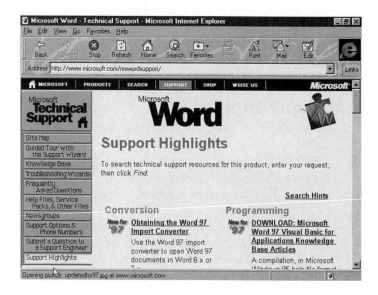

A

You get more than answers to questions from the Web site. You can download extra clips (art, sounds, and movies) and bug fixes (Microsoft does actually try to fix things). The Knowledge Base lets you search for information on specific topics. Troubleshooting wizards guide you through solutions to some of your Word problems. A file for frequently asked questions may include your question. Chances are if it's a common problem, the site will either tell you how to get around it or confirm that it is a known problem and you can't do anything about it until a bug fix is issued.

Newsgroups can be as helpful as any other portion of the online helps. This is the area where users post their Word problems and other users reply with solutions they've come up with. If you get into the newsgroup section, you can send your own problem to the group to see whether someone can answer it for you. It's like informal chatting, but with people who volunteer their time to post intelligent answers to questions.

Questions in the newsgroups are broken down into categories such as drawings and graphics, mail merge and fields, and page layout. You can go directly to an area where you might find answers rather than wading through a lot of topics that don't relate to your problem. Browsing the newsgroups is a good way to learn about known problems and possible solutions.

INDEX

MACMILLAN COMPUTER PUBLISHING USA

A VIACOM COMPANY

Support:

If you need assistance with the information in this book or with a CD/Disk accompanying the book, please access the Knowledge Base on our Web site at **http://www.superlibrary.com/general/support**. Our most Frequently Asked Questions are answered there. If you do not find the answer to your questions on our Web site, you may contact Macmillan Technical Support **(317) 581-3833** or e-mail us at **support@mcp.com**.

Teach Yourself Microsoft PowerPoint 97 in 24 Hours

Alexandria Haddad and Christopher Haddad

Teach Yourself Microsoft PowerPoint 97 in 24 Hours is an introductory tutorial that enables the reader to quickly create dynamic, captivating presentations. Beginning users will quickly learn how to utilize the new features of PowerPoint 97 with the easy, task-oriented format—the material is presented in manageable one-hour lessons. Practical, easy-to-follow exercises walk the reader through the concepts. Sections on free informational resources (templates, graphics, and so on) are included.

Price: $19.99 USA/$28.95 CDN   *User level: New–Casual*
ISBN: 0-672-31117-8   *400 pages*

Teach Yourself Microsoft Excel 97 in 24 Hours

Lois Patterson

Teach Yourself Microsoft Excel 97 in 24 Hours uses a task-oriented format to help the reader become productive in this spreadsheet application with just 24 one-hour lessons. Many new features of Excel 97, including increased connectivity and the enhanced Chart wizard, are covered in this book, making it a tutorial for those who are upgrading from previous versions of Excel. Accomplished users will find tips to help increase their productivity. This book includes numerous illustrations and figures that demonstrate how to operate Excel's key features as well as more mathematical and scientific examples than many texts.

Price: $19.99 USA/$28.95 CDN   *User level: New–Casual*
ISBN: 0-672-31116-X   *400 pages*

Teach Yourself Access 97 in 24 Hours

Timothy Buchanan, David Nielsen, and Rob Newman

As organizations and end users continue to upgrade to NT Workstation and Windows 95, a surge in 32-bit productivity applications, including Microsoft Office 97, is expected. Using an easy-to-follow approach, this book teaches the fundamentals of a key component in the Microsoft Office 97 package, Access 97. Users will learn how to use and manipulate existing databases, create databases with wizards, and build databases from scratch in 24 one-hour lessons.

Price: $19.99 USA/$28.95 CDN   *User level: New–Casual*
ISBN: 0-672-31027-9   *400 pages*

Teach Yourself Microsoft Outlook 97 in 24 Hours

Brian Proffitt and Kim Spilker

Microsoft Office, the leading application productivity suite available, will have Outlook as a personal information manager in its next version. Using step-by-step instructions and real-world examples, readers will explore the new features of Outlook and learn how to successfully and painlessly integrate Outlook with other Office 97 applications. Each lesson focuses on working with Outlook as a single user as well as in a group setting.

Price: $19.99 USA/$28.95 CDN   *User level: New–Casual*
ISBN: 0-672-31044-9   *400 pages*

Microsoft Office 97 Unleashed

Paul McFedries and Sue Charlesworth

Microsoft has brought the Web to its Office suite of products. Hyperlinking, Office Assistants, and Active Document Support lets users publish documents to the Web or an intranet site. It also completely integrates with Microsoft FrontPage, making it possible to point and click a Web page into existence. This book details each of the Office products—Excel, Access, PowerPoint, Word, and Outlook—and shows the estimated 22 million registered users how to create presentations and Web documents. The CD-ROM that accompanies the book includes powerful utilities and two best-selling books in HTML format.

Price: $39.99 USA/$56.95 CDN *User level: Accomplished–Expert*
ISBN: 0-672-31010-4 *1,200 pages*

Paul McFedries' Windows 95 Unleashed, Professional Reference Edition

Paul McFedries

Paul McFedries' Windows 95 Unleashed, Professional Reference Edition takes readers beyond the basics, exploring all facets of this operating system, including installation, the Internet, customization, optimization, networking multimedia, plug-and-play, and the new features of the Windows Messaging System for communications. It includes coverage of Internet Explorer 4.0, bringing the "active desktop" to Windows 95. The accompanying CD-ROM contains 32-bit software designed for Windows 95 and an easy-to-search online chapter on troubleshooting for Windows 95.

Price: $59.99 USA/$84.95 CDN *User level: Accomplished–Expert*
ISBN: 0-672-31039-2 *1,750 pages*

Teach Yourself Web Publishing with Microsoft Office 97 in a Week

Michael Larson

Microsoft Office is taking the market by storm. With this book's clear, step-by-step approach and practical examples, users will learn how to effectively use components of Microsoft Office to publish attractive, well-designed documents for the World Wide Web or intranet. This book focuses on the Web publishing features of the latest versions of Word, Excel, Access, and PowerPoint, and explains the basics of Internet/intranet technology, the Microsoft Internet Explorer browser, and HTML. The accompanying CD-ROM is loaded with Microsoft Internet Explorer 3.0 and an extensive selection of additional graphics, templates, scripts, ActiveX controls, and multimedia clips to enhance Web pages.

Price: $39.99 USA/$56.95 CDN *User level: New–Casual–Accomplished*
ISBN: 1-57521-232-3 *464 pages*

Teach Yourself Microsoft FrontPage 97 in a Week

Donald Doherty

FrontPage is the number one Web site creation program in the market, and this book explains how to use it. Everything from adding Office 97 documents to a Web site to using Java, HTML, wizards, VBScript, and JavaScript in a Web page is covered. With this book, readers will learn all the nuances of Web design and will have, through the included step-by-step examples, created an entire Web site using FrontPage 97. The accompanying CD-ROM includes Microsoft Internet Explorer 3.0, ActiveX and HTML development tools, plus additional ready-to-use templates, graphics, scripts, Java applets, and more.

Price: $29.99 USA/$42.95 CDN *User level: New–Casual*
ISBN: 1-57521-225-0 *500 pages*